PENGUIN TWENTIETH

THE CROWDED DAN

Virginia Woolf is now recognized as a major twentieth-century author, a great novelist and essayist, and a key figure in literary history as a feminist and modernist. Born in 1882, she was the daughter of the editor and critic Leslie Stephen, and suffered a traumatic adolescence after the deaths of her mother, in 1895, and her step-sister Stella, in 1897, leaving her subject to breakdowns for the rest of her life. Her father died in 1904 and two years later her favourite brother Thoby died suddenly of typhoid. With her sister, the painter Vanessa Bell, she was drawn into the company of writers and artists such as Lytton Strachey and Roger Fry, later known as the Bloomsbury Group. Among them she met Leonard Woolf, whom she married in 1912, and together they founded the Hogarth Press in 1917, which was to publish the work of T. S. Eliot, E. M. Forster and Katherine Mansfield as well as the earliest translations of Freud. Woolf lived an energetic life among friends and family, reviewing and writing, and dividing her time between London and the Sussex Downs. In 1941, fearing another attack of mental illness, she drowned herself.

Her first novel, *The Voyage Out*, appeared in 1915, and she then worked through the transitional *Night and Day* (1919) to the highly experimental and impressionistic *Jacob's Room* (1922). From then on her fiction became a series of brilliant and extraordinarily varied experiments, each one searching for a fresh way of presenting the relationship between individual lives and the forces of society and history. She was particularly concerned with women's experience, not only in her novels but also in her essays and her two books of feminist polemic, *A Room of One's Own* (1929) and *Three Guineas* (1938). Her major novels include *Mrs Dalloway* (1925), the historical fantasy *Orlando* (1928), written for Vita Sackville-West, the extraordinarily poetic vision of *The Waves* (1931), the family saga of *The Years* (1937), and *Between the Acts* (1941). All these are published by Penguin, as are her *Diaries*, Volumes I–V, and selections from her essays and short stories.

Rachel Bowlby is Reader in English at Sussex University. She is the author of *Just Looking* (1985), *Virginia Woolf: Feminist Destinations* (1988), *Still Crazy After All These Years: Women, Writing and Psychoanalysis* (1992) and *Shopping with Freud* (1993).

Julia Briggs is General Editor for the works of Virginia Woolf in Penguin Twentieth-Century Classics.

THE CROWDED DANCE OF MODERN LIFE

SELECTED ESSAYS: VOLUME TWO

VIRGINIA WOOLF

EDITED WITH AN INTRODUCTION
AND NOTES BY RACHEL BOWLBY

PENGUIN BOOKS

PENGUIN BOOKS

Published by the Penguin Group
Penguin Books Ltd, 27 Wrights Lane, London w8 5tz, England
Penguin Books USA Inc., 375 Hudson Street, New York, New York 10014, USA
Penguin Books Australia Ltd, Ringwood, Victoria, Australia
Penguin Books Canada Ltd, 10 Alcorn Avenue, Toronto, Ontario, Canada m4v 3b2
Penguin Books (NZ) Ltd, 182–190 Wairau Road, Auckland 10, New Zealand

Penguin Books Ltd, Registered Offices: Harmondsworth, Middlesex, England

This collection first published 1993
1 3 5 7 9 10 8 6 4 2

Selection, introduction and notes copyright © Rachel Bowlby, 1993
All rights reserved

The moral right of the author has been asserted

Typeset by Datix International Limited, Bungay, Suffolk
Filmset in 10/12 pt Monophoto Garamond
Printed in England by Clays Ltd, St Ives plc

Except in the United States of America, this book is sold subject
to the condition that it shall not, by way of trade or otherwise, be lent,
resold, hired out, or otherwise circulated without the publisher's
prior consent in any form of binding or cover other than that in
which it is published and without a similar condition including this
condition being imposed on the subsequent purchaser

CONTENTS

Bibliographical Note vii
Introduction ix
Further Reading xxxi
A Note on the Texts xxxiii

THE CROWDED DANCE OF MODERN LIFE   1
The War from the Street   3
Modern Fiction   5
The Royal Academy   13
Gothic Romance   19
How it Strikes a Contemporary   23
To Spain   32
Thunder at Wembley   39
On Being Ill   43
The Cinema   54
How Should One Read a Book?   59
Street Haunting: A London Adventure   70
Evening over Sussex: Reflections in a Motor Car   82
The Sun and the Fish   86
The Niece of an Earl   92
Foreword to *Recent Paintings by Vanessa Bell*   97
Professions for Women   101
The London Scene: 107
I   The Docks of London   107
II   Oxford Street Tide   113
III   Great Men's Houses   117
IV   Abbeys and Cathedrals   122
V   'This is the House of Commons'   127
Why Art Today Follows Politics   133
Craftsmanship   137
The Art of Biography   144

CONTENTS

Reviewing 152
The Dream 164
Thoughts on Peace in an Air Raid 168
Ellen Terry 173
The Death of the Moth 179

Notes 183

Bibliographical Note

The following is a list of abbreviated titles used in this edition.

Diary: *The Diary of Virginia Woolf*, 5 vols, ed. Anne Olivier Bell (Hogarth Press, 1977; Penguin Books, 1979).
Letters: *The Letters of Virginia Woolf*, 6 vols, ed. Nigel Nicolson and Joanne Trautmann (Hogarth Press, 1975–80).
Passionate Apprentice: *A Passionate Apprentice: The Early Journals, 1897–1909*, ed. Mitchell A. Leaska (Hogarth Press, 1990).
Essays: *The Essays of Virginia Woolf*, 3 vols (to be six vols), ed. Andrew McNeillie (Hogarth Press, 1986).
CE: *Collected Essays*, 4 vols, ed. Leonard Woolf (Hogarth Press, 1966, 1967).

Introduction
The Crowded Dance of Modern Life

'New forms for our new sensations': this is how Woolf captures or captions a question she struggles with and plays with throughout her essays, whether she is giving a quick-fire reviewer's response to the latest novel, or meandering more slowly between books and modern life, or between words and the world they shape. The phrase occurs in an essay called 'Hours in a Library', when she is wondering about the 'amazing' appeal of some contemporary works in contrast to the tried and tested classics.[1] 'Sensations' is itself a word with modern connotations in this usage, and calls to mind the *fin de siècle* aesthetics of Walter Pater, of whom Woolf was an avid reader.[2] In his 'Conclusion' to *Studies in the History of the Renaissance*, Pater had argued, scandalously and in a radical and deliberate separation of present sensations from lasting forms, for an aesthetics dependent on obtaining from each moment the maximum of experience:

> It is with this movement, with the passage and dissolution of impressions, images, sensations, that analysis leaves off . . .
> . . . Every moment some form grows perfect in hand or face; some tone on the hills or the sea is choicer than the rest; some mood of passion or insight or intellectual excitement is irresistibly real and attractive to us – for that moment only.[3]

Where Pater is interested in the succession of pointed, separate moments, with forms no sooner perceptible than surpassed, Woolf begins with the assumption that forms for sensations are what is needed. And whereas Pater's focus is on personal psychology, not treated as historically variable, Woolf's repeated 'new' and collective 'our' implies that there may be differences in culture, including the psychology of those who live in it, between one period and another. Woolf thus at once takes up as significant a question about change and newness – literature cannot be the same for every age or culture – and, at the same time, suggests, unlike Pater, that sensations should be shaped into forms – that there should be continuity and stability.

INTRODUCTION

Within this tiny quotation lies the germ of Woolf's maddeningly and delightfully ambivalent response to modern life, 'the modern mind',[4] and modern writing. On the one hand, she will seem to take in joyfully and passively the pleasures of a book, a walk, a sensation of some kind; on the other, and in a second move, which is meant to supersede the first, she will pull back and insist without more ado that there must be judgement, or order, or permanence, or depth.

A case in point is the essay from which the title quotation to this volume is taken. In 'Life and the Novelist', Woolf is reviewing a novel called *A Deputy Was King*, by G. B. Stern. In the course of four brief pages, Woolf runs through a whole philosophy of the double movement of the process of writing for novelists and of the experience and understanding of modern culture. The novelist, unlike other artists, is someone who takes his or her material from that fluid, unstructured something called 'life':

> Taste, sound, movement, a few words here, a gesture there, a man coming in, a woman going out, even the motor that passes in the street or the beggar who shuffles along the pavement, and all the reds and blues and lights and shades of the scene claim his attention and rouse his curiosity. He can no more cease to receive impressions than a fish in mid-ocean can cease to let the water rush through his gills.[5]

The novelist is both naturalistically passive (like a fish in water), and solicited by a scene put on for him, to 'claim his attention and rouse his curiosity'. The impressions he drinks in address all kinds of sense – taste, sound, sight – and comprise a random sequence of disconnected details, with abstract and concrete subjects – taste, gesture, woman, beggar, motor, reds – all occupying the same level, undifferentiated.

Woolf continues, however, with a firm 'But' which moves with determination – as she claims to be stating what is obvious – from passivity of receptiveness to firm control:

> But if this sensibility is one of the conditions of the novelist's life, it is obvious that all writers whose books survive have known how to master it and make it serve their purposes . . . they have mastered their perceptions, hardened them, and changed them into the fabrics of their art.

... Life is subjected to a thousand disciplines and exercises. It is curbed; it is killed. It is mixed with this, stiffened with that, brought into contrast with something else ... There emerges from the mist something stark, something formidable and enduring, the bone and substance upon which our rush of indiscriminating emotion was founded.[6]

The language of rock-like hardness and discipline – 'a thousand disciplines', no less – applies both to the required exercises of the writer and to the enduring qualities of the finished work. 'Indiscriminating emotion' must be transposed into something both functional and subordinate ('make it serve their purposes'), as the making of literature is abruptly shifted between the two extremes of passive impressionability to maximum mastery: what life did to the novelist, the novelist now turns around and does to life.

In the next paragraph, Woolf describes the first of 'these two processes' as 'undoubtedly the easier, the simpler, and the pleasanter'. There is thus a work ethic underlying the commanding requirement of subsequent discipline, its 'rigours' stressed all the more sharply by their explicit differentiation from the pleasanter enjoyment of the 'preliminary emotion'.[7] Woolf then goes on, after this principled introduction, to a description of the high-society, cosmopolitan story of *A Deputy Was King*, with its 'up to date' portrayal of the life of a fashionable extended family in 1921. After this, she moves into a summary of the reader's response, which reproduces the first stage of the writing process, that of passive receptiveness:

We have been letting ourselves bask in appearances ... We have sat receptive and watched, with our eyes rather than with our minds, as we do at the cinema, what passes on the screen in front of us ... This hand-to-mouth method, this ladling out of sentences which have the dripping brilliance of words that live upon real lips, is admirable for one purpose, disastrous for another. All is fluent and graphic; but no character or situation emerges cleanly.[8]

The assumption here that for films, as opposed to books, there is only uncritical reception, is not, as we shall see, one that Woolf always makes; but in this place, it is interesting that the analogy enables her to make the cinema's screen into a figure for the depthlessness of the unreflective novel, which is all surface. The imagery of the second part of the quotation introduces a taste of Woolf's aesthetics of literary and other forms of production and consumption: a bad novel is like slopped soup; things should emerge cleanly, no mess, whatever the assortment of ingredients that may originally have gone into the pan.

But towards the end of the essay, the distinctions become less severe:

> This kind of work requires great dexterity and nimbleness, and gratifies a real desire. To know the outside of one's age, its dresses and its dances and its catchwords, has an interest and even a value which the spiritual adventures of a curate, or the aspirations of a high-minded schoolmistress, solemn as they are, for the most part lack. It might well be claimed, too, that to deal with the crowded dance of modern life so as to produce the illusion of reality needs far higher literary skill than to write a serious essay upon the poetry of John Donne or the novels of M. Proust.[9]

Even though she will pull back from this once again, Woolf lets an attraction break through here, which has the effect of cancelling, or at least detracting from, the overt argument about the greater importance of the novel with values and permanence. Here, the lasting novel is implicitly the dull Victorian tale of a curate or schoolmistress, while 'its dresses and its dances and its catchwords' have a thoroughly twenties swing, which no critical statement can stop. By this time, it is coming to seem as if 'the crowded dance of modern life', in what is acknowledged as being its gratification of 'a real desire', is continuing to claim attention against the austerities of the disciplined work.

It is significant that, in the essay we have been looking at, the novelist and the life he tries to capture are revealingly gendered, with 'life' taking the floor as an endlessly attractive and attracting modern woman:

> Stridently, clamorously, life is forever pleading that she is the proper end of fiction and that the more he sees of her and catches of her the better his book will be. She does not add, however, that she is grossly impure; and that the side she flaunts uppermost is often, for the novelist, of no value whatever. Appearance and movement are the lures she trails to entice him after her, as if these were her essence, and by catching them he gained his goal.[10]

As in the case of comparable passages where literature or language are also gendered as an impossible woman who cannot be pinned down,[11] so here the disruptive impurity is represented as feminine, and the secondary force of control as masculine.

The identification with this disciplinary function, set against the elusive, unstructured materials upon which it works, always seems arbitrary in Woolf's many deployments of the sequence. Precisely because they are represented as what is not controlled, not willed, the details and the pleasures of modern life can come to seem more interesting and more suggestive in Woolf's writings about culture and literature than the contrary type of statement, where she is expressly putting all that at the distance of a preliminary stage or emotion, to be overcome by disciplined hard work. They seem to have an insuppressible fascination, which the attempt at suppression only shows up more clearly.

But it is in her essays about reading, writing and the literary tradition, much more than in her essays about aspects of modern culture, that the insistence on the two-part movement, from the formless and passive to the need to bring order and assert control, seems most marked. It is as though when dealing with literature, and perhaps under pressure of the very genre of the essay about literature, Woolf was more compelled to assert and affirm the importance of fixity; whereas when she was out and about, roaming among subjects that were not marked out in the same way, she let herself lose track more of the standards, so that this kind of essay could itself become like the elusive, undisciplined 'life' that so fascinates the writer. Yet this is to make the distinction too simply, for in the same way that many of the most open speculations about modern life and historical changes occur in the midst of literary prescriptions (as in 'Life and the Novelist'), so the essays on non-literary topics are often interesting also for the ways in which they reveal underlying assumptions and fixities in Woolf's thinking about norms of human psychology and values.

'The London Scene', a series of five short pieces narrating an imaginary stroll around different areas and aspects of the city, contains some wonderful passages about Oxford Street as epitomizing the ephemerality of modernity, as contrasted with a traditional emphasis on solidity and permanence; and the sentences themselves here start to sound like pastiches of a rhyming advertising slogan:

> The charm of modern London is that it is not built to last; it is built to pass ... Their pride required the illusion of permanence. Ours, on the contrary, seems to delight in proving that we can make stone and brick as transitory as our own desires. (pp. 115–16)

When she writes about the architecture of department stores, Woolf sounds indistinguishable from much later definitions in the 1980s of postmodern architecture as the playful quotation of earlier styles:

> The palaces of Oxford Street ignore what seemed good to the Greeks, to the Elizabethan, to the eighteenth-century nobleman; they are overwhelmingly conscious that unless they can devise an architecture that shows off the dressing-case, the Paris frock, the cheap stockings and the jar of bath salts to perfection, their palaces, their mansions and motor cars and the little villas out at Croydon and Surbiton where their shop assistants live, not so badly after all, with a gramophone and wireless, and money to spend at the movies – all this will be swept to ruin. Hence they stretch stone fantastically; crush together in one wild confusion the styles of Greece, Egypt, Italy, America; and boldly attempt an air of lavishness, opulence, in their effort to persuade the multitude that here unending beauty, ever fresh, ever new, very cheap and within the reach of everybody, bubbles up every day of the week from an inexhaustible well. The mere thought of age, of solidity, of lasting for ever is abhorrent to Oxford Street. (p. 116)

Unlike many similar sequels to letting a passage run wild into lists of pleasures or random experiences, Woolf does not in this case pull back or call a halt in the following paragraph, adopting a regulatory stance. As if to emphasize this difference, a figure called the 'moralist' is brought on only to be dismissed as out of place, out of his depth amid those 'somehow keeping afloat on the bounding, careless, remorseless tide of the street' (p. 117), involved directly, not at a distance, with the delights or the needs of material things.

The listing of articles for sale reproduces the shopper's hurried glance, one thing after another, then more, and nothing draws them together beyond the significant fact that they are all items of feminine adornment. Woolf's Oxford Street is characterized by 'passing': the passing of its buildings, of the people strolling along

INTRODUCTION

in its tide, and of the short-lived bits and pieces that succeed one another in the shop windows with such speed. The shopping street becomes a place that seems to draw out Baudelaire's famous nineteenth-century definition of modernity – any modernity, not just the present age – as 'the transitory, the fleeting, the contingent'. For Baudelaire this is only 'half of art, of which the other half is the eternal and the immovable',[12] and generally this is the case for Woolf too, as she situates and stabilizes the loosenesses of fragmentary experience in terms of a second-stage order. Here, though, it is as if transitoriness had itself become a norm, after an earlier time when lasting values predominated.

The quotations suggest a question about the nature of the shopper's interest. The store owners are engaged in a perpetual 'effort to persuade the multitude' of the existence of a continuous stream of new things available to all; 'as transitory as our own desires' suggests that the ephemerality of Oxford Street's displays is responding to a disposition already there in human nature, whether or not it has only developed alongside the transient buildings and commodities that match it. There is a perfect fit between the offers and the demand. In the first of the five London scenes, on the docklands, Woolf had indicated this adjustment from the other side, going so far as to imply that the market and its range of available products is entirely dependent on consumer demand:

> It is we – our tastes, our fashions, our needs – that make the cranes dip and swing, that call the ships from the sea. Our body is their master. We demand shoes, furs, bags, stoves, oil, rice puddings, candles; and they are brought us. Trade watches us anxiously to see what new desires are beginning to grow in us, what new dislikes. (p. 112).

This touching fantasy of the spontaneous generation of desires that 'trade' – like an over-indulgent parent waiting 'anxiously' to see what the child will want next – asks no more than to satisfy, culminates in what sounds like a truly personal example: 'Because one chooses to light a cigarette, all those barrels of Virginian tobacco are swung on shore (p. 112). Here indeed is a faultlessly matched arrangement of supply and demand, with the carrying of Virginian tobacco to Virginia.

INTRODUCTION

The model of the perfect fit occurs in the docklands section too, but this time with rather different implications for psychology than was the case with new, and perpetually growing, consumer desires. Here, the stress is not on endless additions to given supplies, but instead on the maintenance of a perfect whole in the careful avoidance of waste:

> None of all the multitudinous products and waste products of the earth but has been tested and found some possible use for. The bales of wool that are being swung from the hold of an Australian ship are girt, to save space, with iron hoops; but the hoops do not litter the floor; they are sent to Germany and made into safety razors ... Not a burr, not a tuft of wool, not an iron hoop is unaccounted for. And the aptness of everything to its purpose, the forethought and readiness which have provided for every process, come, as if by the back door, to provide that element of beauty which nobody in the docks has ever given half a second of thought to. (p. 111).

Rather than endless surplus, desires continually emerging and continually fulfilled, this is a fantasy of perfect static functioning, nothing left over and everything 'found some possible use for' – a matter of thrift as opposed to excess. When Woolf makes this into an aesthetics of function – fitness of itself leading to beauty – the correspondence becomes apparent in the way she discusses the relation between life and the forms of art, as we saw in 'Life and the Novelist'. Unlike the superfluities of the writer who pours it all out from her ladle indiscriminately, the true novelist should be economical in this sense of having every element serve a purpose.

This aestheticization of waste-free efficiency can be related to other discussions where Woolf treats reading and other artistic activities in terms of their psychological uses and significance. In 'The Dream', she is talking about a popular novelist of the nineteenth century and points out, despite a condemnation of the aesthetic qualities of the works of Marie Corelli, that they may have had their uses:

> [I]f her books saved one working man from suicide, or allowed a dressmaker's drudge here and there to dream that she, too, was Thelma or Mavis Clare, there were no films then to sustain them with plush and glow and rapture after the day's work. (p. 166)

This assumes a literally saving power for art – and second-rate art at that – and also the constancy of a psychological need for fantasy as both relaxation (after work) and compensation (dressmakers' 'drudges' are not Thelma).

The description contrasts interestingly with the one habitually applied in relation to genuine art where, as for the writer in 'Life and the Novelist', the sequence goes in the other direction, from distracted passivity to work. In 'How Should One Read a Book?', the pattern is equally explicit. After an initial indulgence in 'the delight of rubbish-reading' comes the second moment, as though by natural exhaustion: 'we tire of rubbish-reading in the long run' (pp. 63–4). Both the material and the attitude change, as we shift from biography to poetry, with a series of samples barely commented on in the manner of Matthew Arnold's 'touchstone' lines. In its selectiveness, as opposed to the diffuse expansiveness of the novels and the 'rubbish', poetry itself symbolizes the refining of the second moment:

> We must pass judgement upon these multitudinous impressions; we must make of these fleeting shapes one that is hard and lasting. (p. 66)

This contrast is also made in terms of a move from food to thought, via a pun on the notion of taste:

> But as time goes on perhaps we can train our taste; perhaps we can make it submit to some control. When it has fed greedily and lavishly upon books of all sorts – poetry, fiction, history, biography – and has stopped reading and looked for long spaces upon the variety, the incongruity of the living world, we shall find that it is changing a little; it is not so greedy, it is more reflective. (pp. 67–8)

Such food metaphors, like the 'ladled' quantities of life discussed above – are frequent when Woolf is discussing aspects of the 'consumption' of books or the 'taking in' of impressions from the world. They sometimes, as here, imply an excess, a crude abundance that will need to be sorted out; and sometimes the stress is rather on eating as a basic need, an impulse or instinct that must be satisfied. In 'Memories of a Working Women's Guild', both are combined:

> [T]hey read with the indiscriminate greed of a hungry appetite,

that crams itself with toffee and beef and tarts and vinegar and champagne all in one gulp.[13]

The grotesqueness of this image of stuffing, reinforced by the champagne, completely incongruous next to the more vulgar fare, goes along with a class distance that is certainly present in much of Woolf's writing about the consumption of literature and other cultural produce. But for all her insistence on the distinctions of high and low, and between the raw and the cooked stages of reading and writing, she nevertheless also wants to hold on to the pleasures of junk food, 'the delight of rubbish-reading'. Whatever the sternness or forcedness, in both senses, of the reiterated need to 'submit to some control', the sweet and low pleasures of the ephemeral and the random are always coming to the fore.

Woolf's essays raise questions about the psychology of cultural consumption, which she also sees in historical terms. She refers – for instance in 'Reading' and in 'On Not Knowing Greek' – to the significance of the change from public to private contexts of reading; which is related, in turn, to what she describes as an increased preoccupation of the past two hundred years with the individual. The development of biography and autobiography is one symptom of this, discussed in essays such as 'The Art of Biography' and 'The New Biography'; so is the increasing interest in personal psychology, both in itself and as a focus within many literary genres. 'Freudian Fiction', perhaps the most tantalizingly entitled of all Woolf's essays, argues for the maintenance of a separation between literature and science: novels should not be applied psychology. Woolf did not in fact read any Freud until late in her life, despite the direct involvement in it of a number of her friends and the publication of James Strachey's English translation literally out of her own basement; but the many references to psychoanalysis and psychology in her essays testify to a recognition of the ways in which these areas of study exemplified and enabled new questions about the modern experience, and in particular about the history and writing of literature.[14]

A fascinating passage in 'Reading' (of which another version appears in 'The Elizabethan Lumber Room') brings together all these questions about the relation of general accounts of psychology to historical differences. It is a description of a tale of sexual misunderstanding:

> Here is a story of the savage caught somewhere off the coast of Labrador, taken to England and shown about like a wild beast. Next year they bring him back and fetch a woman savage on board to keep him company. When they see each other they blush; they blush profoundly; the sailor notices it but knows not why it is. And later the two savages set up house together on board ship, she attending to his wants, he nursing her in sickness, but living, as the sailors note, in perfect chastity. The erratic searchlight cast by these records falling for a second upon those blushing cheeks three hundred years ago, among the snow, sets up that sense of communication which we are apt to get only from fiction. We seem able to guess why they blushed; the Elizabethans would notice it, but it has waited over three hundred years for us to interpret it.[15]

The understanding between 'us' assumed here is so assured that Woolf does not herself make the interpretation that is now taken as obvious, as though spelling it out might simply repeat the crude colonial gestures that provoked the first blush on the part of those treated as uncomplicated animals.

The references to communication across the ages and to a contemporary interpretation not available to the Elizabethans might suggest that the underlying assumption is one of a transhistorically constant human nature, changing only through advances in knowledge (we know more than they did). But it is significant, first of all, that Woolf takes the waywardness of fiction as likely to be a better source of historical enlightenment than chronicles. Reconstructing a story that only comes into being from the perspective of contemporary interests (the image of the 'erratic searchlight' happening upon and then refocusing on a detail barely noted, but noted none the less) sets up a complex double time of historical understanding, which is more than simply chronological or progressive in its orientation. The blush itself can now – but only now – be seen as having been an unspoken and unspeakable commentary about the sexual and racial power relations of the sixteenth-century voyages of discovery.

Woolf sometimes groups the psychological interests of the present alongside technological innovations as symptomatic of the new features that will have to find their way into fiction and other representations – 'new forms for our new sensations'. This is from the piece entitled 'Gothic Romance':

> [T]he desire to widen our boundaries, to feel excitement without danger, and to escape as far as possible from the facts of life drive us perpetually to trifle with the risky ingredients of the mysterious and the unknown. Science ... will modify the Gothic romance of the future with the aeroplane and the telephone. Already the bolder of our novelists have made use of psychoanalysis to startle and dismay. (p. 21)

This begins with an appeal to what are taken to be some general psychological needs that give rise to certain types of fictional fantasy; and then goes on to consider how these will be inflected by specific things and ideas that will alter through history. In passages like this one, Woolf is a long way from the high tones of her assertions about the necessity of strict controls and timeless literary standards.

She does not, further, see the objects or the ideas as inertly awaiting a mouthpiece in novels that would simply take them up, or take them in, unmodified (this was her criticism of the novel reviewed in 'Freudian Fiction'). Instead, she is speculating about how new things, as well as new ideas, may both develop out of distinctive ways of thinking and, in their turn, have effects on the possibilities of how we think. One tiny example is a moment at the beginning of 'The London Scene', when a ship coming up the estuary is likened to 'a car on a parking ground'. By reversing (and the verb 'reversing' begs the same question) the literary norm whereby the logical order of the comparison would follow the historical sequence of appearance (the car like a ship), Woolf slips in a suggestion about how new things, with their accompanying uses and associations, retroactively come to operate upon the ways in which things that antedate them are represented too.

In essays such as 'Flying over London', 'The Cinema' and 'Evening over Sussex: Reflections in a Motor Car', such possibilities are developed in relation to new objects of interest and fantasies of identity. 'The Cinema' begins as though it is going to condemn the new medium as hopelessly crude by comparison with literature, and answering only to the most basic of popular appetites for distraction.

Once again there is the naturalization of a crudely instinctive, infantile taste here attributed to 'the savages of the twentieth century watching the pictures' (p. 54):

> [A]t first sight, the art of the cinema seems simple, even stupid ... The eye licks it all up instantaneously, and the brain, agreeably titillated, settles down to watch things happening without bestirring itself to think. For the ordinary eye, the English unaesthetic eye, is a simple mechanism, which takes care that the body does not fall down coal-holes, provides the brain with toys and sweetmeats to keep it quiet, and can be trusted to go on behaving like a competent nursemaid until the brain comes to the conclusion that it is time to wake up. (p. 54)

And later, there are some despairing comments on the reductiveness of attempts to translate novels into films. Yet the chief interest that emerges in the piece is not in the simplifying qualities of cinema, but in the ways in which it has the potential to be a medium for evoking the pathos of time having passed, or the complexity of modern experience.

The first occurs through the way that film can actually reproduce, before our eyes, and 'as it was', what happened years ago; and the force of this for Woolf lies now in the absolutely irremediable and unprecedented crack in historical continuity that was the 1914–18 war (she frequently uses the word 'chasm' in this connection):

> The war sprung its chasm at the feet of all this innocence and ignorance, but it was thus that we danced and pirouetted, toiled and desired, thus that the sun shone and the clouds scudded up to the very end. (p. 55)

The pleasant, pirouetting climate of the pre-war expanse of time now seems to act as a backcloth for a lack of simple orders and pleasures, which is also the condition of modern life itself. Here too, Woolf thinks that the cinema could be the medium to show this up, as a form of 'visual emotion' (she was writing before the invention of sound cinema):

> We should see violent changes of emotion produced by their collision. The most fantastic contrasts could be flashed before us with a speed which the writer can only toil after in vain; the dream architecture of arches and battlements, of cascades falling and

fountains rising, which sometimes visits us in sleep or shapes itself in half-darkened rooms, could be realized before our waking eyes. No fantasy could be too far-fetched or insubstantial . . .

How all this is to be attempted, much less achieved, no one at the moment can tell us. We get intimations only in the chaos of the streets, perhaps, when some momentary assembly of colour, sound, movement suggests that here is a scene waiting a new art to be transfixed. (p. 58)

'Transfixed' is a striking word here, literally: it suggests a violent hit or arrest quite unlike the bland settlement that more often seems to be connoted when Woolf appeals to an idea of artistic form. The collision of emotions and the speed of their change lead associatively to the shocks of the street, appearing as a rush of sense impressions that can only be seized in an imageless flash of 'colour, sound, movement', not unified but held apart. Emotions are thus themselves perceived as analogous to the modern street, which appears as a rapid series of abstract paintings: real life is itself already the scene of a film. The street thus takes the place occupied by nature in an earlier literary tradition: Wordsworth's 'intimations of immortality'[16] from the child's view of the grandeur of mountain landscapes have become 'intimations' of the opposite, a fantasy not of natural form but of urban chaos. And nature itself is now a surreal, internal dreamworld of night-time, fantastical fears, rather than the source, outside the perceiving self, of a sense of permanent forms.

In her sense of the aptness of the new visual media as (formless) forms for new ways of seeing, Woolf is close to some of the insights given at the same time, though in a different intellectual tradition, by Walter Benjamin. Benjamin, too, saw that the very precision of the camera, able to register each and every image separately, made it the perfect instrumental analogue for the multiplicity and discontinuity of modern sensations – for the fragmentary, transitory, fleeting moments of an experience infinitely divisible but not capable of integration, whether psychologically or artistically, in the same old ways.

In an essay called 'A Small History of Photography', Benjamin speculated about the relation of photography's capacity to enlarge – to see what the naked eye could not – to the psychoanalytic discovery or invention of an unconscious as the previously invisible substructure secretly underlying all our thoughts and doings.[17] From Benjamin's essay, which takes as its example the slow-motion exposure of the processes of taking a step, it would follow that the fact that we can now see imaged an infinite number of hitherto unknown motions that go to make up the process of walking alters our attitude (itself a metaphor of posture) to that movement, even as the capacity or wish to investigate it must also be related to other cultural developments. A comparable linking of the visual to the minutiae of psychology in their new scientific modes occurs also in one of Woolf's essays entitled 'Royalty'. Hovering between parody and serious analysis, as if this were the only conceivable form for the sensations it takes as its subject, this short piece examines the fascination with royalty and aristocracy, hyperbolically assuming it to be universal. Speaking of snobbery with tongue in cheek, or nose very pointedly in the air, Woolf alleges – in a structure that has come by now to be familiar in her writing – that the media merely cater to an appetite or demand that is there to begin with:

> We too want to see the Dukes and Kings. There is no denying it, for the picture papers show us what we want to see, and the picture papers are full of Dukes and Kings.[18]

Like the other 'Royalty' essay, a review of Princess Marie's autobiography,[19] this piece identifies a turn in the direction of ordinariness, with the royals becoming recognizably like ourselves. But here, this is seen not as a chance for democracy but as the inevitable end of the 'very complex emotion' of snobbish interest that depends on a perceptible difference of class (quite simply, in these terms, Mrs Simpson, the American divorcée with the same name as a well-known London department store, just will not do).

But then, as so often when she is writing about the needs and pleasures of reading, Woolf takes for granted a constancy of psychological structure, such that the function formerly served by the spectacle of the royals will have to be supplied in some other way:

> If therefore Royalty fails to gratify our need of Royalty, the Protestant religion is not going to come to our help. The desire will have to find some other outlet. And the picture papers, in which we see the reflection of so many desires, are already hinting at a possible substitute.[20]

Amazingly enough, the answer turns out to be a caterpillar, as Woolf launches into a panegyric for the capacity of the magazines' new close-up photographic techniques to show science's view of the natural world as a wonder:

> If the picture papers then would come to our help, we might dream a new dream, acquire a new snobbery; we might see the coral insect at work; the panda alone in his forest; the wild yet controlled dance of the atoms which makes, it is said, the true being of the kitchen table; and spend our curiosity upon them. The camera has an immense power in its eye, if it would only turn that eye in rather a different direction.[21]

Nothing could so perfectly evoke the future successes of phenomena, natural and unnatural, like the *National Geographic* or television nature documentary programmes. Here, where she is not on her own territory, wanting to keep the factual and the poetic strictly separate as she complains about the piling up of sociological description in the novels of Arnold Bennett or H. G. Wells, Woolf glimpses the surprising possibilities not of fantasy as opposed to science, but of science *as* fantasy:[22] new sensations alongside our new forms.

The question about the camera's direction at the end of the last quotation points us towards still other ways in which Woolf explored the relationship between psychology and the media of writing and seeing. In 'The Art of Biography', she links recent changes in this genre to developments in the mass media and publishing fashions, themselves indicated metonymically by one of their principal technical instruments:

> [S]ince we live in an age when a thousand cameras are pointed, by newspapers, letters, and diaries, at every character from every angle, [the biographer] must be prepared to admit contradictory versions of the same face. Biography will enlarge its scope by hanging up looking-glasses at odd corners. (pp. 149–50)

The saturation of personal information in various types of publication is thus seen not as a levelling out, but as the means to a greater diversity and complexity in the way that a face is viewed. Further, the placing of the optical instrument, whether camera or mirror, is seen to play a crucial part in the image that will be developed of the biography's subject. If it is a matter of 'hanging up looking-glasses at odd corners', deliberately looking for the eccentric angle, then the 'life' becomes not something statically and simply there to be registered objectively, but quite openly a matter of a choice of perspective that implicates the viewer and that might have been a different one.

It is notable, too, that this extension of views is connected to what Woolf identifies as an unequivocally positive, and positivist, change in the understanding of sexuality. In the previous paragraph, she writes:

> What was thought a sin is now known, by the light of facts won for us by the psychologists, to be perhaps a misfortune; perhaps a curiosity; perhaps neither one nor the other, but a trifling foible of no great importance ... The accent on sex has changed within living memory. This leads to the destruction of a great deal of dead matter still obscuring the true features of the human face. Many of the old chapter headings – life at college, marriage, career – are shown to be very arbitrary and artificial distinctions. (p. 149)

It is striking in this that the discovery of artificiality and arbitrariness is directly correlated to the discovery of a definite, non-arbitrary truth about the significance of sex. This means that the new generic indeterminacy, rendering obsolete 'the old chapter headings', as Woolf herself showed in the fictional biography *Jacob's Room*, is itself represented as a definite truth, predicated on the correction of errors and the advancement of knowledge. The psychologists are conquerors who have 'won for us' facts for all time and lifted the veil of 'dead matter still obscuring the true features of the human face'. We are reminded here of the savages' blush, and the tension in Woolf's retelling of that tale between a story of modern enlightenment (we now know better than they did) and one that depends on a sense of how differently human behaviour is interpreted in different cultures and historical periods (so that all 'chapter headings' are 'arbitrary and artificial', including those that take the modern view of the significance of sex).

Looked at from the point of view of the subject of biography, not the writer, these looking-glasses hung up at odd corners become the uncertainty and the opportunity of an identity that is never one, and never settled. The notion of a multiplicity of selves – playfully explored in *Orlando*, where the hero(ine) of the pseudo-biography not only changes sex, but moves around between a couple of thousand different selves – appears, too, in many essays. Sometimes, as in 'Street Haunting: A London Adventure', it has to do with the shedding of the respectable self of one's normal, everyday identity in favour of a temporary anonymity that leaves the (non-)self open and permeable to the passing sights and impressions of the city. The street scene becomes a theatre, offering constantly changing sights and imaginary identities to the spectator moving from moment to moment and detached from the ties of responsibility, either to the maintenance of a particular image of her own self, or to the people who happen to lie in her way.

The theatricality of the motif of multiple selves is often literalized, as in the piece on Ellen Terry. This woman's life, oscillating between domesticity and the stage, itself made her more of an actress, because she played out the part of more than one script; but at the same time, in that 'Something of Ellen Terry it seems overflowed every part and remained unacted', not fitting into the stock parts, she became wholly original: 'That was Ellen Terry's fate – to act a new part' (p. 178). Acting has taken priority here as the model for selfhood, so that it is not being compared as the fake or artificial in comparison with some more real or personal self – though it is, by implication, available for copying. The truly original person, therefore, the one who is most herself, is going to be not a non-actor but the actor or actress who makes a new part.

In this mode, when she is universalizing a dramatic model of subjectivity, Woolf sounds like a forerunner of much twentieth-century sociology which has taken as its basis the idea of social behaviour as set-piece role-playing.[23] There is this much in common, that neither sees the everyday acting of parts as a weak or approximate imitation in comparison with some prior or unique core of self: you are your parts, though the scripts and the scope may vary. For Woolf, however, the potential for multiple selves is not a neutral description, but generally valued as an affirmative sign of people's (usually women's) versatility and variation. The most negative way of putting this is that the habitual, everyday self is a source of imprisonment, so that access to other selves (or, as in 'Street

Haunting', to the temporary anonymity of the street) becomes functional, a means of escape and recuperation.

In a piece like 'Evening over Sussex: Reflections in a Motor Car', the disparate reflections of the shifting selves – including a mock-presidential self who takes the others in hand and, at the end, the body, which is a source of 'delicious society' – take on associations with modern speed and progress. Where Woolf habitually compares an urban scene with the prehistoric or feudal landscape that must have preceded it on the same spot, here the move is reversed, as she (or some of her narrator's selves) gaze out on the still, rural Sussex countryside and imagine (in a mock-Wellsian, utopian fantasy) 'the economical, powerful and efficient future when houses will be cleansed by a puff of hot wind' (p. 84). It is as though a modern mobility, of cars or selves, also has effects on the understanding of place and history. The landscape becomes a film passing rapidly outside the car windows, and just as its images change constantly, so each one comes to seem unstable: the modern must have been ancient, the still ancient is about to disappear from view.

Perhaps the most daring and surprising appearance of multiple selves is in 'On Being Ill', in which Woolf proposes – once again with that wayward mixture of the ironic and the serious – that illness, as a rich source of fantasy life, should be elevated alongside 'love and battle and jealousy among the prime themes of literature' (p. 43). Woolf creates a new version of the Wordsworthian child's descent from immortal intimations into the worldly prison-house, suggesting that illness provides the possibility of recovering – a word that acquires a second sense here – those potential selves that the process of maturation has had to push out of the way: 'to live and live till we have lived out those embryo lives which attend about us in early youth until "I" suppressed them' (p. 49). The inconsistency of tense in this suggests the incompatible kinds of time that accompany the two stages indicated here. Youth is like an eternal present, a paradise filled with endless possibilities, but this phase is always over already – 'until "I" suppressed them'. The fantasy for the future thus becomes a replica of the fantasy of what has been lost, conditional upon the abandonment of the 'I' whose tenuous hold is marked by the inverted commas that point it out as questionable. The two equivalent temporal words – 'till' and 'until'

– reflect this exact correspondence between the imagined past and the potential selves that fan backwards and forwards from the unstably fixed present of 'I'.

This mutability and multiplicity of selves is connected, as we have seen, with a conception of the rapid, fragmentary 'dance of modern life', which draws in every facet of personal experience to its new steps. However much she may deplore the absence of solid, permanent values in theory, whenever this dance appears Woolf's essays seem to be carried away by its attractive movements, leaving behind the stable literary orders for the looser possibilities – pleasures and fears and risks – of changing identities, changing sights, changing places. The mobility of the modern dance is made literal in the regular focusing in these essays on scenes of modern transport (the car, the Tube, the aeroplane) and tourism ('To Spain'). And language too is drawn into this drift, as part of the heterogeneous world encapsulated by 'its dresses and its dances and its catchwords'. In 'Craftsmanship', which was written as a radio talk, words are granted value not in themselves, but only in so far as their meaning is not determinate, not useful (the routinely factual or informational should be relegated, she suggests, to some other, less equivocal kind of notation, to avoid words' inherent ambiguity). In illustrating this, it seems perfectly apt that Woolf chooses a notice from the underground, something that ought to be perfectly functional:

> When we travel on the Tube, for example, when we wait on the platform for a train, there, hung up in front of us, on an illuminated signboard, are the words 'Passing Russell Square'. We look at those words; we repeat them; we try to impress that useful fact upon our minds; the next train will pass Russell Square. We say over and over again as we pace, 'Passing Russell Square, passing Russell Square'. And then as we say them, the words shuffle and change, and we find ourselves saying, 'Passing away saith the world, passing away . . .' (pp. 137–8)

With its words flashing on and off and its actual citing of the 'passing' word, this sign looks as though it might have been made (as well as to guide the traveller on the Tube) to illustrate Baudelaire's definition of the modern as 'the transitory, the fleeting, the contingent', completed, as it comes to be in the narrator's associations, by 'the other half . . . the eternal and the immovable' by the biblical connection (see 'Craftsmanship', note 2, p. 210). Here in the underground station, with the latest electronic writing joining some of the oldest words in the world, is a juxtaposition of permanence and the passing moment, itself flashed out or fleshed out literally under the sign of 'passing'. In a thoroughly modern fashion, the would-be functional sign becomes, for a moment, a work of art, read as though unfamiliar and linking itself to past words and traditions. This then could stand – but just for a moment – as the sign of Woolf's ceaseless fascination with the surprising connections and clashes amid the discontinuous movements of modern life.

Rachel Bowlby 1990

The editor would like to thank Bet Inglis and the Sussex University Library for help in obtaining material, and Julia Briggs for her contribution to the notes.

NOTES

1. 'Hours in a Library', *CE*, II, p. 39.
2. For a detailed study of Woolf's relation to Pater, see Perry Meisel, *The Absent Father: Virginia Woolf and Walter Pater* (Yale University Press, 1980)
3. Walter Pater, *Studies in the History of the Renaissance* (1873), Conclusion'.
4. A phrase she uses frequently in 'The Narrow Bridge of Art', *CE*, II, pp. 218–29.
5. 'Life and the Novelist', *CE*, II, p. 131.
6. ibid., pp. 131–2.
7. ibid., p. 132.
8. ibid., pp. 133–4.
9. ibid., p. 136.
10. ibid., p. 135.
11. See the discussion of some of these in the 'Introduction' to *A Woman's Essays*, Penguin Books, 1992.
12. Charles Baudelaire, *The Painter of Modern Life* (1863), ch. 4, 'Modernity'.

13. 'Memories of a Working Women's Guild'; see *A Woman's Essays*, Penguin Books, 1992, p. 144.
14. James Strachey's translations of Freud, which became the Standard Edition, were published by the Hogarth Press, run by Leonard and Virginia Woolf. For a stimulating account of Woolf's relation to psychoanalysis, see Elizabeth Abel, *Virginia Woolf and the Fictions of Psychoanalysis* (University of Chicago Press, 1989), esp. ch. 1.
15. 'Reading', *CE*, II, p. 20. Another version of this passage appears in 'The Elizabethan Lumber Room', *CE*, I, p. 48.
16. The allusion is to Wordsworth's 'Ode: Intimations of Immortality from Recollections of Early Childhood'.
17. Walter Benjamin, 'A Small History of Photography', in *One-Way Street and Other Writings*, trans. Edward Jephcott and Kingsley Shorter (New Left Books, 1979), pp. 240–57.
18. 'Royalty', *CE*, IV, p. 212.
19. See *A Woman's Essays*, Penguin Books, 1992, pp. 154–8.
20. 'Royalty', *CE*, IV, p. 214.
21. ibid., p. 215.
22. The phrase is used frequently in *Picture Post*.
23. For sociology and psychology that use metaphors of acting and role-play, see for example Erving Goffman, *The Presentation of Self in Everyday Life*; Eric Berne, *Games People Play*.

Further Reading

PRIMARY

The Essays of Virginia Woolf, 3 vols (to be 6 vols), ed. Andrew McNeillie (Hogarth Press, 1986).
Collected Essays, 4 vols, ed. Leonard Woolf (Hogarth Press, 1966, 1967).
Moments of Being: Unpublished Autobiographical Writings of Virginia Woolf, ed. Jeanne Schulkind (2nd edn, Hogarth Press, 1985).
The Diary of Virginia Woolf, 5 vols, ed. Anne Olivier Bell (Hogarth Press, 1977; Penguin Books, 1979).
A Passionate Apprentice: The Early Journals, 1897-1909, ed. Mitchell A. Leaska (Hogarth Press, 1990).
The Letters of Virginia Woolf, 6 vols, ed. Nigel Nicolson and Joanne Trautmann (Hogarth Press, 1975-80).
The Complete Shorter Fiction of Virginia Woolf, ed. Susan Dick (2nd edn, Hogarth Press, 1989).
The Pargiters, ed. Mitchell A. Leaska (Hogarth Press, 1977).

SECONDARY

Michèle Barrett, 'Introduction' to Virginia Woolf, *Women and Writing* (Women's Press, 1979).
Gillian Beer, *Arguing With the Past* (Routledge, 1989).
Quentin Bell, *Virginia Woolf: A Biography*, 2 vols (Hogarth Press, 1972).
Edward L. Bishop, 'Metaphor and the Subversive Process of Virginia Woolf's Essays', in *Style*, vol. 21, no. 4, (Winter 1987), pp. 573-89).
Rachel Bowlby, *Virginia Woolf: Feminist Destinations* (Basil Blackwell, 1988).
Rachel Bowlby, 'Walking, Women and Writing: Virginia Woolf as Flâneuse', in *Still Crazy After All These Years* (Routledge, 1992).
George Lukács, 'On the Nature and Form of the Essay: A Letter to

Leo Popper', in *Soul and Form*, trans. Anna Bostock (M.I.T. Press, 1974).

Jane Marcus, *Virginia Woolf and the Languages of Patriarchy* (Indiana University Press, 1987).

Perry Meisel, *The Absent Father: Virginia Woolf and Walter Pater* (Yale University Press, 1980).

Brenda R. Silver, *Virginia Woolf's Reading Notebooks* (Princeton University Press, 1983).

Elizabeth Steele, *Virginia Woolf's Literary Sources and Allusions: A Guide to the Essays* (Garland, 1983).

Alex Zwerdling, *Virginia Woolf and the Real World* (University of California Press, 1986).

A Note on the Texts

The text of each essay reproduced here is that of first publication except where essays were reprinted in *The Common Reader* or *The Common Reader: Second Series*; in these cases the revised texts have been preferred. The provenance of individual items is indicated at the start of each essay. Three essays are reprinted from Hogarth Press pamphlets ('On Being Ill', 'Foreword to *Recent Paintings by Vanessa Bell*' and 'Reviewing'), and five further essays that were first published posthumously in England in *The Death of the Moth* (Hogarth Press, 1942) are reproduced from there. For more detailed publication histories readers are referred to Andrew McNeillie's authoritative six-volume edition of *The Essays of Virginia Woolf* (Hogarth Press), published from 1986 onwards; this supersedes the *Collected Essays* edited in four volumes by Leonard Woolf (Hogarth Press, 1966, 1967), since these are incomplete and the provision of dates and other details is erratic and sometimes inaccurate.

This collection of essays is intended as a companion to the earlier volume, *A Woman's Essays*, published by Penguin Books in 1992. The two books, together with their introductions, are meant to be taken as a pair, though this volume focuses particularly on Woolf's cultural and political writings. In addition to some of her best-known and most influential writings, this volume makes available some less familiar texts.

THE CROWDED DANCE
OF MODERN LIFE

The War from the Street

A review of D. Bridgman Metchim's *Our Own History of the War: From a South London View* (Arthur G. Stockwell, 1918), first published in *The Times Literary Supplement*, 9 January 1919.

Mr Metchim has discovered the very important truth that the history of the war is not and never will be written from our point of view. The suspicion that this applies to wars in the past also has been much increased by living through four years almost entirely composed of what journalists call 'historic days.' No one who has taken stock of his own impressions since August 4, 1914,[1] can possibly believe that history as it is written closely resembles history as it is lived; but as we are for the most part quiescent, and, if sceptical ourselves, content to believe that the rest of mankind believes, we have no right to complain if we are fobbed off once more with historians' histories. Less sluggish or less cynical, Mr Metchim here records the history of the war as it appeared to a gentleman living in South London so far as the body is concerned, but populating the whole of England spiritually, constituting, in fact, that anonymous monster the Man in the Street. He is not an individual himself, nor is the anonymous 'you' who merges into the gentleman in South London an individual; both together compose a vast, featureless, almost shapeless jelly of human stuff taking the reflection of the things[2] that individuals do, and occasionally wobbling this way or that as some instinct of hate, revenge, or admiration bubbles up beneath it.

They, the individuals, the generals, the statesmen, the people with names, proclaim war.

> How and why, date, &c., will be found in any reliable history ... You felt frightfully strawlike about that time ... You bolted each edition of your paper red-hot as it came out ... You saw [the Russians] yourself pass through London ... You read several versions of The Truth about Neuve Chapelle, and Real Facts

about Neuve Chapelle, and heard many personal tales against people in high positions, and you cursed the Government.

So it goes on. The individuals do the thing, and you in a muddled way reflect what they do in blurred pictures half obliterating each other; little particles of you get somehow broken off and turned into soldiers and sent to France, to reflect rather different things out there, while you, in your vast quivering bulk, remain at home. Soon your mind, if one may distinguish one part of the jelly from another, has had certain inscriptions scored upon it so repeatedly that it believes that it has originated them; and you begin to have violent opinions of your own, which are reinforced by those varieties of you, Jones, Livermore and Algernon Shaw, so that there is a very marked sameness of opinion throughout the jelly. There is a little latitude allowed upon certain points, as, for example, 'the curious incident of the Angels of Mons ... Jones said that probably wreaths of smoke had been mistaken for Angels; Shaw said that the British soldier was not a fanciful man, and would be far more likely to mistake Angels for wreaths of smoke. You were prepared to open your mind on the matter.' But to have opinions is not your business; for four years and more you are nothing but a vast receptacle for the rumours of other people's opinions and deeds. There has been a great naval battle in the North Sea; they have won; we have won – so at least a friend of somebody's cook says. Your conviction that nothing is ever going to touch you is profound; it is obviously not in the nature of things that you should be touched. But the quality that distinguishes you from your French or Italian counterpart is your humour; all your feelings come out wearing the same livery. The humour of death is much the same as the humour of the allotment garden. But by this time we are analysing you with admiration, and therefore you are not us; and therefore the history is, as it is always fated to be, your history, not ours.

Modern Fiction

A slightly revised version, taken from *The Common Reader*, of
an essay first published as 'Modern Novels' in *The Times Literary
Supplement*, 10 April 1919.

In making any survey, even the freest and loosest, of modern fiction, it is difficult not to take it for granted that the modern practice of the art is somehow an improvement upon the old.[1] With their simple tools and primitive materials, it might be said, Fielding did well and Jane Austen even better, but compare their opportunities with ours! Their masterpieces certainly have a strange air of simplicity. And yet the analogy between literature and the process, to choose an example, of making motor cars[2] scarcely holds good beyond the first glance. It is doubtful whether in the course of the centuries, though we have learnt much about making machines, we have learnt anything about making literature. We do not come to write better; all that we can be said to do is to keep moving, now a little in this direction, now in that, but with a circular tendency should the whole course of the track be viewed from a sufficiently lofty pinnacle. It need scarcely be said that we make no claim to stand, even momentarily, upon that vantage ground. On the flat, in the crowd, half blind with dust, we look back with envy to those happier warriors, whose battle is won and whose achievements wear so serene an air of accomplishment that we can scarcely refrain from whispering that the fight was not so fierce for them as for us. It is for the historian of literature to decide; for him to say if we are now beginning or ending or standing in the middle of a great period of prose fiction, for down in the plain little is visible. We only know that certain gratitudes and hostilities inspire us; that certain paths seem to lead to fertile land, others to the dust and the desert; and of this perhaps it may be worth while to attempt some account.

Our quarrel, then, is not with the classics, and if we speak of quarrelling with Mr Wells, Mr Bennett, and Mr Galsworthy,[3] it is partly that by the mere fact of their existence in the flesh their work has a living, breathing, everyday imperfection which bids us take what liberties with it we choose. But it is also true that, while we thank them for a thousand gifts, we reserve our unconditional gratitude for Mr Hardy, for Mr Conrad, and in a much lesser degree for the Mr Hudson of *The Purple Land*, *Green Mansions*, and *Far Away and Long Ago*.[4] Mr Wells, Mr Bennett, and Mr Galsworthy have excited so many hopes and disappointed them so persistently that our gratitude largely takes the form of thanking them for having shown us what they might have done but have not done; what we certainly could not do, but as certainly, perhaps, do not wish to do. No single phrase will sum up the charge or grievance which we have to bring against a mass of work so large in its volume and embodying so many qualities, both admirable and the reverse. If we tried to formulate our meaning in one word we should say that these three writers are materialists. It is because they are concerned not with the spirit but with the body that they have disappointed us, and left us with the feeling that the sooner English fiction turns its back upon them, as politely as may be, and marches, if only into the desert, the better for its soul. Naturally, no single word reaches the centre of three separate targets. In the case of Mr Wells it falls notably wide of the mark. And yet even with him it indicates to our thinking the fatal alloy in his genius, the great clod of clay that has got itself mixed up with the purity of his inspiration. But Mr Bennett is perhaps the worst culprit of the three, inasmuch as he is by far the best workman. He can make a book so well constructed and solid in its craftsmanship that it is difficult for the most exacting of critics to see through what chink or crevice decay can creep in. There is not so much as a draught between the frames of the windows, or a crack in the boards. And yet – if life should refuse to live there? That is a risk which the creator of *The Old Wives' Tale*, George Cannon, Edwin Clayhanger,[5] and hosts of other figures, may well claim to have surmounted. His characters live abundantly, even unexpectedly, but it remains to ask how do they live, and what do they live for? More and more they seem to us, deserting even the well-built villa in the Five Towns, to spend their time in some softly padded first-class railway carriage, pressing bells and buttons innumerable; and the destiny to which they travel so luxuriously becomes more and more unquestionably an eternity of bliss spent in the very best hotel in Brighton. It can scarcely be said of Mr Wells that he is a materialist in the sense that he takes too much delight in the solidity of his fabric. His mind is too generous in its sympathies to allow him to spend much time in making things shipshape and substantial. He is a materialist from sheer goodness of heart, taking upon his shoulders the work that ought to have been discharged by government officials, and in the plethora of his ideas and facts scarcely having leisure to realize, or forgetting to think important, the crudity and coarseness of his human beings. Yet what more damaging criticism can there be both of his earth and of his Heaven than that they are to be inhabited here and hereafter by his Joans and his Peters?[6] Does not the inferiority of their natures tarnish whatever institutions and ideals may be provided for them by the generosity of their creator? Nor, profoundly though we respect the integrity and humanity of Mr Galsworthy, shall we find what we seek in his pages.

If we fasten, then, one label on all these books, on which is one word materialists, we mean by it that they write of unimportant things; that they spend immense skill and immense industry making the trivial and the transitory appear the true and the enduring.

We have to admit that we are exacting, and, further, that we find it difficult to justify our discontent by explaining what it is that we exact. We frame our question differently at different times. But it reappears most persistently as we drop the finished novel on the crest of a sigh – Is it worth while? What is the point of it all? Can it be that, owing to one of those little deviations which the human spirit seems to make from time to time, Mr Bennett has come down with his magnificent apparatus for catching life just an inch or two on the wrong side? Life escapes; and perhaps without life nothing else is worth while. It is a confession of vagueness to have to make use of such a figure as this, but we scarcely better the matter by speaking, as critics are prone to do, of reality. Admitting the vagueness which afflicts all criticism of novels, let us hazard the opinion that for us at this moment the form of fiction most in vogue more often misses than secures the thing we seek. Whether we call it life or spirit, truth or reality, this, the essential thing, has moved off, or on, and refuses to be contained any longer in such ill-fitting vestments as we provide. Nevertheless, we go on perseveringly conscientiously, constructing our two and thirty chapters after a design which more and more ceases to resemble the vision in our minds. So much of the enormous labour of proving the solidity, the likeness to life, of the story is not merely labour thrown away but labour misplaced to the extent of obscuring and blotting out the light of the conception. The writer seems constrained, not by his own free will but by some powerful and unscrupulous tyrant who has him in thrall, to provide a plot, to provide comedy, tragedy, love interest, and an air of probability embalming the whole so impeccable that if all his figures were to come to life they would find themselves dressed down to the last button of their coats in the fashion of the hour. The tyrant is obeyed; the novel is done to a turn. But sometimes, more and more often as time goes by, we suspect a momentary doubt, a spasm of rebellion, as the pages fill themselves in the customary way. Is life like this? Must novels be like this?

Look within and life, it seems, is very far from being 'like this'. Examine for a moment an ordinary mind on an ordinary day. The mind receives a myriad impressions – trivial, fantastic, evanescent, or engraved with the sharpness of steel. From all sides they come, an incessant shower of innumerable atoms; and as they fall, as they shape themselves into the life of Monday or Tuesday,[7] the accent falls differently from of old; the moment of importance came not here but there; so that, if a writer were a free man and not a slave, if he could write what he chose, not what he must, if he could base his work upon his own feeling and not upon convention, there would be no plot, no comedy, no tragedy, no love interest or catastrophe in the accepted style, and perhaps not a single button sewn on as the Bond Street tailors would have it. Life is not a series of gig lamps[8] symmetrically arranged; life is a luminous halo, a semi-transparent envelope surrounding us from the beginning of consciousness to the end. Is it not the task of the novelist to convey this varying, this unknown and uncircumscribed spirit, whatever aberration or complexity it may display, with as little mixture of the alien and external as possible? We are not pleading merely for courage and sincerity; we are suggesting that the proper stuff of fiction is a little other than custom would have us believe it.

It is, at any rate, in some such fashion as this that we seek to define the quality which distinguishes the work of several young writers, among whom Mr James Joyce is the most notable, from that of their predecessors. They attempt to come closer to life, and to preserve more sincerely and exactly what interests and moves them, even if to do so they must discard most of the conventions which are commonly observed by the novelist. Let us record the atoms as they fall upon the mind in the order in which they fall, let us trace the pattern, however disconnected and incoherent in appearance, which each sight or incident scores upon the consciousness. Let us not take it for granted that life exists more fully in what is commonly thought big than in what is commonly thought small. Any one who has read *The Portrait of the Artist as a Young Man* or, what promises to be a far more interesting work, *Ulysses*, now appearing in the *Little Review*,[9] will have hazarded some theory of this nature as to Mr Joyce's intention. On our part, with such a fragment before us, it is hazarded rather than affirmed; but whatever the intention of the whole, there can be no question but that it is of the utmost sincerity and that the result, difficult or unpleasant as we may judge it, is undeniably important. In contrast with those whom we have called materialists, Mr Joyce is spiritual; he is concerned at all costs to reveal the flickerings of that innermost flame which flashes its messages through the brain, and in order to preserve it he disregards with complete courage whatever seems to him adventitious, whether it be probability, or coherence, or any other of these signposts which for generations have served to support the imagination of a reader when called upon to imagine what he can neither touch nor see. The scene in the cemetery, for instance, with its brilliancy, its sordidity, its incoherence, its sudden lightning flashes of significance, does undoubtedly come so close to the quick of the mind that, on a first reading at any rate, it is difficult not to acclaim a masterpiece. If we want life itself, here surely we have it. Indeed, we find ourselves fumbling rather awkwardly if we try to say what else we wish, and for what reason a work of such originality yet fails to compare, for we must take high examples, with *Youth* or *The Mayor of Casterbridge*.[10] It fails because of the comparative poverty of the writer's mind, we might say simply and have done with it. But it is possible to press a little further and wonder whether we may not refer our sense of being in a bright yet narrow room, confined and shut in, rather than enlarged and set free, to some limitation imposed by the method as well as by the mind. Is it the method that inhibits the creative power? Is it due to the method that we feel neither jovial nor magnanimous, but centred in a self which, in spite of its tremor of susceptibility, never embraces or creates what is outside itself and beyond? Does the emphasis laid, perhaps didactically, upon indecency, contribute to the effect of something angular and isolated? Or is it merely that in any effort of such originality it is much easier, for contemporaries especially, to feel what it lacks than to name what it gives? In any case it is a mistake to stand outside examining 'methods'. Any method is right, every method is right, that expresses what we wish to express, if we are writers; that brings us closer to the novelist's intention if we are readers. This method has the merit of bringing us closer to what we were prepared to call life itself; did not the reading of *Ulysses* suggest how much of life is excluded or ignored, and did it not come with a shock to open *Tristram Shandy* or even *Pendennis*[11] and be by them convinced that there are not only other aspects of life, but more important ones into the bargain.

However this may be, the problem before the novelist at present, as we suppose it to have been in the past, is to contrive means of being free to set down what he chooses. He has to have the courage to say that what interests him is no longer 'this' but 'that': out of 'that', alone must he construct his work. For the moderns 'that', the point of interest, lies very likely in the dark places of psychology. At once, therefore, the accent falls a little differently; the emphasis is upon something hitherto ignored; at once a different outline of form becomes necessary, difficult for us to grasp, incomprehensible to our predecessors. No one but a modern, no one perhaps but a Russian, would have felt the interest of the situation which Tchekov has made into the short story which he calls 'Gusev'.[12] Some Russian soldiers lie ill on board a ship which is taking them back to Russia. We are given a few scraps of their talk and some of their thoughts; then one of them dies and is carried away; the talk goes on among the others for a time, until Gusev himself dies, and looking 'like a carrot or a radish' is thrown overboard. The emphasis is laid upon such unexpected places that at first it seems as if there were no emphasis at all; and then, as the eyes accustom themselves to twilight and discern the shapes of things in a room we see how complete the story is, how profound, and how truly in obedience to his vision Tchekov has chosen this, that, and the other, and placed them together to compose something new. But it is impossible to say 'this is comic', or 'that is tragic', nor are we certain, since short stories, we have been taught, should be brief and conclusive, whether this, which is vague and inconclusive, should be called a short story at all.

The most elementary remarks upon modern English fiction can hardly avoid some mention of the Russian influence, and if the Russians are mentioned one runs the risk of feeling that to write of any fiction save theirs is waste of time. If we want understanding of the soul and heart where else shall we find it of comparable profundity? If we are sick of our own materialism the least considerable of their novelists has by right of birth a natural reverence for the human spirit. 'Learn to make yourself akin to people . . . But let this sympathy be not with the mind – for it is easy with the mind – but with the heart, with love towards them.'[13] In every great Russian writer we seem to discern the features of a saint, if sympathy for the sufferings of others, love towards them, endeavour to reach some goal worthy of the most exacting demands of the spirit constitute saintliness. It is the saint in them which confounds us with a feeling of our own irreligious triviality, and turns so many of our famous novels to tinsel and trickery. The conclusions of the Russian mind, thus comprehensive and compassionate, are inevitably, perhaps, of the utmost sadness. More accurately indeed we might speak of the inconclusiveness of the Russian mind. It is the sense that there is no answer, that if honestly examined life presents question after question which must be left to sound on and on after the story is over in hopeless interrogation that fills us with a deep, and finally it may be with a resentful, despair. They are right perhaps; unquestionably they see further than we do and without our gross impediments of vision. But perhaps we see something that escapes them, or why should this voice of protest mix itself with our gloom? The voice of protest is the voice of another and an ancient civilization which seems to have bred in us the instinct to enjoy and fight rather than to suffer and understand. English fiction from Sterne to Meredith[14] bears witness to our natural delight in humour and comedy, in the beauty of earth, in the activities of the intellect, and in the splendour of the body. But any deductions that we may draw from the comparison of two fictions so immeasurably far apart are futile save indeed as they flood us with a view of the infinite possibilities of the art and remind us that there is no limit to the horizon, and that nothing – no 'method', no experiment, even of the wildest – is forbidden, but only falsity and pretence. 'The proper stuff of fiction' does not exist; everything is the proper stuff of fiction, every feeling, every thought; every quality of brain and spirit is drawn upon; no perception comes amiss. And if we can imagine the art of fiction come alive and standing in our midst, she would undoubtedly bid us break her and bully her, as well as honour and love her, for so her youth is renewed and her sovereignty assured.

The Royal Academy

First published in the *Athenaeum*, 22 August 1919.

'The motor cars of Empire – the bodyguard of Europe – the stainless knight of Belgium'[1] – such is our English romance that nine out of ten of those passing from the indiscriminate variety of Piccadilly to the courtyard of Burlington House do homage to the embattled tyres and the kingly presence of Albert on his high-minded charger with some nonsense of this sort. They are, of course, only the motor cars of the rich grouped round a statue; but whether the quadrangle in which they stand radiates back the significance of everything fourfold, so that King Albert and the motor cars exude the essence of kingliness and the soul of vehicular traffic, or whether the crowd is the cause of it, or the ceremonious steps leading up, the swing-doors admitting and the flunkeys fawning, it is true that, once you are within the precincts, everything appears symbolic, and the state of mind in which you ascend the broad stairs to the picture galleries is both heated and romantic.

Whatever visions we may have indulged, we find ourselves on entering confronted by a lady in full evening dress. She stands at the top of a staircase, one hand loosely closed round a sheaf of lilies, while the other is about to greet someone of distinction who advances towards her up the stairs. Not a hair is out of place. Her lips are just parted. She is about to say, 'How nice of you to come!' But such is the skill of the artist that one does not willingly cross the range of her cordial and yet condescending eye. One prefers to look at her obliquely. She said, 'How nice of you to come!' so often and so graciously while I stood there that at last my eye wandered off in search of people of sufficient distinction for her to say it to. There was no difficulty in finding them. Here was a nobleman in a kilt, the Duke of R——; here a young officer in khaki, and, to keep him company, the head and shoulders of a young girl, whose upturned eyes and pouting lips appear to be entreating the sky to be bluer, roses to be redder, ices to be sweeter, and men to be manlier for her sake. To do her justice, the gallant youth seemed to respond. As they stepped up the staircase to the lady in foaming white he vowed that come what might – the flag of England – sweet chimes of home – a woman's honour – an Englishman's word – only a scrap of paper – for your sake, Alice – God save the King – and all the rest of it. The range of her vocabulary was more limited. She kept her gaze upon the sky or the ice or whatever it might be with a simple sincerity which was enforced by a single row of pearls and a little drapery of white tulle about the shoulders.

'How nice of you to come!' said the hostess once more. But immediately behind them stumped the Duke, a bluff nobleman, 'more at home on the brae-side than among these kickshaws and knick-knacks, my lady. Splendid sport. Twenty antlers and a Buck Royal.[2] Clean between the eyes, eh what? Out all day. Never know when I'm done. Cold bath, hard bed, glass of whisky. A mere nothing. Damned foreigners. Post of duty. The Guard dies, but never surrenders. The ladies of our family – Up, Guards, and at them! Gentlemen –' and, as he utters the last words in a voice choked with emotion, the entire company swing round upon their heels, displaying only a hind view of their perfectly fitting mess-jackets, since there are some sights that it is not good for a man to look upon.[3]

The scene, though not all the phrases, come from a story by Rudyard Kipling.[4] But scenes from Rudyard Kipling must take place with astonishing frequency at these parties in order that the English maidens and gallant officers may have occasion to insist upon their chastity on the one hand and protect it on the other, without which, so far as one can see, there would be no reason for their existence. Therefore it was natural to look about me, a little shyly, for the sinister person of the seducer. There is, I can truthfully say, no such cur in the whole of the Royal Academy; and it was only when I had gone through the rooms twice and was about to inform the maiden that her apprehensions, though highly creditable, were in no way necessary that my eye was caught by the white underside of an excessively fine fish. 'The Duke caught that!' I exclaimed, being still within the radius of the ducal glory. But I was wrong. Though fine enough, the fish, as a second glace put it beyond a doubt, was not ducal; its triangular shape, let alone the fact that a small urchin in corduroys held it suspended by the tail, was enough to start me in the right direction. Ah, yes – the harvest of the sea, toilers of the deep, a fisherman's home, nature's bounty – such phrases formed themselves with alarming rapidity – but to descend to details. The picture, no. 306,[5] represents a young woman holding a baby on her knee. The child is playing with the rough model of a ship; the large fish is being dangled before his eyes by a brother a year or two older in a pair of corduroys which have been cut down from those worn by the fisherman engaged in cleaning cod on the edge of the waves. Judging from the superb rosiness, fatness, and blueness of every object depicted, even the sea itself wearing the look of a prize animal tricked out for a fair, it seemed certain that the artist intended a compliment in a general way to the island race. But something in the woman's eye arrested me. A veil of white dimmed the straightforward lustre. It is thus that painters represent the tears that do not fall. But what, we asked, had this great hulk of a matron surrounded by fish, any one of which was worth eighteenpence the pound, to cry for? Look at the little boy's breeches. They are not, if you look closely, of the same pattern as the fisherman's. Once that fact is grasped, the story reels itself out like a line with a salmon on the end of it. Don't the waves break with a sound of mockery on the beach? Don't her eyes cloud with memories at the sight of a toy boat? It is not always summer. The sea has another voice than this; and, since her husband will never want his breeches any more – but the story when written out is painful, and rather obvious into the bargain.

The point of a good Academy picture is that you can search the canvas for ten minutes or so and still be doubtful whether you have extracted the whole meaning. There is, for example, no. 248, *Cocaine*. A young man in evening dress lies, drugged, with his head upon the pink satin of a woman's knee. The ornamental clock assures us that it is exactly eleven minutes to five. The burning lamp proves that it is dawn. He, then, has come home to find her waiting? She has interrupted his debauch? For my part, I prefer to imagine what in painters' language (a tongue well worth separate study) would be called 'a dreary vigil.' There she has sat since eight-thirty, alone, in pink satin. Once she rose and pressed the photograph in the silver frame to her lips. She might have married that man (unless it is her father, of which one cannot be sure). She was a thoughtless girl, and he left her to meet his death on the field of battle. Through her tears she gazes at the next photograph – presumably that of a baby (again the painter has been content with a suggestion). As she looks a hand fumbles at the door. 'Thank God!' she cries as her husband staggers in and falls helpless across her knees, 'thank God our Teddy died!' So there she sits, staring disillusionment in the eyes, and whether she gives way to temptation, or breathes a vow to the photographs, or gets him to bed before the maid comes down, or sits there for ever, must be left to the imagination of the onlooker.

But the queer thing is that one wants to be her. For a moment one pretends that one sits alone, disillusioned, in pink satin. And then people in the little group of gazers begin to boast that they have known sadder cases themselves. Friends of theirs took cocaine. 'I myself as a boy for a joke –' 'No, George – but how fearfully rash!' Everyone wished to cap that story with a better, save for one lady who, from her expression, was acting the part of consoler, had got the poor thing to bed, undressed her, soothed her, and even spoken with considerable sharpness to that unworthy brute, unfit to be a husband, before she moved on in a pleasant glow of self-satisfaction. Every picture before which one of these little groups had gathered seemed to radiate the strange power to make the beholder more heroic and more romantic; memories of childhood, visions of possibilities, illusions of all kinds poured down upon us from the walls. In a cooler mood one might accuse the painters of some exaggeration. There must be well over ten thousand delphiniums in the Royal Academy, and not one is other than a perfect specimen. The condition of the turf is beyond praise. The sun is exquisitely adapted to the needs of the sundials. The yew hedges are irreproachable; the manor house a miracle of timeworn dignity; and as for the old man with a scythe, the girl at the well, the village donkey, the widow lady, the gipsies' caravan, the boy with a rod, each is not only the saddest, sweetest, quaintest, most picturesque, tenderest, jolliest of its kind, but has a symbolical meaning much to the credit of England. The geese are English geese, and even the polar bears, though they have not that advantage, seem, such is the persuasion of the atmosphere, to be turning to carriage rugs as we look at them.

It is indeed a very powerful atmosphere; so charged with manliness and womanliness, pathos and purity, sunsets and Union Jacks, that the shabbiest and most suburban catch a reflection of the rosy glow. 'This is England! these are the English!' one might exclaim if a foreigner were at hand. But one need not say that to one's compatriots. They are, perhaps, not quite up to the level of the pictures. Some are meagre; others obese; many have put on what is too obviously the only complete outfit that they possess. But the legend on the catalogue explains any such discrepancy in a convincing manner. 'To give unto them beauty for ashes. Isaiah lxi. 3' – that is the office of this exhibition. Our ashes will be transformed if only we expose them openly enough to the benignant influence of the canvas. So we look again at the Lord Chancellor and Mr Balfour,[6] at the Lady B., at the Duke of R., at Mr Ennever of the Pelman Institute, at officers of all descriptions, architects, surgeons, peers, dentists, doctors, lawyers, archbishops, roses, sundials, battlefields, fish and Skye terriers. From wall to wall, glowing with colour, glistening with oil, framed in gilt, and protected by glass, they ogle and elevate, inspire and command. But they overdo it. One is not altogether such a bundle of ashes as they suppose, or sometimes the magic fails to work. A large picture by Mr Sargent called *Gassed*[7] at last pricked some nerve of protest, or perhaps of humanity. In order to emphasize his point that the soldiers wearing bandages round their eyes cannot see, and therefore claim our compassion, he makes one of them raise his leg to the level of his elbow in order to mount a step an inch or two above the ground. This little piece of over-emphasis was the final scratch of the surgeon's knife which is said to hurt more than the whole operation. After all, one had been jabbed and stabbed, slashed and sliced for close on two hours. The lady began it, the Duke continued it; little children had wrung tears; great men extorted veneration. From first to last each canvas had rubbed in some emotion, and what the paint failed to say the catalogue had enforced in words. But Mr Sargent was the last straw. Suddenly the great rooms rang like a parrot-house with the intolerable vociferations of gaudy and brainless birds. How they shrieked and gibbered! How they danced and sidled! Honour, patriotism, chastity, wealth, success, importance, position, patronage, power – their cries rang and echoed from all quarters. 'Anywhere, anywhere, out of this world!' was the only exclamation with which one could stave off the brazen din as one fled downstairs, out of doors, round the motor cars, beneath the disdain of the horse and its rider, and so out into the comparative sobriety of Piccadilly. No doubt the reaction was excessive; and I must leave it to Mr Roger Fry[8] to decide whether the emotions here recorded are the proper result of one thousand six hundred and seventy-four works of art.

Gothic Romance

A review of Edith Birkhead's The Tale of Terror: A Study of the Gothic Romance *(Constable, 1921), first published in* The Times Literary Supplement, *5 May 1921.*

It says much for Miss Birkhead's natural good sense that she has been able to keep her head where many people would have lost theirs. She has read a great many books without being suffocated. She has analysed a great many plots without being nauseated. Her sense of literature has not been extinguished by the waste-paper baskets[1] full of old novels so courageously heaped on top of it. For her 'attempt to trace in outline the origin of the Gothic romance and the tale of terror' has necessarily led her to grope in basements and attics where the light is dim and the dust is thick. To trace the course of one strand in the thick skein of our literature is well worth doing. But perhaps Miss Birkhead would have increased the interest of her work if she had enlarged her scope to include some critical discussion of the aesthetic value of shock and terror,[2] and had ventured some analysis of the taste which demands this particular stimulus.[3] But her narrative is quite readable enough to supply the student with material for pushing the inquiry a little further.

Since it is held that Gothic romance was introduced by Horace Walpole's *Castle of Otranto*, in the year 1764, there is no need to confound it with the romance of Spenser or of Shakespeare. It is a parasite, an artificial commodity, produced half in joke in reaction against the current style, or in relief from it. If we run over the names of the most famous of the Gothic romancers – Clara Reeve, Mrs Radcliffe, Monk Lewis, Charles Maturin, Sarah Wilkinson[4] – we shall smile at the absurdity of the visions which they conjure up. We shall, perhaps, congratulate ourselves upon our improvement. Yet since our ancestors bought two thousand copies of Mrs Bennett's *Beggar Girl and her Benefactors*, on the day of publication,[5] at a cost of thirty-six shillings for the seven volumes, there must have been something in the trash that was appetizing, or something in the appetites that was coarse. It is only polite to give our ancestors the benefit of the doubt. Let us try to put ourselves in their places. The books that formed part of the ordinary library in the year 1764 were, presumably, Johnson's *Vanity of Human Wishes*, Gray's Poems, Richardson's *Clarissa*, Addison's *Cato*, Pope's *Essay on Man*.[6] No one could wish for a more distinguished company. At the same time, as literary critics are too little aware, a love of literature is often roused and for the first years nourished not by the good books but by the bad. It will be an ill day when all the reading is done in libraries and none of it in Tubes. In the eighteenth century there must have been a very large public which found no delight in the peculiar literary merits of the age; and if we reflect how long the days were and how empty of distraction, we need not be surprised to find a school of writers grown up in flat defiance of the prevailing masters. Horace Walpole, Clara Reeve, and Mrs Radcliffe [7] all turned their backs upon their time and plunged into the delightful obscurity of the Middle Ages, which were so much richer than the eighteenth century in castles, barons, moats, and murders.

What Horace Walpole began half in fun was continued seriously and with considerable power by Mrs Radcliffe. That she had a conscience in the matter is evident from the pains she is at to explain her mysteries when they have done their work. The human body 'decayed and disfigured by worms, which were visible in the features and hands,' turns out to be a waxen image credibly placed there in fulfilment of a vow. But there is little wonder that a novelist perpetually on the stretch first to invent mysteries and then to explain them had no leisure for the refinements of the art. 'Mrs Radcliffe's heroines,' says Miss Birkhead, 'resemble nothing more than a composite photograph in which all distinctive traits are merged into an expressionless type.' The same fault can be found with most books of sensation and adventure, and is, after all, inherent in the subject: for it is unlikely that a lady confronted by a male body stark naked, wreathed in worms, where she had looked, maybe, for a pleasant landscape in oils, should do more than give a loud cry and drop senseless. And women who give loud cries and drop senseless do it in much the same way. That is one of the reasons why it is extremely difficult to write a tale of terror which continues to shock and does not first become insipid and later ridiculous. Even Miss Wilkinson, who wrote that 'Adeline Barnett was fair as a lily, tall as the pine, her fine dark eyes sparkling as diamonds, and she moved with the majestic air of a goddess,' had to ridicule her own favourite style before she had done. Scott, Jane Austen, and Peacock[8] stooped from their heights to laugh at the absurdity of the convention and drove it, at any rate, to take refuge underground. For it flourished subterraneously all through the nineteenth century, and for sixpence you can buy today at the bookstall the recognizable descendant of the *Mysteries of Udolpho*. Nor is Adeline Barnett by any means defunct. She is probably an earl's daughter at the present moment; vicious, painted; in society. But if you call her Miss Wilkinson's Adeline she will have to answer none the less.

It would be a fine exercise in discrimination to decide the precise point at which romance becomes Gothic and imagination moonshine. Coleridge's lines in 'Kubla Khan' about the woman wailing for her demon lover are a perfect example of the successful use of emotion.[9] The difficulty, as Miss Birkhead shows, is to know where to stop. Humour is comparatively easy to control; psychology is too toilsome to be frequently overdone; but a gift for romance easily escapes control and cruelly plunges its possessor into disrepute. Maturin and Monk Lewis heaped up horrors until Mrs Radcliffe herself appeared calm and composed. And they have paid the penalty. The skull-headed lady, the vampire gentleman, the whole troop of monks and monsters who once froze and terrified now gibber in some dark cupboard of the servants' hall. In our day we flatter ourselves the effect is produced by subtler means. It is at the ghosts within us that we shudder, and not at the decaying bodies of barons or the subterranean activities of ghouls. Yet the desire to widen our boundaries, to feel excitement without danger, and to escape as far as possible from the facts of life drive us perpetually to trifle with the risky ingredients of the mysterious and the unknown. Science, as Miss Birkhead suggests, will modify the Gothic romance of the future with the aeroplane and the telephone. Already the bolder of our novelists have made use of psychoanalysis to startle and dismay. And already – such perils attend the use of the abnormal in fiction – the younger generation has been heard to complain that the horror of the *Turn of the Screw*[10] is altogether too tame and conventional to lift a hair of their heads. But can we possibly say that Henry James was a Goth?

How it Strikes a Contemporary[1]

A revised version, published in *The Common Reader*, of an essay that first appeared in *The Times Literary Supplement*, 5 April 1923.

In the first place a contemporary can scarcely fail to be struck by the fact that two critics at the same table at the same moment will pronounce completely different opinions about the same book. Here, on the right, it is declared a masterpiece of English prose; on the left, simultaneously, a mere mass of waste-paper which, if the fire could survive it, should be thrown upon the flames. Yet both critics are in agreement about Milton and about Keats. They display an exquisite sensibility and have undoubtedly a genuine enthusiasm. It is only when they discuss the work of contemporary writers that they inevitably come to blows. The book in question, which is at once a lasting contribution to English literature and a mere farrago of pretentious mediocrity, was published about two months ago. That is the explanation; that is why they differ.

The explanation is a strange one. It is equally disconcerting to the reader who wishes to take his bearings in the chaos of contemporary literature and to the writer who has a natural desire to know whether his own work, produced with infinite pains and in almost utter darkness, is likely to burn for ever among the fixed luminaries of English letters or, on the contrary, to put out the fire. But if we identify ourselves with the reader and explore his dilemma first, our bewilderment is short-lived enough. The same thing has happened so often before. We have heard the doctors disagreeing about the new and agreeing about the old twice a year on the average, in spring and autumn, ever since Robert Elsmere, or was it Stephen Phillips,[2] somehow pervaded the atmosphere, and there was the same disagreement among grown-up people about these books too. It would be much more marvellous, and indeed much more upsetting, if, for a wonder, both gentlemen agreed, pronounced Blank's book an undoubted masterpiece, and thus faced us with the necessity of deciding whether we should back their judgement to the extent of ten and sixpence.³ Both are critics of reputation; the opinions tumbled out so spontaneously here will be starched and stiffened into columns of sober prose which will uphold the dignity of letters in England and America.

It must be some innate cynicism, then, some ungenerous distrust of contemporary genius, which determines us automatically as the talk goes on that, were they to agree – which they show no signs of doing – half a guinea is altogether too large a sum to squander upon contemporary enthusiasms, and the case will be met quite adequately by a card to the library. Still the question remains, and let us put it boldly to the critics themselves. Is there no guidance nowadays for a reader who yields to none in reverence for the dead, but is tormented by the suspicion that reverence for the dead is vitally connected with understanding of the living? After a rapid survey both critics are agreed that there is unfortunately no such person. For what is their own judgement worth where new books are concerned? Certainly not ten and sixpence. And from the stores of their experience they proceed to bring forth terrible examples of past blunders; crimes of criticism which, if they had been committed against the dead and not against the living, would have lost them their jobs and imperilled their reputations. The only advice they can offer is to respect one's own instincts, to follow them fearlessly and, rather than submit them to the control of any critic or reviewer alive, to check them by reading and reading again the masterpieces of the past.

Thanking them humbly, we cannot help reflecting that it was not always so. Once upon a time, we must believe, there was a rule, a discipline, which controlled the great republic of readers in a way which is now unknown. That is not to say that the great critic – the Dryden, the Johnson, the Coleridge, the Arnold[4] – was an impeccable judge of contemporary work, whose verdicts stamped the book indelibly and saved the reader the trouble of reckoning the value for himself. The mistakes of these great men about their own contemporaries are too notorious to be worth recording. But the mere fact of their existence had a centralizing influence. That alone, it is not fantastic to suppose, would have controlled the disagreements of the dinner-table and given to random chatter about some book just out an authority now entirely to seek. The diverse schools would have debated as hotly as ever, but at the back of every reader's mind would have been the consciousness that there was at least one man who kept the main principles of literature closely in view: who, if you had taken to him some eccentricity of the moment, would have brought it into touch with permanence and tethered it by his own authority in the contrary blasts of praise and blame.*5 But when it comes to the making of a critic, nature must be generous and society ripe. The scattered dinner-tables of the modern world, the chase and eddy of the various currents which compose the society of our time, could only be dominated by a giant of fabulous dimensions. And where is even the very tall man whom we have the right to expect? Reviewers we have but no critic;[6] a million competent and incorruptible policemen but no judge. Men of taste and learning and ability are forever lecturing the young and celebrating the dead. But the too frequent result of their able and industrious pens is a desiccation of the living tissues of literature into a network of little bones. Nowhere shall we find the downright vigour of a Dryden, or Keats with his fine and natural bearing, his profound insight and sanity, or Flaubert and the tremendous power of his fanaticism, or Coleridge,[7] above all, brewing in his head the whole of poetry and letting issue now and then one of those profound general statements which are caught up by the mind when hot with the friction of reading as if they were of the soul of the book itself.

And to all this, too, the critics generously agree. A great critic, they say, is the rarest of beings. But should one miraculously appear, how should we maintain him, on what should we feed him? Great critics, if they are not themselves great poets, are bred from the profusion of the age. There is some great man to be vindicated, some school to be founded or destroyed. But our age is meagre to

---

* How violent these are two quotations will show. 'It [*Told by an Idiot*] should be read as *The Tempest* should be read, and as *Gulliver's Travels* should be read, for if Miss Macaulay's poetic gift happens to be less sublime than those of the author of *The Tempest*, and if her irony happens to be less tremendous than that of the author of *Gulliver's Travels*, her justice and wisdom are no less noble than theirs.' – The *Daily News*.

The next day we read: 'For the rest one can only say that if Mr Eliot had been pleased to write in demotic English *The Waste Land* might not have been, as it just is to all but anthropologists, and literati, so much waste-paper.' – The *Manchester Guardian*.

the verge of destitution. There is no name which dominates the rest. There is no master in whose workshop the young are proud to serve apprenticeship. Mr Hardy has long since withdrawn from the arena, and there is something exotic about the genius of Mr Conrad[8] which makes him not so much an influence as an idol, honoured and admired, but aloof and apart. As for the rest, though they are many and vigorous and in the full flood of creative activity, there is none whose influence can seriously affect his contemporaries, or penetrate beyond our day to that not very distant future which it pleases us to call immortality. If we make a century our test, and ask how much of the work produced in these days in England will be in existence then, we shall have to answer not merely that we cannot agree upon the same book, but that we are more than doubtful whether such a book there is. It is an age of fragments. A few stanzas, a few pages, a chapter here and there, the beginning of this novel, the end of that, are equal to the best of any age or author. But can we go to posterity with a sheaf of loose pages, or ask the readers of those days, with the whole of literature before them, to sift our enormous rubbish-heaps for our tiny pearls? Such are the questions which the critics might lawfully put to their companions at table, the novelists and poets.

At first the weight of pessimism seems sufficient to bear down all opposition. Yes, it is a lean age, we repeat, with much to justify its poverty; but, frankly, if we pit one century against another the comparison seems overwhelmingly against us. *Waverley*, *The Excursion*, 'Kubla Khan', *Don Juan*, Hazlitt's Essays, *Pride and Prejudice*, *Hyperion*, and *Prometheus Unbound*[9] were all published between 1800 and 1821. Our century has not lacked industry; but if we ask for masterpieces it appears on the face of it that the pessimists are right. It seems as if an age of genius must be succeeded by an age of endeavour; riot and extravagance by cleanliness and hard work. All honour, of course, to those who have sacrificed their immortality to set the house in order. But if we ask for masterpieces, where are we to look? A little poetry, we may feel sure, will survive; a few poems by Mr Yeats, by Mr Davies, by Mr de la Mare. Mr Lawrence, of course, has moments of greatness, but hours of something very different. Mr Beerbohm, in his way, is perfect, but it is not a big way. Passages in *Far Away and Long Ago* will undoubtedly go to posterity entire. *Ulysses*[10] was a memorable catastrophe – immense in daring, terrific in disaster. And so, picking and choosing, we select now this, now that, hold it up for display, hear it defended or derided, and finally have to meet the objection that even so we are only agreeing with the critics that it is an age incapable of sustained effort, littered with fragments, and not seriously to be compared with the age that went before.

But it is just when opinions universally prevail and we have added lip service to their authority that we become sometimes most keenly conscious that we do not believe a word that we are saying. It is a barren and exhausted age, we repeat; we must look back with envy to the past. Meanwhile it is one of the first fine days of spring. Life is not altogether lacking in colour. The telephone, which interrupts the most serious conversations and cuts short the most weighty observations, has a romance of its own. And the random talk of people who have no chance of immortality and thus can speak their minds out has a setting, often, of lights, streets, houses, human beings, beautiful or grotesque, which will weave itself into the moment for ever. But this is life; the talk is about literature. We must try to disentangle the two, and justify the rash revolt of optimism against the superior plausibility, the finer distinction, of pessimism.

Our optimism, then, is largely instinctive. It springs from the fine day and the wine and the talk; it springs from the fact that when life throws up such treasures daily, daily suggests more than the most voluble can express, much though we admire the dead, we prefer life as it is. There is something about the present which we would not exchange, though we were offered a choice of all past ages to live in. And modern literature, with all its imperfections, has the same hold on us and the same fascination. It is like a relation whom we snub and scarify daily, but, after all, cannot do without. It has the same endearing quality of being that which we are, that which we have made, that in which we live, instead of being something, however august, alien to ourselves and beheld from the outside. Nor has any generation more need than ours to cherish its contemporaries. We are sharply cut off from our predecessors. A shift in the scale – the war, the sudden slip of masses held in position for ages – has shaken the fabric from top to bottom, alienated us from the past and made us perhaps too vividly conscious of the present. Every day we find ourselves doing, saying, or thinking things that would have been impossible to our fathers. And we feel the differences which have not been noted far more keenly than the resemblances which have been very perfectly expressed. New books lure us to read them partly in the hope that they will reflect this re-arrangement of our attitude – these scenes, thoughts, and apparently fortuitous groupings of incongruous things which impinge upon us with so keen a sense of novelty – and, as literature does, give it back into our keeping, whole and comprehended. Here indeed there is every reason for optimism. No age can have been more rich than ours in writers determined to give expression to the differences which separate them from the past and not to the resemblances which connect them with it. It would be invidious to mention names, but the most casual reader dipping into poetry, into fiction, into biography can hardly fail to be impressed by the courage, the sincerity, in a word, by the widespread originality of our time. But our exhilaration is strangely curtailed. Book after book leaves us with the same sense of promise unachieved, of intellectual poverty, of brilliance which has been snatched from life but not transmuted into literature. Much of what is best in contemporary work has the appearance of being noted under pressure, taken down in a bleak shorthand[11] which preserves with astonishing brilliance the movements and expressions of the figures as they pass across the screen. But the flash is soon over, and there remains with us a profound dissatisfaction. The irritation is as acute as the pleasure was intense.

After all, then, we are back at the beginning, vacillating from extreme to extreme, at one moment enthusiastic, at the next pessimistic, unable to come to any conclusion about our contemporaries. We have asked the critics to help us, but they have deprecated the task. Now, then, is the time to accept their advice and correct these extremes by consulting the masterpieces of the past. We feel ourselves indeed driven to them, impelled not by calm judgement but by some imperious need to anchor our instability upon their security. But, honestly, the shock of the comparison between past and present is at first disconcerting. Undoubtedly there is a dullness in great books. There is an unabashed tranquillity in page after page of Wordsworth and Scott and Miss Austen which is sedative to the verge of somnolence. Opportunities occur and they neglect them. Shades and subtleties accumulate and they ignore them. They seem deliberately to refuse to gratify those senses which are stimulated so briskly by the moderns; the senses of sight, of sound, of touch – above all, the sense of the human being, his depth and the variety of his perceptions, his complexity, his confusion, his self, in short. There is little of all this in the works of Wordsworth and Scott and Jane Austen. From what, then, arises that sense of security which gradually, delightfully, and completely overcomes us? It is the power of their belief – their conviction, that imposes itself upon us. In Wordsworth, the philosophic poet, this is obvious enough. But it is equally true of the careless Scott, who scribbled masterpieces to build castles before breakfast, and of the modest maiden lady who wrote furtively and quietly simply to give pleasure. In both there is the same natural conviction that life is of a certain quality. They have their judgement of conduct. They know the relations of human beings towards each other and towards the universe. Neither of them probably has a word to say about the matter outright, but everything depends on it. Only believe, we find ourselves saying, and all the rest will come of itself. Only believe, to take a very simple instance which the recent publication of *The Watsons*[12] brings to mind, that a nice girl will instinctively try to soothe the feelings of a boy who has been snubbed at a dance, and then, if you believe it implicitly and unquestioningly, you will not only make people a hundred years later feel the same thing, but you will make them feel it as literature. For certainty of that kind is the condition which makes it possible to write. To believe that your impressions hold good for others is to be released from the cramp and confinement of personality. It is to be free, as Scott was free, to explore with a vigour which still holds us spell-bound the whole world of adventure and romance. It is also the first step in that mysterious process in which Jane Austen was so great an adept. The little grain of experience once selected, believed in, and set outside herself, could be put precisely in its place, and she was then free to make of it, by a process which never yields its secrets to the analyst, into that complete statement which is literature.

So then our contemporaries afflict us because they have ceased to believe. The most sincere of them will only tell us what it is that happens to himself. They cannot make a world, because they are not free of other human beings. They cannot tell stories because they do not believe that stories are true. They cannot generalize. They depend on their senses and emotions, whose testimony is trustworthy, rather than on their intellects whose message is obscure. And they have perforce to deny themselves the use of some of the most powerful and some of the most exquisite of the weapons of their craft. With the whole wealth of the English language at the back of them, they timidly pass about from hand to hand and book to book only the meanest copper coins. Set down at a fresh angle of the eternal prospect they can only whip out their notebooks and record with agonized intensity the flying gleams, which light on what? and the transitory splendours, which may, perhaps, compose nothing whatever. But here the critics interpose, and with some show of justice.

If this description holds good, they say, and is not, as it may well be, entirely dependent upon our position at the table and certain purely personal relationships to mustard pots and flower vases, then the risks of judging contemporary work are greater than ever before. There is every excuse for them if they are wide of the mark; and no doubt it would be better to retreat, as Matthew Arnold advised, from the burning ground of the present to the safe tranquillity of the past. 'We enter on burning ground,' wrote Matthew Arnold, 'as we approach the poetry of times so near to us, poetry like that of Byron, Shelley, and Wordsworth, of which the estimates are so often not only personal, but personal with passion,'[13] and this, they remind us, was written in the year 1880. Beware, they say, of putting under the microscope one inch of a ribbon which runs many miles; things sort themselves out if you wait; moderation, and a study of the classics are to be recommended. Moreover, life is short; the Byron centenary[14] is at hand; and the burning question of the moment is, did he or did he not, marry his sister? To sum up, then – if indeed any conclusion is possible when everybody is talking at once and it is time to be going – it seems that it would be wise for the writers of the present to renounce the hope of creating masterpieces. Their poems, plays, biographies, novels are not books but notebooks, and Time, like a good schoolmaster, will take them in his hands, point to their blots and scrawls and erasions, and tear them across; but he will not throw them into the waste-paper basket. He will keep them because other students will find them very useful. It is from notebooks of the present[15] that the masterpieces of the future are made. Literature, as the critics were saying just now, has lasted long, has undergone many changes, and it is only a short sight and a parochial mind that will exaggerate the importance of these squalls, however they may agitate the little boats now tossing out at sea. The storm and the drenching are on the surface; continuity and calm are in the depths.

As for the critics whose task it is to pass judgement upon the books of the moment, whose work, let us admit, is difficult, dangerous, and often distasteful, let us ask them to be generous of encouragement, but sparing of those wreaths and coronets which are so apt to get awry, and fade, and make the wearers, in six months time, look a little ridiculous. Let them take a wider, a less personal view of modern literature, and look indeed upon the writers as if they were engaged upon some vast building, which being built by common effort, the separate workmen may well remain anonymous. Let them slam the door upon the cosy company where sugar is cheap and butter plentiful, give over, for a time at least, the discussion of that fascinating topic – whether Byron married his sister – and, withdrawing, perhaps, a hand's breadth from the table where we sit chattering, say something interesting about literature. Let us buttonhole them as they leave, and recall to their memory that gaunt aristocrat, Lady Hester Stanhope,[16] who kept a milk-white horse in her stable in readiness for the Messiah and was forever scanning the mountain tops, impatiently but with confidence, for signs of his approach, and ask them to follow her example; scan the horizon; see the past in relation to the future; and so prepare the way for masterpieces to come.

To Spain

First published in the *Nation and Athenaeum*, 5 May 1923, and later in *New Republic*, New York, 6 June 1923.

You, who cross the Channel yearly, probably no longer see the house at Dieppe,[1] no longer feel, as the train moves slowly down the street, one civilization fall, another rise – from the ruin and chaos of British stucco this incredible pink-and-blue phoenix, four stories high, with its flower-pots, its balconies, its servant girl leaning on the window-sill, indolently looking out. Quite unmoved you sit reading – Thomas Hardy, perhaps – bridging abysses, preserving continuity, a little contemptuous of the excitement which is moving those who feel themselves liberated from one civilization, launched upon another to such odd gestures, such strange irreticences. But reflect how much they have already gone through. Try to recall the look of London streets seen very early, perhaps very young, from a cab window on the way to Victoria. Everywhere there is the same intensity, as if the moment, instead of moving, lay suddenly still, became suddenly solemn, fixed the passers-by in their most transient aspects eternally. They do not know how important they have become. If they did, perhaps they would cease to buy newspapers and scrub doorsteps. But we who are about to leave them feel all the more moved that they should continue to do these homely things on the brink of that precipice – our departure. Therefore it is natural that those who have survived the crossing, with its last scrutiny of passing faces so like a little rehearsal of death, should be shaken; should move handbags; start conversations; and tremble for one intoxicating moment upon the brink of that ideal society where everyone without fear or hesitation reveals the depths of his soul.

But it is only for a moment. Next, the disembodied spirit fluttering at the window desires above all things to be admitted to the new society where the houses are painted in lozenges of pale pink and blue; women wear shawls; trousers are baggy; there are crucifixes on hilltops; yellow mongrel dogs; chairs in the street; cobbles – gaiety, frivolity, drama, in short. 'I'm awfully sorry for Agnes, because now they can't be married till he gets a job in London. It's too far to get back from the works for midday dinner. I should have thought the father would have done something for them.' These detached sentences, spoken a little brokenly (for they are frowning into tiny mirrors and drawing combs intently through fair bobbed hair) by two English girls, fall like the bars of a prison-house heavily across the mind. It is from them that we must escape; the hours, the works, the divisions, rigid and straight, of the old British week. Already, as the train moved out of Dieppe, these obstructions seemed bubbling and boiling in the cauldron of a more congenial civilization. The days of the week diminished; the hours disappeared. It was five o'clock, but no banks had simultaneously shut their doors, nor from innumerable lifts had millions of citizens emerged in time for dinner, or in the poorer suburbs for slices of cold meat and Swiss roll laid orderly in shallow glass dishes. There must be divisions, even for the French, but where they fall we cannot tell, and the lady in the corner, so pale, so plump, so compact, seemed as she sat smiling to be riding life over ditches and boundaries smoothed out by the genius of the Latin race.

She rose to go to the dining car. As she sat down she took a small frying-pan from her handbag and hid it discreetly beneath a tent made from a copy of *Le Temps*. Deftly, as each dish was served, she secreted a portion in the absence of the waiter. Her husband smiled. Her husband approved. We only knew that she was brave. They might be poor. The helpings were large. The French have mothers. To redress perpetually the extravagances of life, and make the covering fit the fact instead of bulging in ostentatious emptiness, was part, no doubt, of the French genius for living. Still, when it comes to the thick, yellow rind of a not fresh cheese — Ironically smiling, she condescended, in that exquisite tongue which twinkles like diamonds with all its accents, to explain that she kept a dog. But she might have kept – anything. 'Life is so simple,' she seemed to say.

'Life is so simple – life is so simple,' said the wheels of the Sud Express[2] all night long in that idiotic or ironic way they have, for any message less appropriate to the uneasy darkness, the clank of chains, the anguished cries of railwaymen, and, in the dawn, the misery of the unrested body could scarcely be imagined. But travellers are much at the mercy of phrases. Taken from home, which, like a shell, has made them hard, separate, individual, vast generalizations formulate in their exposed brains; the stress of wheel or window-blind beats into rhythm idiotic sayings of false profundity about life, repeats to distraction fragments of prose, and makes them stare with ferocious melancholy at the landscape, which, in the middle of France, is dull enough. The French are methodical; but life is simple; the French are prosaic; the French have roads. Yes, they have roads which strike from that lean poplar there to Vienna, to Moscow; pass Tolstoy's house, climb mountains, then march, all shop decorated, down the middle of famous cities. But in England the road runs out on to a cliff; wavers into sand at the edge of the sea. It begins to seem dangerous to live in England. Here actually one could build a house and have no neighbours; go for a walk along this eternal white road for two, three, four miles, and meet only one black dog and one old woman who, depressed perhaps by the immensity of the landscape and the futility of locomotion, has sat herself down on a bank, attached her cow to her by a rope, and there sits, unmoved, incurious, monumental. Could our English poets for a moment share her seat and think her thoughts, forget the parish, the pansy, and the sparrow's egg, and concentrate (as she appears to do) upon the fate of man!

But as the country grows larger and larger outside Bordeaux the concentration which is needed to produce even the simplest of little thoughts is rent as a glove is torn by the thrust of a large hand. Blessed are painters with their brushes, paints, and canvases. But words are flimsy things. They turn tail at the first approach of visual beauty. They let one down in the most literal sense into a chaotic, an alarming chasm, filled – for the eye pours it all in – with white towns, with mules in single file, with solitary farms, with enormous churches, with vast fields crumbling at evening into pallor, with fruit-trees blazing askew like blown matches, and trees burning with oranges, and clouds and storms. Beauty seems to have closed overhead, and one washes this way and that in her waters. It is always on the shoulders of a human being that one climbs out; a profile in the corridor; a lady in deep mourning who steps into a motor car and drives across an arid plain – where and why? a child in Madrid throwing confetti effusively upon the figure of Christ; an Englishman discussing, while his hat obscures half the Sierra Nevada,[3] Mr Churchill's last article in *The Times*. 'No,' one says to beauty – as one rebukes an importunate dog – 'down, down; let me look at you through the eyes of human beings.'

But the Englishman's hat is no measure of the Sierra Nevada. Setting out next day upon foot and mule-back, this wrinkled red-and-white screen, this background for hats, this queer comment (especially at sunset) upon Mr Churchill's article in *The Times*, is found to consist of stones, olive trees, goats, asphodels, irises, bushes, ridges, shelves, clumps, tufts, and hollows innumerable, indescribable, unthinkable. The mind's contents break into short sentences. It is hot; the old man; the frying-pan; it is hot; the image of the Virgin; the bottle of wine; it is time for lunch; it is only half-past twelve; it is hot. And then over and over again come all those objects – stones, olives, goats, asphodels, dragon-flies, irises, until by some trick of the imagination they run into phrases of command, exhortation, and encouragement such as befit soldiers marching, sentinels on lonely nights, and leaders of great battalions. But must one give up the struggle? Must one relinquish the game? Yes, for the clouds are drifting across the pass; mules mind not what they carry; mules never stumble; they know the way. Why not leave everything to them?

Riders, as night comes on (and the pass was very misty), seem to be riding out of life towards some very enticing prospect, while the four legs of their beasts carry on all necessary transactions with the earth. Riders are at rest; on they go, and on and on. And, they muse, what does it all matter; and what harm can come to a good man (behold two priests stepping out of the drizzle, bowing and disappearing) in life or after death? And then, since a fox has crossed the path, which is on turf and must be nearly at the top of the mountain, how strangely it seems as if they were riding in England, a long day's journey, hundreds of years ago, and the danger is over, and they see the lights of the inn, and the hostess comes into the courtyard and bids them sit round the fire while she cooks dinner, which they do, half-dreaming, while clumsy boys and girls with red flowers pass and repass in the background, and the mother suckles her baby, and the old man, who never speaks, breaks tufts from the brushwood and throws them on the fire, which blazes up, and the whole company stares.

But, good heavens! One never knows what days follow what nights. Good heavens again! 'Don Fernando had a passion for pigeon pie, and so kept pigeons up here' – on his roof, that is, from which one has this astonishing, this strange, this disturbing view of the Alpujarras. 'He died last summer in Granada.' Did he, indeed? It is the light, of course; a million razor-blades have shaved off the bark and the dust, and out pours pure colour; whiteness from fig-trees; red and green and again white from the enormous, the humped, the everlasting landscape. But listen to the sounds on the roof – first the fluttering pigeons; then water rushing; then an old man crying chickens for sale; then a donkey braying in the valley far below. Listen; and as one listens this random life begins to be issued from the heart of a village which has faced the African coast with a timeless and aristocratic endurance for a thousand years. But how say this (as one descends from the blaze) to the Spanish peasant woman who bids one enter her room, with its lilies and its washing, and smiles and looks out of the window as if she too had looked for a thousand years?

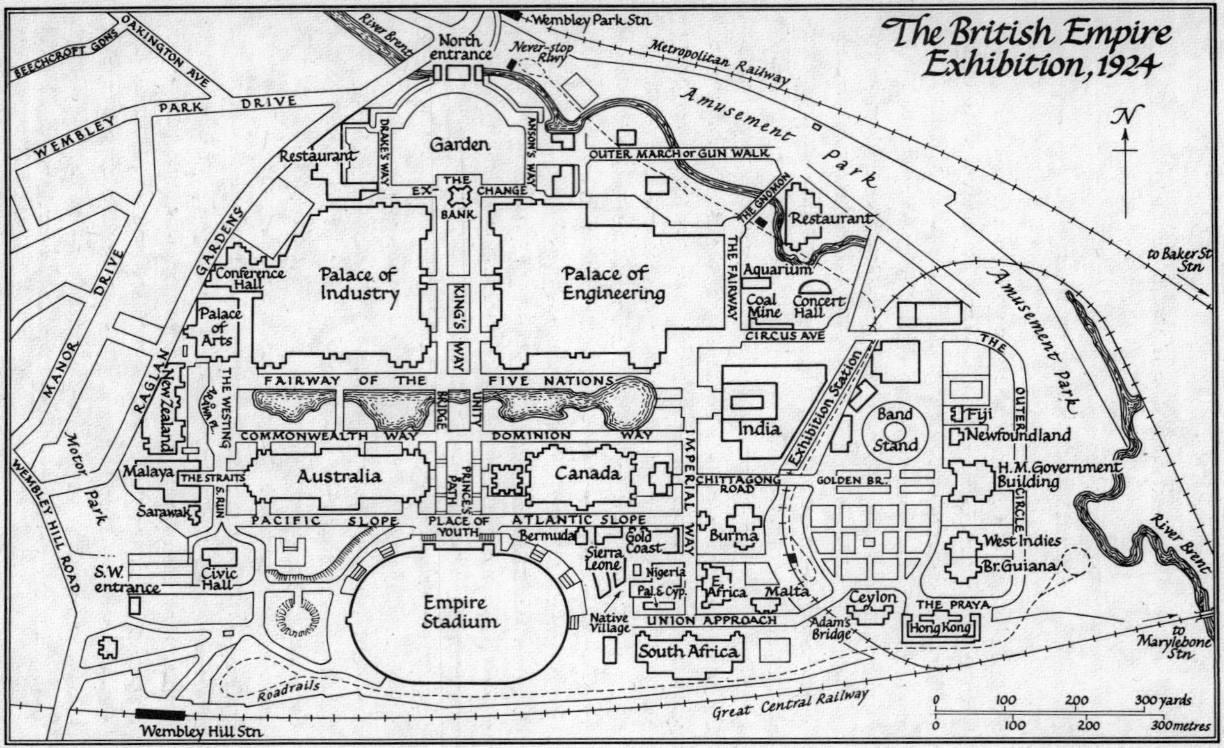
The British Empire Exhibition, 1924
N
Wembley Park Stn
Metropolitan Railway
Amusement Park
to Baker St Stn
Amusement Park
River Brent
to Marylebone Stn
Great Central Railway
Wembley Hill Stn
Roadrails
North entrance
Never-stop Rlwy
BEECHCROFT GDNS
OAKINGTON AVE
PARK DRIVE
WEMBLEY
MANOR DRIVE
RAGLAN GARDENS
WEMBLEY HILL ROAD
Motor Park
S.W. entrance
Garden
Restaurant
DRAKE'S WAY
ANSON'S WAY
OUTER MARCH or GUN WALK
THE EX-CHANGE
BANK
THE GNOMON
Restaurant
Palace of Industry
Palace of Engineering
KING'S WAY
THE FAIRWAY
Aquarium
Coal Mine
Concert Hall
CIRCUS AVE
Conference Hall
Palace of Arts
New Zealand
THE WESTING
ARAWA PL.
FAIRWAY OF THE FIVE NATIONS
UNITY BRIDGE
COMMONWEALTH WAY
DOMINION WAY
Malaya
THE STRAITS
S. RUN
Sarawak
Australia
PRINCE'S PATH
Canada
IMPERIAL WAY
PACIFIC SLOPE
PLACE OF YOUTH
ATLANTIC SLOPE
Bermuda
Gold Coast
Sierra Leone
Nigeria
Pal. & Cyp.
Native Village
Civic Hall
Empire Stadium
India
Exhibition Station
Band Stand
CHITTAGONG ROAD
GOLDEN BR.
Burma
E. Africa
Malta
UNION APPROACH
South Africa
Adam's Bridge
Ceylon
THE PRAYA
Hong Kong
THE OUTER CIRCLE
Fiji
Newfoundland
H.M. Government Building
West Indies
Br. Guiana
0 100 200 300 yards
0 100 200 300 metres

Thunder at Wembley

First published in the *Nation and Athenaeum*, 28 June 1924.

It is nature that is the ruin of Wembley;[1] yet it is difficult to see what steps Lord Stevenson, Lieut.-General Sir Travers Clarke, and the Duke of Devonshire[2] could have taken to keep her out. They might have eradicated the grass and felled the chestnut trees; even so the thrushes would have got in, and there would always have been the sky. At Earl's Court and the White City, so far as memory serves, there was little trouble from this source. The area was too small; the light too brilliant.[3] If a single real moth strayed in to dally with the arc lamps he was at once transformed into a dizzy reveller; if a laburnum tree shook her tassels, spangles of limelight floated in the violet and crimson air. Everything was intoxicated and transformed. But at Wembley nothing is changed and nobody is drunk. They say, indeed, that there is a restaurant where each diner is forced to spend a guinea[4] upon his dinner. What vistas of cold ham that statement calls forth! What pyramids of rolls! What gallons of tea and coffee! For it is unthinkable that there should be champagne, plovers' eggs, or peaches at Wembley. And for six and eightpence two people can buy as much ham and bread as they need. Six and eightpence is not a large sum; but neither is it a small sum. It is a moderate sum, a mediocre sum. It is the prevailing sum at Wembley. You look through an open door at a regiment of motor cars aligned in avenues. They are not opulent and powerful; they are not flimsy and cheap.[5] Six and eightpence seems to be the price of each of them. It is the same with the machines for crushing gravel. One can imagine better; one can imagine worse. The machine before us is a serviceable type, and costs, inevitably, six and eightpence. Dress fabrics, rope, table linen, old masters,[6] sugar, wheat, filigree silver, pepper, birds' nests (edible, and exported to Hong Kong), camphor, bees-wax, rattans,[7] and the rest – why trouble to ask the price? One knows beforehand – six and eightpence. As for the buildings themselves, those vast, smooth, grey palaces, no vulgar riot of ideas tumbled expensively in their architect's head; equally, cheapness was abhorrent to him, and vulgarity anathema. Per perch, rod, or square foot, however ferro-concrete palaces are sold, they too work out at six and eightpence.

But then, just as one is beginning a little wearily to fumble with those two fine words – democracy, mediocrity – nature asserts herself where one would least look to find her – in clergymen, schoolchildren, girls, young men, invalids in bath-chairs. They pass, quietly, silently, in coveys, in groups, sometimes alone. They mount the enormous staircases; they stand in queues to have their spectacles rectified gratis; to have their fountain pens filled gratis; they gaze respectfully into sacks of grain; glance reverently at mowing machines[8] from Canada; now and again stoop to remove some paper bag or banana skin and place it in the receptacles provided for that purpose at frequent intervals along the avenues. But what has happened to our contemporaries? Each is beautiful; each is stately. Can it be that one is seeing human beings for the first time? In streets they hurry; in houses they talk; they are bankers in banks; sell shoes in shops. Here against the enormous background of ferro-concrete Britain, of rosy Burma,[9] at large, unoccupied, they reveal themselves simply as human beings, creatures of leisure, civilization, and dignity; a little languid perhaps, a little attenuated, but a product to be proud of. Indeed, they are the ruin of the Exhibition. The Duke of Devonshire and his colleagues should have kept them out. As you watch them trailing and flowing, dreaming and speculating, admiring this coffee-grinder, that milk-and-cream separator; the rest of the show becomes insignificant. And what, one asks, is the spell it lays upon them? How, with all this dignity of their own, can they bring themselves to believe in that?

But this cynical reflection, at once so chill and so superior, was made, of course, by the thrush. Down in the Amusement Compound by some grave oversight on the part of the Committee several trees and rhododendron bushes have been allowed to remain; and these, as anybody could have foretold, attract the birds. As you wait your turn to be hoisted into mid-air, it is impossible not to hear the thrush singing. You look up, and discover a whole chestnut tree with its blossoms standing; you look down, and see ordinary grass, scattered with petals, harbouring insects, sprinkled with stray wild flowers. The gramophone does its best; they light a horse-shoe of fairy lamps above the Jack and Jill; a man bangs a bladder and implores you to come and tickle monkeys; boatloads of serious men are poised on the heights of the scenic railway; but all is vain. The cry of ecstasy that should have split the sky as the boat dropped to its doom patters from leaf to leaf, dies, falls flat, while the thrush proceeds with his statement. And then some woman, in the row of red-brick villas outside the grounds, comes out and wrings a dish-cloth in her backyard. All this the Duke of Devonshire should have prevented.

The problem of the sky, however, remains. Is it, one wonders, lying back limp but acquiescent in a green deck-chair, part of the Exhibition? Is it lending itself with exquisite tact to show off to the best advantage snowy Palestine, ruddy Burma, sand-coloured Canada, and the minarets and pagodas of our possessions in the East? So quietly it suffers all these domes and palaces to melt into its breast; receives them with such sombre and tender discretion; so exquisitely allows the rare lamps of Jack and Jill and the Monkey-Teasers to bear themselves like stars. But even as we watch and admire what we would fain credit to the forethought of Lieut.-General Sir Travers Clarke, a rushing sound is heard. Is it the wind or is it the British Empire Exhibition? It is both. The wind is rising and shuffling along the avenues; the Massed Bands of Empire are assembling and marching to the Stadium. Men like pincushions, men like pouter pigeons, men like pillar-boxes pass in procession. Dust swirls after them. Admirably impassive, the Bands of Empire march on. Soon they will have entered the fortress; soon the gates will have clanged. But let them hasten! For either the sky has misread her directions or some appalling catastrophe is impending. The sky is livid, lurid, sulphurine. It is in violent commotion. It is whirling water-spouts of cloud into the air; of dust in the Exhibition. Dust swirls down the avenues, hisses and hurries like erected cobras round the corners. Pagodas are dissolving in dust. Ferro-concrete is fallible. Colonies are perishing and dispersing in spray of inconceivable beauty and terror which some malignant power illuminates. Ash and violet are the colours of its decay. From every quarter human beings come flying – clergymen, schoolchildren, invalids in bath-chairs. They fly with outstretched arms, and a vast sound of wailing rolls before them, but there is neither confusion nor dismay. Humanity is rushing to destruction, but humanity is accepting its doom. Canada opens a frail tent of shelter. Clergymen and schoolchildren gain its portals. Out in the open, under a cloud of electric silver, the Bands of Empire strike up. The bagpipes neigh. Clergy, schoolchildren, and invalids group themselves round the Prince of Wales in butter. Cracks like the white roots of trees spread themselves across the firmament. The Empire is perishing; the bands are playing; the Exhibition is in ruins. For that is what comes of letting in the sky.

On Being Ill

This essay was first published in the *New Criterion*, January 1926, as
'Illness: An Unexplored Mine' in *Forum*, New York, April 1926, and
then, in the slightly revised version reprinted here, as a pamphlet
by the Hogarth Press, 1930.

Considering how common illness is,[1] how tremendous the spiritual change that it brings, how astonishing, when the lights of health go down, the undiscovered countries that are then disclosed, what wastes and deserts of the soul a slight attack of influenza brings to view, what precipices and lawns sprinkled with bright flowers a little rise of temperature reveals, what ancient and obdurate oaks are uprooted in us by the act of sickness, how we go down into the pit of death and feel the waters of annihilation close above our heads and wake thinking to find ourselves in the presence of the angels and the harpers when we have a tooth out and come to the surface in the dentist's arm-chair and confuse his 'Rinse the mouth – rinse the mouth' with the greeting of the Deity stooping from the floor of Heaven to welcome us[2] – when we think of this, as we are so frequently forced to think of it, it becomes strange indeed that illness has not taken its place with love and battle and jealousy among the prime themes of literature. Novels, one would have thought, would have been devoted to influenza; epic poems to typhoid; odes to pneumonia; lyrics to tooth-ache. But no; with a few exceptions – De Quincey attempted something of the sort in *The Opium Eater*;[3] there must be a volume or two about disease scattered through the pages of Proust[4] – literature does its best to maintain that its concern is with the mind; that the body is a sheet of plain glass through which the soul looks straight and clear, and, save for one or two passions such as desire and greed, is null, and negligible and non-existent. On the contrary, the very opposite is true. All day, all night the body intervenes; blunts or sharpens, colours or discolours, turns to wax in the warmth of June, hardens to tallow in the murk of February. The creature within can only gaze through the pane – smudged or rosy; it cannot separate off from the body like the sheath of a knife or the pod of a pea for a single instant; it must go through the whole unending procession of changes, heat and cold, comfort and discomfort, hunger and satisfaction, health and illness, until there comes the inevitable catastrophe; the body smashes itself to smithereens, and the soul (it is said) escapes. But of all this daily drama of the body there is no record. People write always of the doings of the mind; the thoughts that come to it; its noble plans; how the mind has civilized the universe. They show it ignoring the body in the philosopher's turret; or kicking the body, like an old leather football, across leagues of snow and desert in the pursuit of conquest or discovery. Those great wars which the body wages with the mind a slave to it, in the solitude of the bedroom against the assault of fever or the oncome of melancholia, are neglected. Nor is the reason far to seek. To look these things squarely in the face would need the courage of a lion tamer; a robust philosophy; a reason rooted in the bowels of the earth. Short of these, this monster, the body, this miracle, its pain, will soon make us taper into mysticism, or rise, with rapid beats of the wings, into the raptures of transcendentalism. The public would say that a novel devoted to influenza lacked plot; they would complain that there was no love in it – wrongly however, for illness often takes on the disguise of love, and plays the same odd tricks. It invests certain faces with divinity, sets us to wait, hour after hour, with pricked ears for the creaking of a stair, and wreathes the faces of the absent (plain enough in health, Heaven knows) with a new significance, while the mind concocts a thousand legends and romances about them for which it has neither time nor taste in health. Finally, to hinder the description of illness in literature, there is the poverty of the language. English, which can express the thoughts of Hamlet and the tragedy of Lear, has no words for the shiver and the headache. It has all grown one way. The merest schoolgirl, when she falls in love, has Shakespeare or Keats to speak her mind for her; but let a sufferer try to describe a pain in his head to a doctor and language at once runs dry. There is nothing ready made for him. He is forced to coin words himself, and, taking his pain in one hand, and a lump of pure sound in the other (as perhaps the people of Babel[5] did in the beginning), so to crush them together that a brand new word in the end drops out. Probably it will be something laughable. For who of English birth can take liberties with the language? To us it is a sacred thing and therefore doomed to die, unless the Americans,[6] whose genius is so much happier in the making of new words than in the disposition of the old, will come to our help and set the springs aflow. Yet it is not only a new language that we need, more primitive, more sensual, more obscene, but a new hierarchy of the passions; love must be deposed in favour of a temperature of 104; jealousy give place to the pangs of sciatica; sleeplessness play the part of villain, and the hero become a white liquid with a sweet taste – that mighty Prince with the moths' eyes and the feathered feet, one of whose names is Chloral.[7]

But to return to the invalid. 'I am in bed with influenza' – but what does that convey of the great experience; how the world has changed its shape; the tools of business grown remote; the sounds of festival become romantic like a merry-go-round heard across far fields; and friends have changed, some putting on a strange beauty, others deformed to the squatness of toads, while the whole landscape of life lies remote and fair, like the shore seen from a ship far out at sea, and he is now exalted on a peak and needs no help from man or God, and now grovels supine on the floor glad of a kick from a housemaid – the experience cannot be imparted and, as is always the way with these dumb things, his own suffering serves but to wake memories in his friends' minds of *their* influenzas, *their* aches and pains which went unwept last February, and now cry aloud, desperately, clamorously, for the divine relief of sympathy.

But sympathy we cannot have. Wisest Fate says no.[8] If her children, weighted as they already are with sorrow, were to take on them that burden too, adding in imagination other pains to their own, buildings would cease to rise; roads would peter out into grassy tracks; there would be an end of music and of painting; one great sigh alone would rise to Heaven, and the only attitudes for men and women would be those of horror and despair. As it is, there is always some little distraction – an organ-grinder at the corner of the hospital, a shop with book or trinket to decoy one past the prison or the workhouse, some absurdity of cat or dog to prevent one from turning the old beggar's hieroglyphic of misery into volumes of sordid suffering; and thus the vast effort of sympathy which those barracks of pain and discipline, those dried symbols of sorrow, ask us to exert on their behalf, is uneasily shuffled off for another time. Sympathy nowadays is dispensed chiefly by the laggards and failures, women for the most part (in whom the obsolete exists so strangely side by side with anarchy and newness),[9] who, having dropped out of the race, have time to spend upon fantastic and unprofitable excursions; C. L.[10] for example, who, sitting by the stale sickroom fire, builds up, with touches at once sober and imaginative, the nursery fender, the loaf, the lamp, barrel organs in the street, and all the simple old wives' tales of pinafores and escapades; A. R., the rash, the magnanimous, who, if you fancied a giant tortoise to solace you or a theorbo[11] to cheer you, would ransack the markets of London and procure them somehow, wrapped in paper, before the end of the day; the frivolous K. T., who, dressed in silks and feathers, powdered and painted (which takes time too) as if for a banquet of Kings and Queens, spends her whole brightness in the gloom of the sickroom, and makes the medicine bottles ring and the flames shoot up with her gossip and her mimicry. But such follies have had their day; civilization points to a different goal; and then what place will there be for the tortoise and the theorbo?

There is, let us confess it (and illness is the great confessional) a childish outspokenness in illness; things are said, truths blurted out, which the cautious respectability of health conceals. About sympathy for example – we can do without it. That illusion of a world so shaped that it echoes every groan, of human beings so tied together by common needs and fears that a twitch at one wrist jerks another, where however strange your experience other people have had it too, where however far you travel in your own mind someone has been there before you – is all an illusion. We do not know our own souls, let alone the souls of others. Human beings do not go hand in hand the whole stretch of the way. There is a virgin forest in each; a snowfield where even the print of birds' feet is unknown. Here we go alone, and like it better so. Always to have sympathy, always to be accompanied, always to be understood would be intolerable. But in health the genial pretence must be kept up and the effort renewed – to communicate, to civilize, to share, to cultivate the desert, educate the native, to work together by day and by night to sport. In illness this make-believe ceases. Directly the bed is called for, or, sunk deep among pillows in one chair, we raise our feet even an inch above the ground on another, we cease to be soldiers in the army of the upright; we become deserters. They march to battle. We float with the sticks on the stream; helter-skelter with the dead leaves on the lawn, irresponsible and disinterested and able, perhaps for the first time for years, to look round, to look up – to look, for example, at the sky.

The first impression of that extraordinary spectacle is strangely overcoming. Ordinarily to look at the sky for any length of time is impossible. Pedestrians would be impeded and disconcerted by a public sky-gazer. What snatches we get of it are mutilated by chimneys and churches, serve as a background for man, signify wet weather or fine, daub windows gold, and, filling in the branches, complete the pathos of dishevelled autumnal plane trees in autumnal squares. Now, lying recumbent, staring straight up, the sky is discovered to be something so different from this that really it is a little shocking. This then has been going on all the time without our knowing it! – this incessant making up of shapes and casting them down, this buffeting of clouds together, and drawing vast trains of ships and waggons from north to south, this incessant ringing up and down of curtains of light and shade, this interminable experiment with gold shafts and blue shadows, with veiling the sun and unveiling it, with making rock ramparts and wafting them away – this endless activity, with the waste of Heaven knows how many million horse power of energy, has been left to work its will year in year out. The fact seems to call for comment and indeed for censure. Ought not someone to write to *The Times*? Use should be made of it. One should not let this gigantic cinema play perpetually to an empty house. But watch a little longer and another emotion drowns the stirrings of civic ardour. Divinely beautiful it is also divinely heartless. Immeasurable resources are used for some purpose which has nothing to do with human pleasure or human profit. If we were all laid prone, stiff, still the sky would be experimenting with its blues and its golds. Perhaps then, if we look down at something very small and close and familiar, we shall find sympathy. Let us examine the rose. We have seen it so often flowering in bowls, connected it so often with beauty in its prime, that we have forgotten how it stands, still and steady, throughout an entire afternoon in the earth. It preserves a demeanour of perfect dignity and self-possession. The suffusion of its petals is of inimitable rightness. Now perhaps one deliberately falls; now all the flowers, the voluptuous purple, the creamy, in whose waxen flesh the spoon has left a swirl of cherry juice; gladioli; dahlias; lilies, sacerdotal, ecclesiastical; flowers with prim cardboard collars tinged apricot and amber, all gently incline their heads to the breeze – all, with the exception of the heavy sunflower, who proudly acknowledges the sun at midday and perhaps at midnight rebuffs the moon. There they stand; and it is of these, the stillest, the most self-sufficient of all things that human beings have made companions; these that symbolize their passions, decorate their festivals, and lie (as if *they* knew sorrow) upon the pillows of the dead. Wonderful to relate,[12] poets have found religion in nature; people live in the country to learn virtue from plants. It is in their indifference that they are comforting. That snowfield of the mind, where man has not trodden, is visited by the cloud, kissed by the falling petal, as, in another sphere, it is the great artists, the Miltons and the Popes, who console not by their thought of us but by their forgetfulness.

Meanwhile, with the heroism of the ant or the bee, however indifferent the sky or disdainful the flowers, the army of the upright marches to battle. Mrs Jones catches her train. Mr Smith mends his motor. The cows are driven home to be milked. Men thatch the roof. The dogs bark. The rooks, rising in a net, fall in a net upon the elm trees. The wave of life flings itself out indefatigably. It is only the recumbent who know what, after all, nature is at no pains to conceal – that she in the end will conquer; heat will leave the world; stiff with frost we shall cease to drag ourselves about the fields; ice will lie thick upon factory and engine; the sun will go out. Even so, when the whole earth is sheeted and slippery, some undulation, some irregularity of surface will mark the boundary of an ancient garden, and there, thrusting its head up undaunted in the starlight, the rose will flower, the crocus will burn. But with the hook of life still in us still we must wriggle. We cannot stiffen peaceably into glassy mounds. Even the recumbent spring up at the mere imagination of frost about the toes and stretch out to avail themselves of the universal hope – Heaven, Immortality. Surely, since men have been wishing all these ages, they will have wished something into existence; there will be some green isle for the mind to rest on even if the foot cannot plant itself there. The co-operative imagination of mankind must have drawn some firm outline. But no. One opens the *Morning Post* and reads the Bishop of Lichfield on Heaven. One watches the church-goers file into those gallant temples where, on the bleakest day, in the wettest fields, lamps will be burning, bells will be ringing, and however the autumn leaves may shuffle and the winds sigh outside, hopes and desires will be changed to beliefs and certainties within. Do they look serene? Are their eyes filled with the light of their supreme conviction? Would one of them dare leap straight into Heaven off Beachy Head?[13] None but a simpleton would ask such questions; the little company of believers lags and drags and strays. The mother is worn; the father tired. As for imagining Heaven, they have no time. Heaven-making must be left to the imagination of the poets. Without their help we can but trifle – imagine Pepys in Heaven,[14] adumbrate little interviews with celebrated people on tufts of thyme, soon fall into gossip about such of our friends as have stayed in Hell, or, worse still, revert again to earth and choose, since there is no harm in choosing, to live over and over, now as man, now as woman, as sea-captain, or court lady, as Emperor or farmer's wife, in splendid cities and on remote moors, at the time of Pericles or Arthur, Charlemagne, or George the Fourth[15] – to live and live till we have lived out those embryo lives which attend about us in early youth until 'I' suppressed them. But 'I' shall not, if wishing can alter it, usurp Heaven too, and condemn us, who have played our parts here as William or Alice to remain William or Alice for ever. Left to ourselves we speculate thus carnally. We need the poets to imagine for us. The duty of Heaven-making should be attached to the office of the Poet Laureate.

Indeed it is to the poets that we turn. Illness makes us disinclined for the long campaigns that prose exacts. We cannot command all our faculties and keep our reason and our judgement and our memory at attention while chapter swings on top of chapter, and, as one settles into place, we must be on the watch for the coming of the next, until the whole structure – arches, towers, and battlements – stands firm on its foundations. *The Decline and Fall of the Roman*

Empire is not the book for influenza, nor *The Golden Bowl* nor *Madame Bovary*.[16] On the other hand, with responsibility shelved and reason in the abeyance – for who is going to exact criticism from an invalid or sound sense from the bed-ridden? – other tastes assert themselves; sudden, fitful, intense. We rifle the poets of their flowers. We break off a line or two and let them open in the depths of the mind:

> and oft at eve
> Visits the herds along the twilight meadows
>
> wandering in thick flocks along the mountains
> Shepherded by the slow unwilling wind.[17]

Or there is a whole three-volume novel to be mused over in a verse of Hardy's or a sentence of La Bruyère.[18] We dip in Lamb's Letters[19] – some prose writers are to be read as poets – and find 'I am a sanguinary murderer of time, and would kill him inchmeal just now. But the snake is vital.' and who shall explain the delight? or open Rimbaud and read

> *O saisons, o châteaux!*
> *Quelle âme est sans défauts?*[20]

and who shall rationalize the charm? In illness words seem to possess a mystic quality. We grasp what is beyond their surface meaning, gather instinctively this, that, and the other – a sound, a colour, here a stress, there a pause – which the poet, knowing words to be meagre in comparison with ideas, has strewn about his page to evoke, when collected, a state of mind which neither words can express nor the reason explain. Incomprehensibility has an enormous power over us in illness, more legitimately perhaps than the upright will allow. In health meaning has encroached upon sound. Our intelligence domineers over our senses. But in illness, with the police off duty, we creep beneath some obscure poem by Mallarmé or Donne,[21] some phrase in Latin or Greek, and the words give out their scent and distil their flavour, and then, if at last we grasp the meaning, it is all the richer for having come to us sensually first, by way of the palate and the nostrils, like some queer odour. Foreigners,[22] to whom the tongue is strange, have us at a disadvantage. The Chinese must know the sound of *Antony and Cleopatra* better than we do.

Rashness is one of the properties of illness – outlaws that we are – and it is rashness that we need in reading Shakespeare. It is not that we should doze in reading him, but that, fully conscious and aware, his fame intimidates and bores, and all the views of all the critics dull in us that thunder clap of conviction which, if an illusion, is still so helpful an illusion, so prodigious a pleasure, so keen a stimulus in reading the great. Shakespeare is getting flyblown;[23] a paternal government might well forbid writing about him, as they put his monument at Stratford beyond the reach of scribbling fingers. With all this buzz of criticism about, one may hazard one's conjectures privately, make one's notes in the margin; but, knowing that someone has said it before, or said it better, the zest is gone. Illness, in its kingly sublimity, sweeps all that aside and leaves nothing but Shakespeare and oneself. What with his overweening power and our overweening arrogance, the barriers go down, the knots run smooth, the brain rings and resounds with *Lear* or *Macbeth*, and even Coleridge himself squeaks[24] like a distant mouse.

But enough of Shakespeare – let us turn to Augustus Hare. There are people who say that even illness does not warrant these transitions; that the author of *The Story of Two Noble Lives* is not the peer of Boswell;[25] and if we assert that short of the best in literature we like the worst – it is mediocrity that is hateful – will have none of that either. So be it. The law is on the side of the normal. But for those who suffer a slight rise of temperature the names of Hare and Waterford and Canning ray out as beams of benignant lustre. Not, it is true, for the first hundred pages or so. There, as so often in these fat volumes, we flounder and threaten to sink in a plethora of aunts and uncles. We have to remind ourselves that there is such a thing as atmosphere; that the masters themselves often keep us waiting intolerably while they prepare our minds for whatever it may be – the surprise, or the lack of surprise. So Hare, too, takes his time; the charm steals upon us imperceptibly; by degrees we become almost one of the family, yet not quite, for our sense of the oddity of it all remains, and share the family dismay when Lord Stuart leaves the room – there was a ball going forward – and is next heard of in Iceland. Parties, he said, bored him – such were

English aristocrats before marriage with intellect had adulterated the fine singularity of their minds. Parties bore them; they are off to Iceland. Then Beckford's mania for castle building[26] attacked him; he must lift a French *château* across the Channel, and erect pinnacles and towers to use as servants' bedrooms at vast expense, upon the borders of a crumbling cliff, too, so that the housemaids saw their brooms swimming down the Solent, and Lady Stuart was much distressed, but made the best of it and began, like the high-born lady that she was, planting evergreens in the face of ruin. Meanwhile the daughters, Charlotte and Louisa, grew up in their incomparable loveliness, with pencils in their hands, forever sketching, dancing, flirting, in a cloud of gauze. They are not very distinct it is true. For life then was not the life of Charlotte and Louisa. It was the life of families, of groups. It was a web, a net, spreading wide and enmeshing every sort of cousin, dependant, and old retainer. Aunts – Aunt Caledon, Aunt Mexborough – grandmothers – Granny Stuart, Granny Hardwicke – cluster in chorus, and rejoice and sorrow and eat Christmas dinner together, and grow very old and remain very upright, and sit in hooded chairs cutting flowers it seems out of coloured paper. Charlotte married Canning and went to India; Louisa married Lord Waterford and went to Ireland. Then letters begin to cross vast spaces in slow sailing ships and communication becomes still more protracted and verbose, and there seems no end to the space and the leisure of those early Victorian days, and faiths are lost and the life of Hedley Vicars revives them; aunts catch cold but recover; cousins marry; there are the Irish famine and the Indian Mutiny, and both sisters remain to their great, but silent, grief without children to come after them. Louisa, dumped down in Ireland with Lord Waterford at the hunt all day, was often very lonely; but she stuck to her post, visited the poor, spoke words of comfort ('I am sorry indeed to hear of Anthony Thompson's loss of mind, or rather of memory; if, however, he can understand sufficiently to trust solely in our Saviour, he has enough') and sketched and sketched. Thousands of notebooks were filled with pen-and-ink drawings of an evening, and then the carpenter stretched sheets for her and she designed frescoes for schoolrooms, had live sheep into her bedroom, draped gamekeepers in blankets, painted Holy Families in abundance, until the great Watts exclaimed that here was

Titian's peer and Raphael's master![27] At that Lady Waterford laughed (she had a generous, benignant sense of humour); and said that she was nothing but a sketcher; had scarcely had a lesson in her life – witness her angel's wings scandalously unfinished. Moreover, there was her father's house forever falling into the sea; she must shore it up; must entertain her friends; must fill her days with all sorts of charities, till her Lord came home from hunting, and then, at midnight often, she would sketch him with his knightly face half hidden in a bowl of soup, sitting with her sketch-book under a lamp beside him. Off he would ride again, stately as a crusader, to hunt the fox, and she would wave to him and think each time, what if this should be the last? And so it was, that winter's morning; his horse stumbled; he was killed. She knew it before they told her, and never could Sir John Leslie forget, when he ran downstairs on the day of the burial, the beauty of the great lady standing to see the hearse depart, nor, when he came back, how the curtain, heavy, mid-Victorian, plush perhaps, was all crushed together where she had grasped it in her agony.

The Cinema

This essay first appeared in the New York journal *Arts*, June 1926.
The version reprinted here was published the following month in
the *Nation and Athenaeum*, 3 July 1926, and later as 'The Movies and
Reality' in *New Republic*, New York, 4 August 1926.

People say that the savage no longer exists in us, that we are at the fag-end of civilization, that everything has been said already, and that it is too late to be ambitious. But these philosophers have presumably forgotten the movies. They have never seen the savages of the twentieth century watching the pictures. They have never sat themselves in front of the screen and thought how, for all the clothes on their backs and the carpets at their feet, no great distance separates them from those bright-eyed, naked men who knocked two bars of iron together and heard in that clangour a foretaste of the music of Mozart.

The bars in this case, of course, are so highly wrought and so covered over with accretions of alien matter that it is extremely difficult to hear anything distinctly. All is hubble-bubble, swarm, and chaos. We are peering over the edge of a cauldron in which fragments of all shapes and savours seem to simmer;[1] now and again some vast form heaves itself up, and seems about to haul itself out of chaos. Yet, at first sight, the art of the cinema seems simple, even stupid. There is the King shaking hands with a football team; there is Sir Thomas Lipton's yacht; there is Jack Horner[2] winning the Grand National. The eye licks it all up instantaneously, and the brain, agreeably titillated, settles down to watch things happening without bestirring itself to think. For the ordinary eye, the English unaesthetic eye, is a simple mechanism, which takes care that the body does not fall down coal-holes, provides the brain with toys and sweetmeats to keep it quiet, and can be trusted to go on behaving like a competent nursemaid until the brain comes to the conclusion that it is time to wake up. What is its surprise, then, to be roused suddenly in the midst of its agreeable somnolence and asked for help? The eye is in difficulties. The eye wants help. The eye says to the brain, 'Something is happening which I do not in the least understand. You are needed.' Together they look at the King, the boat, the horse, and the brain sees at once that they have taken on a quality which does not belong to the simple photograph of real life. They have become not more beautiful, in the sense in which pictures are beautiful, but shall we call it (our vocabulary is miserably insufficient) more real, or real with a different reality from that which we perceive in daily life? We behold them as they are when we are not there. We see life as it is when we have no part in it. As we gaze we seem to be removed from the pettiness of actual existence. The horse will not knock us down. The King will not grasp our hands. The wave will not wet our feet. From this point of vantage, as we watch the antics of our kind, we have time to feel pity and amusement, to generalize, to endow one man with the attributes of the race. Watching the boat sail and the wave break, we have time to open our minds wide to beauty and register on top of it the queer sensation – this beauty will continue, and this beauty will flourish whether we behold it or not. Further, all this happened ten years ago, we are told. We are beholding a world which has gone beneath the waves. Brides are emerging from the abbey – they are now mothers; ushers are ardent – they are now silent; mothers are tearful; guests are joyful; this has been won and that has been lost, and it is over and done with. The war sprung its chasm at the feet of all this innocence and ignorance, but it was thus that we danced and pirouetted, toiled and desired, thus that the sun shone and the clouds scudded up to the very end.

But the picture-makers seem dissatisfied with such obvious sources of interest as the passage of time and the suggestiveness of reality. They despise the flight of gulls, ships on the Thames, the Prince of Wales, the Mile End Road, Piccadilly Circus.[3] They want to be improving, altering, making an art of their own – naturally, for so much seems to be within their scope. So many arts seemed to stand by ready to offer their help. For example, there was literature. All the famous novels of the world, with their well-known characters, and their famous scenes, only asked, it seemed, to be put on the films. What could be easier and simpler? The cinema fell upon its prey with immense rapacity, and to this moment[4] largely subsists upon the body of its unfortunate victim. But the results are disastrous to both. The alliance is unnatural. Eye and brain are torn asunder ruthlessly as they try vainly to work in couples. The eye says: 'Here is Anna Karenina.'[5] A voluptuous lady in black velvet wearing pearls comes before us. But the brain says: 'That is no more Anna Karenina than it is Queen Victoria.' For the brain knows Anna almost entirely by the inside of her mind – her charm, her passion, her despair. All the emphasis is laid by the cinema upon her teeth, her pearls, and her velvet. Then 'Anna falls in love with Vronsky' – that is to say, the lady in black velvet falls into the arms of a gentleman in uniform, and they kiss with enormous succulence, great deliberation, and infinite gesticulation on a sofa in an extremely well-appointed library, while a gardener incidentally mows the lawn. So we lurch and lumber through the most famous novels of the world. So we spell them out in words of one syllable written, too, in the scrawl of an illiterate schoolboy. A kiss is love. A broken cup is jealousy. A grin is happiness. Death is a hearse. None of these things has the least connection with the novel that Tolstoy wrote, and it is only when we give up trying to connect the pictures with the book that we guess from some accidental scene – like the gardener mowing the lawn – what the cinema might do if it were left to its own devices.

But what, then, are its devices? If it ceased to be a parasite, how would it walk erect? At present it is only from hints that one can frame any conjecture. For instance, at a performance of Dr Caligari[6] the other day, a shadow shaped like a tadpole suddenly appeared at one corner of the screen. It swelled to an immense size, quivered, bulged, and sank back again into nonentity. For a moment it seemed to embody some monstrous, diseased imagination of the lunatic's brain. For a moment it seemed as if thought could be conveyed by shape more effectively than by words. The monstrous, quivering tadpole seemed to be fear itself, and not the statement, 'I am afraid.' In fact, the shadow was accidental, and the effect unintentional. But if a shadow at a certain moment can suggest so much more than the actual gestures and words of men and women in a state of fear, it seems plain that the cinema has within its grasp innumerable symbols for emotions that have so far failed to find expression. Terror has, besides its ordinary forms, the shape of a tadpole; it burgeons, bulges, quivers, disappears. Anger is not merely rant and rhetoric, red faces and clenched fists. It is perhaps a black line wriggling upon a white sheet. Anna and Vronsky need no longer scowl and grimace. They have at their command – but what? Is there, we ask, some secret language which we feel and see, but never speak, and, if so, could this be made visible to the eye? Is there any characteristic which thought possesses that can be rendered visible without the help of words? It has speed and slowness; dart-like directness and vaporous circumlocution. But it has also, especially in moments of emotion, the picture-making power, the need to lift its burden to another bearer; to let an image run side by side along with it. The likeness of the thought is, for some reason, more beautiful, more comprehensible, more available than the thought itself. As everybody knows, in Shakespeare the most complex ideas form chains of images through which we mount, changing and turning, until we reach the light of day. But, obviously, the images of a poet are not to be cast in bronze, or traced by pencil. They are compact of a thousand suggestions of which the visual is only the most obvious or the uppermost. Even the simplest image; 'My luve's like a red, red rose, that's newly sprung in June,'[7] presents us with impressions of moisture and warmth and the glow of crimson and the softness of petals inextricably mixed and strung upon the lilt of a rhythm which is itself the voice of the passion and hesitation of the lover. All this, which is accessible to words, and to words alone, the cinema must avoid.

Yet if so much of our thinking and feeling is connected with seeing, some residue of visual emotion which is of no use either to painter or to poet may still await the cinema. That such symbols will be quite unlike the real objects which we see before us seems highly probable. Something abstract, something which moves with controlled and conscious art, something which calls for the very slightest help from words or music[8] to make itself intelligible, yet justly uses them subserviently – of such movements and abstractions the films may, in time to come, be composed. Then, indeed, when some new symbol for expressing thought is found, the film-maker has enormous riches at his command. The exactitude of reality and its surprising power of suggestion are to be had for the asking. Annas and Vronskys – there they are in the flesh. If into this reality he could breathe emotion, could animate the perfect form with thought, then his booty could be hauled in hand over hand. Then, as smoke pours from Vesuvius,[9] we should be able to see thought in its wildness, in its beauty, in its oddity, pouring from men with their elbows on a table; from women with their little handbags slipping to the floor. We should see these emotions mingling together and affecting each other.

We should see violent changes of emotion produced by their collision. The most fantastic contrasts could be flashed before us with a speed which the writer can only toil after in vain; the dream architecture of arches and battlements, of cascades falling and fountains rising, which sometimes visits us in sleep or shapes itself in half-darkened rooms, could be realized before our waking eyes. No fantasy could be too far-fetched or insubstantial. The past could be unrolled, distances annihilated, and the gulfs which dislocate novels (when, for instance, Tolstoy has to pass from Levin to Anna,[10] and in so doing jars his story and wrenches and arrests our sympathies) could, by the sameness of the background, by the repetition of some scene, be smoothed away.

How all this is to be attempted, much less achieved, no one at the moment can tell us. We get intimations only in the chaos of the streets, perhaps, when some momentary assembly of colour, sound, movement suggests that here is a scene waiting a new art to be transfixed. And sometimes at the cinema, in the midst of its immense dexterity and enormous technical proficiency, the curtain parts and we behold, far off, some unknown and unexpected beauty. But it is for a moment only. For a strange thing has happened – while all the other arts were born naked, this, the youngest, has been born fully clothed. It can say everything before it has anything to say. It is as if the savage tribe, instead of finding two bars of iron to play with, had found, scattering the seashore, fiddles, flutes, saxophones, trumpets, grand pianos by Erard and Bechstein, and had begun with incredible energy, but without knowing a note of music, to hammer and thump upon them all at the same time.

How Should One Read a Book?

This essay, first published in the Yale Review, *October 1926, was considerably revised for* The Common Reader: Second Series *(1932), the version reprinted here.*

In the first place, I want to emphasize the note of interrogation at the end of my title.[1] Even if I could answer the question for myself, the answer would apply only to me and not to you. The only advice, indeed, that one person can give another about reading is to take no advice, to follow your own instincts, to use your own reason, to come to your own conclusions. If this is agreed between us, then I feel at liberty to put forward a few ideas and suggestions because you will not allow them to fetter that independence which is the most important quality that a reader can possess. After all, what laws can be laid down about books? The Battle of Waterloo was certainly fought on a certain day; but is *Hamlet* a better play than *Lear*? Nobody can say. Each must decide that question for himself. To admit authorities, however heavily furred and gowned, into our libraries and let them tell us how to read, what to read, what value to place upon what we read, is to destroy the spirit of freedom which is the breath of those sanctuaries. Everywhere else we may be bound by laws and conventions – there we have none.

But to enjoy freedom, if the platitude is pardonable, we have of course to control ourselves. We must not squander our powers, helplessly and ignorantly, squirting half the house in order to water a single rose-bush; we must train them, exactly and powerfully, here on the very spot. This, it may be, is one of the first difficulties that faces us in a library. What is 'the very spot'? There may well seem to be nothing but a conglomeration and huddle of confusion. Poems and novels, histories and memoirs, dictionaries and bluebooks;[2] books written in all languages by men and women of all tempers, races, and ages jostle each other on the shelf. And outside the donkey brays, the women gossip at the pump, the colts gallop across the fields. Where are we to begin? How are we to bring order into this multitudinous chaos and so get the deepest and widest pleasure from what we read?

It is simple enough to say that since books have classes – fiction, biography, poetry – we should separate them and take from each what it is right that each should give us. Yet few people ask from books what books can give us. Most commonly we come to books with blurred and divided minds, asking of fiction that it shall be true, of poetry that it shall be false, of biography that it shall be flattering, of history that it shall enforce our own prejudices. If we could banish all such preconceptions when we read, that would be an admirable beginning. Do not dictate to your author; try to become him. Be his fellow-worker and accomplice. If you hang back, and reserve and criticize at first, you are preventing yourself from getting the fullest possible value from what you read. But if you open your mind as widely as possible, then signs and hints of almost imperceptible fineness, from the twist and turn of the first sentences, will bring you into the presence of a human being unlike any other. Steep yourself in this, acquaint yourself with this, and soon you will find that your author is giving you, or attempting to give you, something far more definite. The thirty-two chapters of a novel – if we consider how to read a novel first – are an attempt to make something as formed and controlled as a building: but words are more impalpable than bricks; reading is a longer and more complicated process than seeing. Perhaps the quickest way to understand the elements of what a novelist is doing is not to read, but to write; to make your own experiment with the dangers and difficulties of words. Recall, then, some event that has left a distinct impression on you – how at the corner of the street, perhaps, you passed two people talking. A tree shook; an electric light danced; the tone of the talk was comic, but also tragic; a whole vision, an entire conception, seemed contained in that moment.

But when you attempt to reconstruct it in words, you will find that it breaks into a thousand conflicting impressions. Some must be subdued; others emphasized; in the process you will lose, probably, all grasp upon the emotion itself. Then turn from your blurred and littered pages to the opening pages of some great novelist – Defoe, Jane Austen, Hardy. Now you will be better able to appreciate their mastery. It is not merely that we are in the presence of a different person – Defoe, Jane Austen, or Thomas Hardy – but that we are living in a different world. Here, in *Robinson Crusoe*,[3] we are trudging a plain high road; one thing happens after another; the fact and the order of the fact is enough. But if the open air and adventure mean everything to Defoe they mean nothing to Jane Austen. Hers is the drawing-room, and people talking, and by the many mirrors of their talk revealing their characters. And if, when we have accustomed ourselves to the drawing-room and its reflections, we turn to Hardy, we are once more spun round. The moors are round us and the stars are above our heads. The other side of the mind is now exposed – the dark side that comes uppermost in solitude, not the light side that shows in company. Our relations are not towards people, but towards Nature and destiny. Yet different as these worlds are, each is consistent with itself. The maker of each is careful to observe the laws of his own perspective, and however great a strain they may put upon us they will never confuse us, as lesser writers so frequently do, by introducing two different kinds of reality into the same book. Thus to go from one great novelist to another – from Jane Austen to Hardy, from Peacock to Trollope, from Scott to Meredith[4] – is to be wrenched and uprooted; to be thrown this way and then that. To read a novel is a difficult and complex art. You must be capable not only of great fineness of perception, but of great boldness of imagination if you are going to make use of all that the novelist – the great artist – gives you.

But a glance at the heterogeneous company on the shelf will show you that writers are very seldom 'great artists'; far more often a book makes no claim to be a work of art at all. These biographies and autobiographies, for example, lives of great men, of men long dead and forgotten, that stand cheek by jowl with the novels and poems, are we to refuse to read them because they are not 'art'? Or shall we read them, but read them in a different way, with a different aim? Shall we read them in the first place to satisfy that curiosity which possesses us sometimes when in the evening we linger in front of a house where the lights are lit and the blinds not yet drawn, and each floor of the house shows us a different section of human life in being?[5] Then we are consumed with curiosity about the lives of these people – the servants gossiping, the gentlemen dining, the girl dressing for a party, the old woman at the window with her knitting. Who are they, what are they, what are their names, their occupations, their thoughts, and adventures?

Biographies and memoirs answer such questions, light up innumerable such houses; they show us people going about their daily affairs, toiling, failing, succeeding, eating, hating, loving, until they die. And sometimes as we watch, the house fades and the iron railings vanish and we are out at sea; we are hunting, sailing, fighting; we are among savages and soldiers; we are taking part in great campaigns. Or if we like to stay here in England, in London, still the scene changes; the street narrows; the house becomes small, cramped, diamond-paned, and malodorous. We see a poet, Donne, driven from such a house because the walls were so thin that when the children cried their voices cut through them. We can follow him, through the paths that lie in the pages of books, to Twickenham; to Lady Bedford's Park,[6] a famous meeting-ground for nobles and poets; and then turn our steps to Wilton, the great house under the downs, and hear Sidney read the *Arcadia* to his sister;[7] and ramble among the very marshes and see the very herons that figure in that famous romance; and then again travel north with that other Lady Pembroke, Anne Clifford, to her wild moors, or plunge into the city and control our merriment at the sight of Gabriel Harvey in his black velvet suit arguing about poetry with Spenser.[8] Nothing is more fascinating than to grope and stumble in the alternate darkness and splendour of Elizabethan London. But there is no staying there. The Temples and the Swifts, the Harleys and the St Johns[9] beckon us on; hour upon hour can be spent disentangling their quarrels and deciphering their characters; and when we tire of them we can stroll on, past a lady in black wearing diamonds, to Samuel Johnson and Goldsmith and Garrick;[10] or cross the Channel, if we like, and meet Voltaire and Diderot, Madame du Deffand;[11] and so back to England and Twickenham – how certain places repeat themselves and certain names! – where Lady Bedford had her Park once and Pope lived later, to Walpole's home at Strawberry Hill.[12] But Walpole introduces us to such a swarm of new acquaintances, there are so many houses to visit and bells to ring that we may well hesitate for a moment, on the Miss Berrys' doorstep, for example, when behold, up comes Thackeray; he is the friend of the woman whom Walpole loved; so that merely by going from friend to friend, from garden to garden, from house to house, we have passed from one end of English literature to another and wake to find ourselves here again in the present, if we can so differentiate this moment from all that have gone before. This, then, is one of the ways in which we can read these lives and letters; we can make them light up the many windows of the past; we can watch the famous dead in their familiar habits and fancy sometimes that we are very close and can surprise their secrets, and sometimes we may pull out a play or a poem that they have written and see whether it reads differently in the presence of the author. But this again rouses other questions. How far, we must ask ourselves, is a book influenced by its writer's life – how far is it safe to let the man interpret the writer? How far shall we resist or give way to the sympathies and antipathies that the man himself rouses in us – so sensitive are words, so receptive of the character of the author? These are questions that press upon us when we read lives and letters, and we must answer them for ourselves, for nothing can be more fatal than to be guided by the preferences of others in a matter so personal.

But also we can read such books with another aim, not to throw light on literature, not to become familiar with famous people, but to refresh and exercise our own creative powers. Is there not an open window on the right hand of the bookcase? How delightful to stop reading and look out! How stimulating the scene is, in its unconsciousness, its irrelevance, its perpetual movement – the colts galloping round the field, the woman filling her pail at the well, the donkey throwing back his head and emitting his long, acrid moan. The greater part of any library is nothing but the record of such fleeting moments in the lives of men, women, and donkeys. Every literature, as it grows old, has its rubbish-heap, its record of vanished moments and forgotten lives told in faltering and feeble accents that have perished. But if you give yourself up to the delight of rubbish-reading you will be surprised, indeed you will be overcome, by the relics of human life that have been cast out to moulder. It may be one letter – but what a vision it gives! It may be a few sentences – but what vistas they suggest! Sometimes a whole story will come together with such beautiful humour and pathos and completeness that it seems as if a great novelist had been at work, yet it is only an old actor, Tate Wilkinson, remembering the strange story of Captain Jones; it is only a young subaltern serving under Arthur Wellesley and falling in love with a pretty girl at Lisbon; it is only Maria Allen letting fall her sewing in the empty drawing-room and sighing how she wishes she had taken Dr Burney's good advice and had never eloped with her Rishy.[13] None of this has any value; it is negligible in the extreme; yet how absorbing it is now and again to go through the rubbish-heaps and find rings and scissors and broken noses buried in the huge past and try to piece them together while the colt gallops round the field, the woman fills her pail at the well, and the donkey brays.

But we tire of rubbish-reading in the long run. We tire of searching for what is needed to complete the half-truth which is all that the Wilkinsons, the Bunburys, and the Maria Allens are able to offer us. They had not the artist's power of mastering and eliminating; they could not tell the whole truth even about their own lives; they have disfigured the story that might have been so shapely. Facts are all that they can offer us, and facts are a very inferior form of fiction. Thus the desire grows upon us to have done with half-statements and approximations; to cease from searching out the minute shades of human character, to enjoy the greater abstractness, the purer truth of fiction. Thus we create the mood, intense and generalized, unaware of detail, but stressed by some regular, recurrent beat, whose natural expression is poetry; and that is the time to read poetry – when we are almost able to write it.

> Western wind, when wilt thou blow?
> The small rain down can rain.
> Christ, if my love were in my arms,
> And I in my bed again![14]

The impact of poetry is so hard and direct that for the moment there is no other sensation except that of the poem itself. What profound depths we visit then – how sudden and complete is our immersion! There is nothing here to catch hold of; nothing to stay us in our flight. The illusion of fiction is gradual; its effects are prepared; but who when they read these four lines stops to ask who wrote them, or conjures up the thought of Donne's house or Sidney's secretary; or enmeshes them in the intricacy of the past and the succession of generations? The poet is always our contemporary.

HOW SHOULD ONE READ A BOOK?

Our being for the moment is centred and constricted, as in any violent shock of personal emotion. Afterwards, it is true, the sensation begins to spread in wider rings through our minds; remoter senses are reached; these begin to sound and to comment and we are aware of echoes and reflections. The intensity of poetry covers an immense range of emotion. We have only to compare the force and directness of

> I shall fall like a tree, and find my grave,
> Only remembering that I grieve,[15]

with the wavering modulation of

> Minutes are numbered by the fall of sands,
> As by an hour glass; the span of time
> Doth waste us to our graves, and we look on it;
> An age of pleasure, revelled out, comes home
> At last, and ends in sorrow; but the life,
> Weary of riot, numbers every sand,
> Wailing in sighs, until the last drop down,
> So to conclude calamity in rest,[16]

or place the meditative calm of

> whether we be young or old,
> Our destiny, our being's heart and home,
> Is with infinitude, and only there;
> With hope it is, hope that can never die,
> Effort, and expectation, and desire,
> And something evermore about to be,[17]

beside the complete and inexhaustible loveliness of

> The moving Moon went up the sky,
> And nowhere did abide:
> Softly she was going up,
> And a star or two beside —[18]

or the splendid fantasy of

> And the woodland haunter
> Shall not cease to saunter
> When, far down some glade,
> Of the great world's burning,

> One soft flame upturning
> Seems, to his discerning,
> Crocus in the shade,[19]

to bethink us of the varied art of the poet; his power to make us at once actors and spectators; his power to run his hand into character as if it were a glove, and be Falstaff or Lear; his power to condense, to widen, to state, once and for ever.

'We have only to compare' – with those words the cat is out of the bag, and the true complexity of reading is admitted. The first process, to receive impressions with the utmost understanding, is only half the process of reading; it must be completed, if we are to get the whole pleasure from a book, by another. We must pass judgement upon these multitudinous impressions; we must make of these fleeting shapes one that is hard and lasting. But not directly. Wait for the dust of reading to settle; for the conflict and the questioning to die down; walk, talk, pull the dead petals from a rose, or fall asleep. Then suddenly without our willing it, for it is thus that Nature undertakes these transitions, the book will return, but differently. It will float to the top of the mind as a whole. And the book as a whole is different from the book received currently in separate phrases. Details now fit themselves into their places. We see the shape from start to finish; it is a barn, a pig-sty, or a cathedral. Now then we can compare book with book as we compare building with building. But this act of comparison means that our attitude has changed; we are no longer the friends of the writer, but his judges; and just as we cannot be too sympathetic as friends, so as judges we cannot be too severe. Are they not criminals, books that have wasted our time and sympathy; are they not the most insidious enemies of society, corrupters, defilers, the writers of false books, faked books, books that fill the air with decay and disease? Let us then be severe in our judgements; let us compare each book with the greatest of its kind. There they hang in the mind the shapes of the books we have read solidified by the judgements we have passed on them – *Robinson Crusoe*, *Emma*, *The Return of the Native*. Compare the novels with these – even the latest and least of novels has a right to be judged with the best. And so with poetry – when the intoxication of rhythm has died down and the splendour of words has faded, a visionary shape will return to us and this must be compared with *Lear*, with *Phèdre*, with *The Prelude*;[20] or if not with these, with whatever is the best or seems to us to be the best in its own kind. And we may be sure that the newness of new poetry and fiction is its most superficial quality and that we have only to alter slightly, not to recast, the standards by which we have judged the old.

It would be foolish, then, to pretend that the second part of reading, to judge, to compare, is as simple as the first – to open the mind wide to the fast flocking of innumerable impressions. To continue reading without the book before you, to hold one shadow-shape against another, to have read widely enough and with enough understanding to make such comparisons alive and illuminating – that is difficult; it is still more difficult to press further and to say, 'Not only is the book of this sort, but it is of this value; here it fails; here it succeeds; this is bad; that is good'. To carry out this part of a reader's duty needs such imagination, insight, and learning that it is hard to conceive any one mind sufficiently endowed; impossible for the most self-confident to find more than the seeds of such powers in himself. Would it not be wiser, then, to remit this part of reading and to allow the critics, the gowned and furred authorities of the library, to decide the question of the book's absolute value for us? Yet how impossible! We may stress the value of sympathy; we may try to sink our own identity as we read. But we know that we cannot sympathize wholly or immerse ourselves wholly; there is always a demon in us who whispers, 'I hate, I love', and we cannot silence him. Indeed, it is precisely because we hate and we love that our relation with the poets and novelists is so intimate that we find the presence of another person intolerable. And even if the results are abhorrent and our judgements are wrong, still our taste, the nerve of sensation that sends shocks through us, is our chief illuminant; we learn through feeling; we cannot suppress our own idiosyncrasy without impoverishing it. But as time goes on perhaps we can train our taste; perhaps we can make it submit to some control. When it has fed greedily and lavishly upon books of all sorts – poetry, fiction, history, biography – and has stopped reading and looked for long spaces upon the variety, the incongruity of the living world, we shall find that it is changing a little; it is not so greedy, it is more reflective. It will begin to bring us not merely judgements on particular books, but it will tell us that there is a quality common to certain books. Listen, it will say, what shall we call *this*? And it will read us perhaps *Lear* and then perhaps the *Agamemnon*[21] in order to bring out that common quality. Thus, with our taste to guide us, we shall venture beyond the particular book in search of qualities that group books together; we shall give them names and thus frame a rule that brings order into our perceptions. We shall gain a further and a rarer pleasure from that discrimination. But as a rule only lives when it is perpetually broken by contact with the books themselves – nothing is easier and more stultifying than to make rules which exist out of touch with facts, in a vacuum – now at last, in order to steady ourselves in this difficult attempt, it may be well to turn to the very rare writers who are able to enlighten us upon literature as an art. Coleridge and Dryden and Johnson,[22] in their considered criticism, the poets and novelists themselves in their unconsidered sayings, are often surprisingly relevant; they light up and solidify the vague ideas that have been tumbling in the misty depths of our minds. But they are only able to help us if we come to them laden with questions and suggestions won honestly in the course of our own reading. They can do nothing for us if we herd ourselves under their authority and lie down like sheep in the shade of a hedge. We can only understand their ruling when it comes in conflict with our own and vanquishes it.

If this is so, if to read a book as it should be read calls for the rarest qualities of imagination, insight, and judgement, you may perhaps conclude that literature is a very complex art and that it is unlikely that we shall be able, even after a lifetime of reading, to make any valuable contribution to its criticism. We must remain readers; we shall not put on the further glory that belongs to those rare beings who are also critics. But still we have our responsibilities as readers and even our importance. The standards we raise and the judgements we pass steal into the air and become part of the atmosphere which writers breathe as they work. An influence is created which tells upon them even if it never finds its way into print. And that influence, if it were well instructed, vigorous and individual and sincere, might be of great value now when criticism is necessarily in abeyance; when books pass in review, like the procession of animals in a shooting gallery, and the critic has only one second in which to load and aim and shoot and may well be pardoned if he mistakes rabbits for tigers, eagles for barndoor fowls, or misses altogether and wastes his shot upon some peaceful cow grazing in a further field. If behind the erratic gunfire of the press the author felt that there was another kind of criticism, the opinion of people reading for the love of reading, slowly and unprofessionally, and judging with great sympathy and yet with great severity, might this not improve the quality of his work? And if by our means books were to become stronger, richer, and more varied, that would be an end worth reaching.

Yet who reads to bring about an end, however desirable? Are there not some pursuits that we practise because they are good in themselves, and some pleasures that are final? And is not this among them? I have sometimes dreamt, at least, that when the Day of Judgement dawns and the great conquerors and lawyers and statesmen come to receive their reward – their crowns, their laurels, their names carved indelibly upon imperishable marble – the Almighty will turn to Peter and will say, not without a certain envy when he sees us coming with our books under our arms, 'Look, these need no reward. We have nothing to give them here. They have loved reading.'

Street Haunting: A London Adventure

This essay was first published in the Yale Review, *October 1927,
and then as a pamphlet in a limited edition by the Westgate Press,
San Francisco in May 1930; the version reprinted here was published
posthumously in* The Death of the Moth, *1942.*

No one perhaps has ever felt passionately towards a lead pencil. But there are circumstances in which it can become supremely desirable to possess one; moments when we are set upon having an object, an excuse for walking half across London between tea and dinner. As the foxhunter hunts in order to preserve the breed of foxes, and the golfer plays in order that open spaces may be preserved from the builders, so when the desire comes upon us to go street rambling the pencil does for a pretext, and getting up we say: 'Really I must buy a pencil,' as if under cover of this excuse we could indulge safely in the greatest pleasure of town life in winter – rambling the streets of London.[1]

The hour should be the evening and the season winter, for in winter the champagne brightness of the air and the sociability of the streets are grateful.[2] We are not then taunted as in the summer by the longing for shade and solitude and sweet airs from the hayfields. The evening hour, too, gives us the irresponsibility which darkness and lamplight bestow. We are no longer quite ourselves. As we step out of the house on a fine evening between four and six, we shed the self our friends know us by and become part of that vast republican army of anonymous trampers, whose society is so agreeable after the solitude of one's own room. For there we sit surrounded by objects which perpetually express the oddity of our own temperaments and enforce the memories of our own experience. That bowl on the mantelpiece, for instance, was bought at Mantua on a windy day. We were leaving the shop when the sinister old woman plucked at our skirts and said she would find herself starving one of these days, but, 'Take it!' she cried, and thrust the blue-and-white china bowl into our hands as if she never wanted to be reminded of her quixotic generosity. So, guiltily, but suspecting nevertheless how badly we had been fleeced, we carried it back to the little hotel where, in the middle of the night, the innkeeper quarrelled so violently with his wife that we all leant out into the courtyard to look, and saw the vines laced about among the pillars and the stars white in the sky. The moment was stabilized, stamped like a coin indelibly among a million that slipped by imperceptibly. There, too, was the melancholy Englishman, who rose among the coffee cups and the little iron tables and revealed the secrets of his soul – as travellers do. All this – Italy, the windy morning, the vines laced about the pillars, the Englishman and the secrets of his soul – rise up in a cloud from the china bowl on the mantelpiece. And there, as our eyes fall to the floor, is that brown stain on the carpet. Mr Lloyd George[3] made that. 'The man's a devil!' said Mr Cummings, putting the kettle down with which he was about to fill the teapot so that it burnt a brown ring on the carpet.

But when the door shuts on us, all that vanishes. The shell-like covering which our souls have excreted[4] to house themselves, to make for themselves a shape distinct from others, is broken, and there is left of all these wrinkles and roughnesses a central oyster of perceptiveness, an enormous eye. How beautiful a street is in winter! It is at once revealed and obscured. Here vaguely one can trace symmetrical straight avenues of doors and windows; here under the lamps are floating islands of pale light through which pass quickly bright men and women, who, for all their poverty and shabbiness, wear a certain look of unreality, an air of triumph, as if they had given life the slip, so that life, deceived of her prey, blunders on without them. But, after all, we are only gliding smoothly on the surface. The eye is not a miner, not a diver, not a seeker after buried treasure. It floats us smoothly down a stream; resting, pausing, the brain sleeps perhaps as it looks.

How beautiful a London street is then, with its islands of light, and its long groves of darkness, and on one side of it perhaps some tree-sprinkled, grass-grown space where night is folding herself to sleep naturally and, as one passes the iron railing, one hears those little cracklings and stirrings of leaf and twig which seem to suppose the silence of fields all round them, an owl hooting, and far away the rattle of a train in the valley. But this is London, we are reminded; high among the bare trees are hung oblong frames of reddish-yellow light – windows; there are points of brilliance burning steadily like low stars – lamps; this empty ground, which holds the country in it and its peace, is only a London square, set about by offices and houses where at this hour fierce lights burn over maps, over documents, over desks where clerks sit turning with wetted forefinger the files of endless correspondences; or more suffusedly the firelight wavers and the lamplight falls upon the privacy of some drawing-room, its easy chairs, its papers, its china, its inlaid table, and the figure of a woman, accurately measuring out the precise number of spoons of tea which— She looks at the door as if she heard a ring downstairs and somebody asking, is she in?

But here we must stop peremptorily. We are in danger of digging deeper than the eye approves; we are impeding our passage down the smooth stream by catching at some branch or root. At any moment, the sleeping army may stir itself and wake in us a thousand violins and trumpets in response; the army of human beings may rouse itself and assert all its oddities and sufferings and sordidities. Let us dally a little longer, be content still with surfaces only – the glossy brilliance of the motor omnibuses; the carnal splendour of the butchers' shops with their yellow flanks and purple steaks; the blue and red bunches of flowers burning so bravely through the plate glass of the florists' windows.

For the eye has this strange property: it rests only on beauty; like a butterfly it seeks colour and basks in warmth. On a winter's night like this, when nature has been at pains to polish and preen herself, it brings back the prettiest trophies, breaks off little lumps of emerald and coral as if the whole earth were made of precious stone. The thing it cannot do (one is speaking of the average unprofessional eye) is to compose these trophies in such a way as to bring out the more obscure angles and relationships. Hence after a prolonged diet of this simple, sugary fare, of beauty pure and uncomposed, we become conscious of satiety. We halt at the door of the boot shop and make some little excuse, which has nothing to do with the real reason, for folding up the bright paraphernalia of the streets and withdrawing to some duskier chamber of the being where we may ask, as we raise our left foot obediently upon the stand: 'What, then, is it like to be a dwarf?'

She came in escorted by two women who, being of normal size, looked like benevolent giants beside her. Smiling at the shop girls, they seemed to be disclaiming any lot in her deformity and assuring her of their protection. She wore the peevish yet apologetic expression usual on the faces of the deformed. She needed their kindness, yet she resented it. But when the shop girl had been summoned and the giantesses, smiling indulgently, had asked for shoes for 'this lady' and the girl had pushed the little stand in front of her, the dwarf stuck her foot out with an impetuosity which seemed to claim all our attention. Look at that! Look at that! she seemed to demand of us all, as she thrust her foot out, for behold it was the shapely, perfectly proportioned foot of a well-grown woman. It was arched; it was aristocratic. Her whole manner changed as she looked at it resting on the stand. She looked soothed and satisfied. Her manner became full of self-confidence. She sent for shoe after shoe; she tried on pair after pair. She got up and pirouetted before a glass which reflected the foot only in yellow shoes, in fawn shoes, in shoes of lizard skin. She raised her little skirts and displayed her little legs. She was thinking that, after all, feet are the most important part of the whole person; women, she said to herself, have been loved for their feet alone. Seeing nothing but her feet, she imagined perhaps that the rest of her body was of a piece with those beautiful feet. She was shabbily dressed, but she was ready to lavish any money upon her shoes. And as this was the only occasion upon which she was not afraid of being looked at but positively craved attention, she was ready to use any device to prolong the choosing and fitting. Look at my feet, she seemed to be saying, as she took a step this way and then a step that way. The shop girl good-humouredly must have said something flattering, for suddenly her face lit up in ecstasy. But, after all, the giantesses, benevolent though they were, had their own affairs to see to; she must make up her mind; she must decide which to choose. At length, the pair was chosen and, as she walked out between her guardians, with the parcel swinging from her finger, the ecstasy faded, knowledge returned, the old peevishness, the old apology came back, and by the time she had reached the street again she had become a dwarf only.

But she had changed the mood; she had called into being an

atmosphere which, as we followed her out into the street, seemed actually to create the humped, the twisted, the deformed. Two bearded men, brothers, apparently, stone-blind,[5] supporting themselves by resting a hand on the head of a small boy between them, marched down the street. On they came with the unyielding yet tremulous tread of the blind, which seems to lend to their approach something of the terror and inevitability of the fate that has overtaken them. As they passed, holding straight on, the little convoy seemed to cleave asunder the passers-by with the momentum of its silence, its directness, its disaster. Indeed, the dwarf had started a hobbling grotesque dance to which everybody in the street now conformed: the stout lady tightly swathed in shiny sealskin; the feeble-minded boy sucking the silver knob of his stick; the old man squatted on a doorstep as if, suddenly overcome by the absurdity of the human spectacle, he had sat down to look at it – all joined in the hobble and tap of the dwarf's dance.

In what crevices and crannies, one might ask, did they lodge, this maimed company of the halt and the blind? Here, perhaps, in the top rooms of these narrow old houses between Holborn and Soho,[6] where people have such queer names, and pursue so many curious trades, are gold beaters, accordion pleaters, cover buttons, or support life, with even greater fantasticality, upon a traffic in cups without saucers, china umbrella handles, and highly coloured pictures of martyred saints. There they lodge, and it seems as if the lady in the sealskin jacket must find life tolerable, passing the time of day with the accordion pleater, or the man who covers buttons; life which is so fantastic cannot be altogether tragic. They do not grudge us, we are musing, our prosperity; when, suddenly, turning the corner, we come upon a bearded Jew, wild, hunger-bitten, glaring out of his misery; or pass the humped body of an old woman flung abandoned on the step of a public building with a cloak over her like the hasty covering thrown over a dead horse or donkey. At such sights the nerves of the spine seem to stand erect; a sudden flare is brandished in our eyes; a question is asked which is never answered. Often enough these derelicts choose to lie not a stone's throw from theatres, within hearing of barrel organs, almost, as night draws on, within touch of the sequined cloaks and bright legs of diners and dancers. They lie close to those shop windows where commerce offers to a world of old women laid on doorsteps, of blind men, of hobbling dwarfs, sofas which are supported by the gilt necks of proud swans; tables inlaid with baskets of many-coloured fruit; sideboards paved with green marble the better to support the weight of boars' heads; and carpets so softened with age that their carnations have almost vanished in a pale green sea.

Passing, glimpsing, everything seems accidentally but miraculously sprinkled with beauty, as if the tide of trade which deposits its burden so punctually and prosaically upon the shores of Oxford Street[7] had this night cast up nothing but treasure. With no thought of buying, the eye is sportive and generous; it creates; it adorns; it enhances. Standing out in the street, one may build up all the chambers of an imaginary house and furnish them at one's will with sofa, table, carpet. That rug will do for the hall. That alabaster bowl shall stand on a carved table in the window. Our merrymaking shall be reflected in that thick round mirror. But, having built and furnished the house, one is happily under no obligation to possess it; one can dismantle it in the twinkling of an eye, and build and furnish another house with other chairs and other glasses. Or let us indulge ourselves at the antique jewellers, among the trays of rings and the hanging necklaces. Let us choose those pearls, for example, and then imagine how, if we put them on, life would be changed. It becomes instantly between two and three in the morning; the lamps are burning very white in the deserted streets of Mayfair. Only motor cars are abroad at this hour, and one has a sense of emptiness, of airiness, of secluded gaiety. Wearing pearls, wearing silk, one steps out on to a balcony which overlooks the gardens of sleeping Mayfair. There are a few lights in the bedrooms of great peers returned from Court, of silk-stockinged footmen, of dowagers who have pressed the hands of statesmen. A cat creeps along the garden wall. Love-making is going on sibilantly, seductively in the darker places of the room behind thick green curtains. Strolling sedately as if he were promenading a terrace beneath which the shires and counties of England lie sun-bathed, the aged Prime Minister recounts to Lady So-and-So with the curls and the emeralds the true history of some great crisis in the affairs of the land. We seem to be riding on the top of the highest mast of the tallest ship; and yet at the same time we know that nothing of this sort matters; love is not proved thus, nor great achievements completed thus; so that we sport with the moment and preen our feathers in it lightly, as we stand on the balcony watching the moonlit cat creep along Princess Mary's garden wall.[8]

But what could be more absurd? It is, in fact, on the stroke of six; it is a winter's evening; we are walking to the Strand to buy a pencil. How, then, are we also on a balcony, wearing pearls in June? What could be more absurd? Yet it is nature's folly, not ours. When she set about her chief masterpiece, the making of man, she should have thought of one thing only. Instead, turning her head, looking over her shoulder, into each one of us she let creep instincts and desires which are utterly at variance with his main being, so that we are streaked, variegated, all of a mixture; the colours have run. Is the true self this which stands on the pavement in January, or that which bends over the balcony in June? Am I here, or am I there? Or is the true self neither this nor that, neither here nor there, but something so varied and wandering that it is only when we give the rein to its wishes and let it take its way unimpeded that we are indeed ourselves? Circumstances compel unity; for convenience sake a man must be a whole. The good citizen when he opens his door in the evening must be banker, golfer, husband, father; not a nomad wandering the desert, a mystic staring at the sky, a debauchee in the slums of San Francisco, a soldier heading a revolution, a pariah howling with scepticism and solitude. When he opens his door, he must run his fingers through his hair and put his umbrella in the stand like the rest.

But here, none too soon, are the second-hand bookshops. Here we find anchorage in these thwarting currents of being; here we balance ourselves after the splendours and miseries of the streets. The very sight of the bookseller's wife with her foot on the fender, sitting beside a good coal fire, screened from the door, is sobering and cheerful. She is never reading, or only the newspaper; her talk, when it leaves bookselling, which it does so gladly, is about hats; she likes a hat to be practical, she says, as well as pretty. O no, they don't live at the shop; they live in Brixton; she must have a bit of green to look at.[9] In summer a jar of flowers grown in her own garden is stood on the top of some dusty pile to enliven the shop. Books are everywhere; and always the same sense of adventure fills us. Second-hand books are wild books, homeless books; they have come together in vast flocks of variegated feather, and have a charm which the domesticated volumes of the library lack. Besides, in this random miscellaneous company we may rub against some complete stranger who will, with luck, turn into the best friend we have in the world. There is always a hope, as we reach down some greyish-white book from an upper shelf, directed by its air of shabbiness and desertion, of meeting here with a man who set out on horseback over a hundred years ago to explore the woollen market in the Midlands and Wales; an unknown traveller, who stayed at inns, drank his pint, noted pretty girls and serious customs, wrote it all down stiffly, laboriously for sheer love of it (the book was published at his own expense); was infinitely prosy, busy, and matter-of-fact, and so let flow in without his knowing it the very scent of hollyhocks and the hay together with such a portrait of himself as gives him forever a seat in the warm corner of the mind's inglenook. One may buy him for eighteenpence now. He is marked three and sixpence,[10] but the bookseller's wife, seeing how shabby the covers are and how long the book has stood there since it was bought at some sale of a gentleman's library in Suffolk, will let it go at that.

Thus, glancing round the bookshop, we make other such sudden capricious friendships with the unknown and the vanished whose only record is, for example, this little book of poems, so fairly printed, so finely engraved, too, with a portrait of the author. For he was a poet and drowned untimely, and his verse, mild as it is and formal and sententious, sends forth still a frail fluty sound like that of a piano organ played in some back street resignedly by an old Italian organ-grinder in a corduroy jacket. There are travellers, too, row upon row of them, still testifying, indomitable spinsters that they were, to the discomforts that they endured and the sunsets they admired in Greece when Queen Victoria was a girl. A tour in Cornwall with a visit to the tin mines was thought worthy of voluminous record. People went slowly up the Rhine and did portraits of each other in Indian ink, sitting reading on deck beside a coil of rope; they measured the pyramids; were lost to civilization for years; converted negroes in pestilential swamps. This packing up and going off, exploring deserts and catching fevers, settling in India for a lifetime, penetrating even to China and then returning to lead a parochial life at Edmonton, tumbles and tosses upon the dusty floor like an uneasy sea, so restless the English are, with the waves at their very door. The waters of travel and adventure seem to break upon little islands of serious effort and lifelong industry stood in jagged column upon the floor. In these piles of puce-bound[11] volumes with gilt monograms on the back, thoughtful clergymen expound the gospels; scholars are to be heard with their hammers and their chisels chipping clear the ancient texts of Euripides and Aeschylus. Thinking, annotating, expounding goes on at a prodigious rate all around us and over everything, like a punctual, everlasting tide, washes the ancient sea of fiction. Innumerable volumes tell how Arthur loved Laura[12] and they were separated and they were unhappy and then they met and they were happy ever after, as was the way when Victoria ruled these islands.

The number of books in the world is infinite, and one is forced to glimpse and nod and move on after a moment of talk, a flash of understanding, as, in the street outside, one catches a word in passing and from a chance phrase fabricates a lifetime. It is about a woman called Kate that they are talking, how 'I said to her quite straight last night . . . if you don't think I'm worth a penny stamp,[13] I said . . .' But who Kate is, and to what crisis in their friendship that penny stamp refers, we shall never know; for Kate sinks under the warmth of their volubility; and here, at the street corner, another page of the volume of life is laid open by the sight of two men consulting under the lamp-post. They are spelling out the latest wire from Newmarket in the stop press news. Do they think, then, that fortune will ever convert their rags into fur and broadcloth, sling them with watch-chains, and plant diamond pins where there is now a ragged open shirt? But the main stream of walkers at this hour sweeps too fast to let us ask such questions. They are wrapt, in this short passage from work to home, in some narcotic dream, now that they are free from the desk, and have the fresh air on their cheeks. They put on those bright clothes which they must hang up and lock the key upon all the rest of the day, and are great cricketers, famous actresses, soldiers who have saved their country at the hour of need. Dreaming, gesticulating, often muttering a few words aloud, they sweep over the Strand and across Waterloo Bridge[14] whence they will be slung in long rattling trains, to some prim little villa in Barnes or Surbiton where the sight of the clock in the hall and the smell of the supper in the basement puncture the dream.

But we are come to the Strand now, and as we hesitate on the curb, a little rod about the length of one's finger begins to lay its bar across the velocity and abundance of life. 'Really I must – really I must' – that is it. Without investigating the demand, the mind cringes to the accustomed tyrant. One must, one always must, do something or other; it is not allowed one simply to enjoy oneself. Was it not for this reason that, some time ago, we fabricated the excuse, and invented the necessity of buying something? But what was it? Ah, we remember, it was a pencil. Let us go then and buy this pencil. But just as we are turning to obey the command, another self disputes the right of the tyrant to insist. The usual conflict comes about. Spread out behind the rod of duty we see the whole breadth of the river Thames – wide, mournful, peaceful. And we see it through the eyes of somebody who is leaning over the Embankment on a summer evening, without a care in the world. Let us put off buying the pencil; let us go in search of this person – and soon it becomes apparent that this person is ourselves. For if we could stand there where we stood six months ago, should we not be again as we were then – calm, aloof, content? Let us try then. But the river is rougher and greyer than we remembered. The tide is running out to sea. It brings down with it a tug and two barges, whose load of straw is tightly bound down beneath tarpaulin covers. There is, too, close by us, a couple leaning over the balustrade with the curious lack of self-consciousness lovers have, as if the importance of the affair they are engaged on claims without question the indulgence of the human race. The sights we see and the sounds we hear now have none of the quality of the past; nor have we any share in the serenity of the person who, six months ago, stood precisely where we stand now. His is the happiness of death; ours the insecurity of life. He has no future; the future is even now invading our peace. It is only when we look at the past and take from it the element of uncertainty that we can enjoy perfect peace. As it is, we must turn, we must cross the Strand again, we must find a shop where, even at this hour, they will be ready to sell us a pencil.

It is always an adventure to enter a new room; for the lives and characters of its owners have distilled their atmosphere into it, and directly we enter it we breast some new wave of emotion. Here, without a doubt, in the stationer's shop people had been quarrelling. Their anger shot through the air. They both stopped; the old woman – they were husband and wife evidently – retired to a back room; the old man whose rounded forehead and globular eyes would have looked well on the frontispiece of some Elizabethan folio,[15] stayed to serve us. 'A pencil, a pencil,' he repeated, 'certainly, certainly.' He spoke with the distraction yet effusiveness of one whose emotions have been roused and checked in full flood. He began opening box after box and shutting them again. He said that it was very difficult to find things when they kept so many different articles. He launched into a story about some legal gentleman who had got into deep waters owing to the conduct of his wife. He had known him for years; he had been connected with the Temple[16] for half a century, he said, as if he wished his wife in the back room to overhear him. He upset a box of rubber bands. At last, exasperated by his incompetence, he pushed the swing door open and called out roughly: 'Where d'you keep the pencils?' as if his wife had hidden them. The old lady came in. Looking at nobody, she put her hand with a fine air of righteous severity upon the right box. There were pencils. How then could he do without her? Was she not indispensable to him? In order to keep them there, standing side by side in forced neutrality, one had to be particular in one's choice of pencils; this was too soft, that too hard. They stood silently looking on. The longer they stood there, the calmer they grew; their heat was going down, their anger disappearing. Now, without a word said on either side, the quarrel was made up. The old man, who would not have disgraced Ben Jonson's title-page, reached the box back to its proper place, bowed profoundly his good-night to us, and they disappeared. She would get out her sewing; he would read his newspaper; the canary would scatter them impartially with seed. The quarrel was over.

In these minutes in which a ghost has been sought for, a quarrel composed, and a pencil bought, the streets had become completely empty. Life had withdrawn to the top floor, and lamps were lit. The pavement was dry and hard; the road was of hammered silver.

Walking home through the desolation one could tell oneself the story of the dwarf, of the blind men, of the party in the Mayfair mansion, of the quarrel in the stationer's shop. Into each of these lives one could penetrate a little way, far enough to give oneself the illusion that one is not tethered to a single mind, but can put on briefly for a few minutes the bodies and minds of others. One could become a washerwoman, a publican, a street singer. And what greater delight and wonder can there be than to leave the straight lines of personality and deviate into those footpaths that lead beneath brambles and thick tree trunks into the heart of the forest where live those wild beasts, our fellow men?

That is true: to escape is the greatest of pleasures; street haunting in winter the greatest of adventures. Still as we approach our own doorstep again, it is comforting to feel the old possessions, the old prejudices, fold us round; and the self, which has been blown about at so many street corners, which has battered like a moth at the flame of so many inaccessible lanterns, sheltered and enclosed. Here again is the usual door; here the chair turned as we left it and the china bowl and the brown ring on the carpet. And here – let us examine it tenderly, let us touch it with reverence – is the only spoil we have retrieved from all the treasures of the city, a lead pencil.

Evening over Sussex:
Reflections in a Motor Car

> First published posthumously in *The Death of the Moth* (1942), this
> essay was probably written in the late summer of 1927, when the
> Woolfs were enjoying their new motor car.

Evening is kind to Sussex,[1] for Sussex is no longer young, and she is grateful for the veil of evening as an elderly woman is glad when a shade is drawn over a lamp, and only the outline of her face remains. The outline of Sussex is still very fine. The cliffs stand out to sea, one behind another. All Eastbourne, all Bexhill, all St Leonards, their parades and their lodging houses, their bead shops and their sweet shops and their placards and their invalids and char-à-bancs,[2] are all obliterated. What remains is what there was when William came over[3] from France ten centuries ago: a line of cliffs running out to sea. Also the fields are redeemed. The freckle of red villas[4] on the coast is washed over by a thin lucid lake of brown air, in which they and their redness are drowned. It was still too early for lamps; and too early for stars.

But, I thought, there is always some sediment of irritation when the moment is as beautiful as it is now. The psychologists must explain; one looks up, one is overcome by beauty extravagantly greater than one could expect – there are now pink clouds over Battle; the fields are mottled, marbled – one's perceptions blow out rapidly like air balls[5] expanded by some rush of air, and then, when all seems blown to its fullest and tautest, with beauty and beauty and beauty, a pin pricks; it collapses. But what is the pin? So far as I could tell, the pin had something to do with one's own impotency. I cannot hold this[6] – I cannot express this – I am overcome by it – I am mastered. Somewhere in that region one's discontent lay; and it was allied with the idea that one's nature demands mastery over all that it receives; and mastery here meant the power to convey[7] what one saw now over Sussex so that another person could share it. And further, there was another prick of the pin: one was wasting one's chance; for beauty spread at one's right hand, at one's left; at one's back too; it was escaping all the time; one could only offer a thimble to a torrent that could fill baths, lakes.

But relinquish, I said (it is well known how in circumstances like these the self splits up[8] and one self is eager and dissatisfied and the other stern and philosophical), relinquish these impossible aspirations; be content with the view in front of us, and believe me when I tell you that it is best to sit and soak; to be passive; to accept; and do not bother because nature has given you six little pocket knives with which to cut up the body of a whale.

While these two selves then held a colloquy about the wise course to adopt in the presence of beauty, I (a third party now declared itself) said to myself, how happy they were to enjoy so simple an occupation. There they sat as the car sped along, noticing everything: a haystack; a rust-red roof; a pond; an old man coming home with his sack on his back; there they sat, matching every colour in the sky and earth from their colour box, rigging up little models of Sussex barns and farmhouses in the red light that would serve in the January gloom. But I, being somewhat different, sat aloof and melancholy. While they are thus busied, I said to myself: Gone, gone; over, over; past and done with, past and done with. I feel life left behind even as the road is left behind. We have been over that stretch, and are already forgotten. There, windows were lit by our lamps for a second; the light is out now. Others come behind us.

Then suddenly a fourth self (a self which lies in ambush, apparently dormant, and jumps upon one unawares. Its remarks are often entirely disconnected with what has been happening, but must be attended to because of their very abruptness) said: 'Look at that.' It was a light; brilliant, freakish; inexplicable. For a second I was unable to name it. 'A star'; and for that second it held its odd flicker of unexpectedness and danced and beamed. 'I take your meaning,' I said. 'You, erratic and impulsive self that you are, feel that the light over the downs there emerging, dangles from the future. Let us try to understand this. Let us reason it out. I feel suddenly attached not to the past but to the future. I think of Sussex in five hundred years to come. I think much grossness will have evaporated. Things will have been scorched up, eliminated. There will be magic gates.

Draughts fan-blown by electric power will cleanse houses. Lights intense and firmly directed will go over the earth, doing the work. Look at the moving light in that hill; it is the headlight of a car. By day and by night Sussex in five centuries will be full of charming thoughts, quick, effective beams.'

The sun was now low beneath the horizon. Darkness spread rapidly. None of my selves could see anything beyond the tapering light of our headlamps on the hedge. I summoned them together. 'Now,' I said, 'comes the season of making up our accounts. Now we have got to collect ourselves; we have got to be one self. Nothing is to be seen any more, except one wedge of road and bank which our lights repeat incessantly. We are perfectly provided for. We are warmly wrapped in a rug; we are protected from wind and rain. We are alone. Now is the time of reckoning. Now I, who preside over the company, am going to arrange in order the trophies which we have all brought in. Let me see; there was a great deal of beauty brought in today; farmhouses; cliffs standing out to sea; marbled fields; mottled fields; red feathered skies; all that. Also there was disappearance and the death of the individual. The vanishing road and the window lit for a second and then dark. And then there was the sudden dancing light, that was hung in the future. What we have made then today,' I said, 'is this: that beauty; death of the individual; and the future. Look, I will make a little figure for your satisfaction; here he comes. Does this little figure advancing through beauty, through death, to the economical, powerful and efficient future when houses will be cleansed by a puff of hot wind satisfy you? Look at him; there on my knee.' We sat and looked at the figure we had made that day. Great sheer slabs of rock, tree tufted, surrounded him. He was for a second very, very solemn. Indeed it seemed as if the reality of things were displayed there on the rug. A violent thrill ran through us; as if a charge of electricity had entered into us. We cried out together: 'Yes, yes,' as if affirming something, in a moment of recognition.

And then the body who had been silent up to now began its song, almost at first as low as the rush of the wheels: 'Eggs and bacon; toast and tea; fire and a bath; fire and a bath; jugged hare,' it went on, 'and redcurrant jelly; a glass of wine; with coffee to follow, with coffee to follow – and then to bed; and then to bed.'

'Off with you,' I said to my assembled selves. 'Your work is done. I dismiss you. Good-night.'

And the rest of the journey was performed in the delicious society of my own body.

The Sun and the Fish

First published in *Time and Tide*, 3 February 1928, and later in *New Republic*, New York, 8 February 1928.

It is an amusing game especially for a dark winter's morning. One says to the eye Athens; Segesta;[1] Queen Victoria; and one waits, as submissively as possible, to see what will happen next. And perhaps nothing happens, and perhaps a great many things happen, but not the things one might expect. The old lady in horn spectacles – our late Queen – is vivid enough; but somehow she has allied herself with a soldier in Piccadilly who is stooping to pick up a coin; with a yellow camel who is swaying through an archway in Kensington Gardens; with a kitchen chair and a distinguished old gentleman waving his hat. Dropped years ago into the mind, she has become stuck about with all sorts of alien matter. When one says Queen Victoria, one draws up the most heterogeneous collection of objects, which it will take a week at least to sort.[2] On the other hand one may say to oneself Mont Blanc at dawn; the Taj Mahal in the moonlight; and the mind remains a blank. For a sight will only survive in the queer pool in which we deposit our memories if it has the good luck to ally itself with some other emotion by which it is preserved. Sights marry, incongruously, morganatically[3] (like the Queen and the camel) and so keep each other alive. Mont Blanc, the Taj Mahal, sights which we travelled and toiled to see, fade and perish and disappear because they failed to find the right mate. On our death-beds it is possible we shall see nothing more majestic than a cat and an old woman in a sun-bonnet. The great sights will have died for lack of mates.

So, on this dark winter's morning, when the real world has faded, let us see what the eye can do for us. Show me the eclipse,[4] we say to the eye; let us see that strange spectacle again. And we see at once – but the mind's eye is only by courtesy an eye; it is a nerve which hears and smells, which transmits heat and cold, which is attached to the brain and rouses the mind to discriminate and speculate – it is only for brevity's sake that we say that we 'see' at once a railway station at night. A crowd is gathered at a barrier; but how curious a crowd! Mackintoshes are slung over their arms; in their hands they carry little cases. They have a provisional, extemporized look. They have that moving and disturbing unity which comes from the consciousness that they (but here it would be more proper to say 'we') have a purpose in common. Never was there a stranger purpose than that which brought us together that June night in Euston Railway Station.[5] We were come to see the dawn. Trains like ours were starting all over England at that very moment to see the dawn. All noses were pointing north. When for a moment we halted in the depths of the country, there were the pale yellow lights of motor cars also pointing north. There was no sleep, no fixity in England that night. All were travelling north. All were thinking of the dawn. As the night wore on the sky, which was the object of so many million thoughts, assumed greater substance and prominence than usual. The consciousness of the whitish soft canopy above us increased in weight as the hours passed. When in the chill early morning we were turned out on a Yorkshire roadside, our senses had orientated themselves differently from usual. We were no longer in the same relation to people, houses and trees; we were related to the whole world. We had come, not to lodge in the bedroom of an inn; we were come for a few hours of disembodied intercourse with the sky.

Everything was very pale. The river was pale and the fields, brimming with grasses and tasselled flowers which should have been red, had no colour in them, but lay there whispering and waving round colourless farmhouses. Now the farmhouse door would open and out would step to join the procession the farmer and his family in their Sunday clothes, neat, dark and silent as if they were going up hill to church; or sometimes women merely leant on the window-sills of the upper rooms watching the procession pass with amused contempt, it appeared – they have come such hundreds of miles, and for what? they seemed to say – in complete silence. We had an odd sense of keeping an appointment with an actor of such vast proportions that he would come silently and be everywhere.

By the time we were at the meeting-place, on a high fell where the hills stretched their limbs out over the flowing brown moorland below, we had put on too – though we were cold and with our feet stood in red bog water were likely to be still colder, though some of us were squatted on mackintoshes among cups and plates, eating, and others were fantastically accoutred and none were at their best – still we had put on a certain dignity. Rather, perhaps, we had put off the little badges and signs of individuality. We were strung out against the sky in outline and had the look of statues standing prominent on the ridge of the world. We were very, very old; we were men and women of the primeval world come to salute the dawn. So the worshippers at Stonehenge[6] must have looked among tussocks of grass and boulders of rock. Suddenly from the motor car of some Yorkshire Squire, there bounded four large lean, red dogs, hounds of the ancient world, hunting dogs, they seemed, leaping with their noses close to the ground on the track of boar or deer. Meanwhile, the sun was rising. A cloud glowed as a white shade glows when the light is slowly turned up behind it. Golden wedge-shaped streamers fell down from it and marked the trees in the valley green and the villages blue-brown. In the sky behind us there swam white islands in pale blue lakes. The sky was open and free there, but in front of us a soft snow bank had massed itself. Yet, as we looked, we saw it proving worn and thin in patches. The gold momentarily increased, melting the whiteness to a fiery gauze, and this grew frailer and frailer till, for one instant, we saw the sun in full splendour. Then there was a pause. There was a moment of suspense, like that which precedes a race. The starter held his watch in his hand counting the seconds. Now they were off.

The sun had to race through the clouds and to reach the goal, which was a thin transparency to the right, before the sacred seconds were up. He started. The clouds flung every obstacle in his way. They clung, they impeded. He dashed through them. He could be felt flashing and flying, when he was invisible. His speed was tremendous. Here he was out and bright; now he was under and lost. But always one felt him flying and thrusting through the murk to his goal. For one second he emerged and showed himself to us through our glasses, a hollowed sun, a crescent sun. It was a proof perhaps that he was doing his best for us. Now he went under for his last effort. Now he was completely blotted out. The moments passed. Watches were held in hand after hand. The sacred twenty-four seconds were begun. Unless he could win through before the last one was over he was lost. Still one felt him tearing and racing behind the clouds to win free; but the clouds held him. They spread; they thickened; they slackened, they muffled his speed. Of the twenty-four seconds only five remained and still he was obscured. And, as the fatal seconds passed and we realized that the sun was being defeated, had now indeed lost the race, all the colour began to go from the moor. The blue turned to purple; the white became livid as at the approach of a violent but windless storm. Pink faces went green, and it became colder than ever. This was the defeat of the sun then, and this was all, so we thought, turning in disappointment from the dull cloud blanket in front of us to the moors behind. They were livid, they were purple; but suddenly one became aware that something more was about to happen; something unexpected, awful, unavoidable. The shadow growing darker and darker over the moor was like the heeling over of a boat, which, instead of righting itself at the critical moment, turns a little further and then a little further; and suddenly capsizes. So the light turned and heeled over and went out. This was the end. The flesh and blood of the world was dead and only the skeleton was left. It hung beneath us, frail; brown; dead; withered. Then, with some trifling movement, this profound obeisance of the light, this stooping down and abasement of all splendour was over. Lightly, on the other side of the world up it rose; it sprang up as if the one movement, after a second's tremendous pause, completed the other and the light which had died here, rose again elsewhere. Never was there such a sense of rejuvenescence and recovery. All the convalescences[7] and respite of life seemed rolled into one. Yet at first, so pale and frail and strange the light was sprinkled rainbow-like in a hoop of colour, that it seemed as if the earth could never live decked out in such frail tints. It hung beneath us, like a cage, like a hoop, like a globe of glass. It might be blown out; it might be stove in. But steadily and surely our relief broadened and our confidence established itself as the great paint-brush washed in woods, dark on the valley, and massed the hills blue above them. The world became more and more solid; it became populous; it became a place where an infinite number of farmhouses, of villages, of railway lines have lodgement; until the whole fabric of civilization was modelled and moulded. But still the memory endured that the earth we stand on is made of colour; colour can be blown out; and then we stand on a dead leaf; and we who tread the earth securely now have seen it dead.

But the eye has not done with us yet. In pursuit of some logic of its own, which we cannot follow immediately, it now presents us with a picture, or generalized impression rather, of London on a hot summer day, when, to judge by the sense of concussion and confusion the London season is at its height. It takes us a moment to realize first that we are in some public gardens, next from the asphalt and the paper bags strewn about that it must be the Zoological Gardens,[8] and then without further preparation we are presented with the complete and perfect effigy of two lizards. After destruction calm; after ruin, steadfastness – that perhaps is the logic of the eye. At any rate one lizard is mounted immobile on the back of another, with only the twinkle of a gold eyelid or the suction of a green flank to show that they are living flesh, and not made of bronze. All human passion seems furtive and feverish beside this still rapture. Time seems to have stopped and we are in the presence of immortality. The tumult of the world has fallen from us like a crumbling cloud. Tanks cut in the level blackness enclose squares of immortality, worlds of settled sunshine, where there is neither rain nor cloud. There the inhabitants perform for ever evolutions whose intricacy, because it has no reason, seems the more sublime. Blue and silver armies, keeping a perfect distance for all their arrow-like quickness, shoot first this way, then that. The discipline is perfect, the control absolute; reason there is none. The most majestic of human evolutions seems feeble and fluctuating compared with the fishes'. Each of these worlds too, which measures perhaps four feet by five is as perfect in its order as in its method. For forests, they have half a dozen bamboo canes; for mountains, sand-hills; in the curves and crinkles of a sea-shell lie for them all adventure, all romance. The rise of a bubble, negligible elsewhere, is here an event of the highest importance. The silver drop bores its way up a spiral staircase through the water to burst against the sheet of glass which seems laid flat across the top. Nothing exists needlessly. The fish themselves seem to have been shaped deliberately and slipped into the world only to be themselves. They neither work nor weep. In their shape is their reason. For what other purpose, except the sufficient one of perfect existence, can they have been thus made, some so round, some so thin, some with radiating fins upon their backs, others lined with red electric light, others undulating like white pan-cakes on a frying-pan, some armoured in blue mail, some given prodigious claws, some outrageously fringed with huge whiskers? More care has been spent upon half a dozen fish than upon all the races of mankind. Under our tweed and silk is nothing but a monotony of pink nakedness. Poets are not transparent to the backbone as these fish are. Bankers have no claws. Kings and Queens themselves wear neither ruffs nor frills. In short, if we were to be turned naked, into an aquarium – but enough. The eye shuts now. It has shown us a dead world and an immortal fish.

The Niece of an Earl

> First published in *Life and Letters*, October 1928, and reprinted in
> *The Common Reader: Second Series* (1932), in this version.

There is an aspect of fiction of so delicate a nature that less has been said about it than its importance deserves. One is supposed to pass over class distinctions in silence; one person is supposed to be as well born as another; and yet English fiction is so steeped in the ups and downs of social rank that without them it would be unrecognizable. When Meredith, in *The Case of General Ople and Lady Camper*,[1] remarks, 'He sent word that he would wait on Lady Camper immediately, and betook himself forthwith to his toilette. She was the niece of an Earl', all of British blood accept the statement unhesitatingly, and know that Meredith is right. A General in those circumstances would certainly have given his coat an extra brush. For though the General might have been, we are given to understand that he was not, Lady Camper's social equal. He received the shock of her rank upon a naked surface. No earldom, baronetage, or knighthood protected him. He was an English gentleman merely, and a poor one at that. Therefore, to British readers even now it seems unquestionably fitting that he should 'betake himself to his toilette' before appearing in the lady's presence.

It is useless to suppose that social distinctions have vanished. Each may pretend that he knows no such restrictions, and that the compartment in which he lives allows him the run of the world. But it is an illusion. The idlest stroller down summer streets may see for himself the charwoman's shawl shouldering its way among the silk wraps of the successful; he sees shop girls pressing their noses against the plate glass of motor cars; he sees radiant youth and august age waiting their summons within to be admitted to the presence of King George. There is no animosity, perhaps, but there is no communication. We are enclosed, and separate, and cut off. Directly we see ourselves in the looking-glass of fiction we know that this is so. The novelist, and the English novelist in particular knows and delights, it seems, to know that Society is a nest of glass boxes one separate from another, each housing a group with special habits and qualities of its own. He knows that there are Earls and that Earls have nieces; he knows that there are Generals and that Generals brush their coats before they visit the nieces of Earls. But this is only the A B C of what he knows. For in a few short pages, Meredith makes us aware not only that Earls have nieces, but that Generals have cousins; that the cousins have friends; that the friends have cooks; that the cooks have husbands, and that the husbands of the cooks of the friends of the cousins of the Generals are carpenters. Each of these people lives in a glass box of his own, and has peculiarities of which the novelist must take account. What appears superficially to be the vast equality of the middle classes is, in truth, nothing of the sort. All through the social mass run curious veins and streakings separating man from man and woman from woman; mysterious prerogatives and disabilities too ethereal to be distinguished by anything so crude as a title impede and disorder the great business of human intercourse. And when we have threaded our way carefully through all these grades from the niece of the Earl to the friend of the cousin of the General, we are still faced with an abyss; a gulf yawns before us; on the other side are the working classes. The writer of perfect judgement and taste, like Jane Austen, does no more than glance across the gulf; she restricts herself to her own special class and finds infinite shades within it. But for the brisk, inquisitive, combative writer like Meredith, the temptation to explore is irresistible. He runs up and down the social scale; he chimes one note against another; he insists that the Earl and the cook, the General and the farmer shall speak up for themselves and play their part in the extremely complicated comedy of English civilized life.

It was natural that he should attempt it. A writer touched by the comic spirit relishes these distinctions keenly; they give him something to take hold of; something to make play with. English fiction without the nieces of Earls and the cousins of Generals would be an arid waste. It would resemble Russian fiction. It would have to fall back upon the immensity of the soul and upon the brotherhood of man. Like Russian fiction, it would lack comedy. But while we realize the immense debt that we owe the Earl's niece and the

General's cousin, we doubt sometimes whether the pleasure we get from the play of satire on these broken edges is altogether worth the price we pay. For the price is a high one. The strain upon a novelist is tremendous. In two short stories Meredith gallantly attempts to bridge all gulfs, and to take half a dozen different levels in his stride. Now he speaks as an Earl's niece; now as a carpenter's wife. It cannot be said that his daring is altogether successful. One has a feeling (perhaps it is unfounded) that the blood of the niece of an Earl is not quite so tart and sharp as he would have it. Aristocracy is not, perhaps, so consistently high and brusque and eccentric as, from his angle, he would represent it. Yet his great people are more successful than his humble. His cooks are too ripe and rotund; his farmers too ruddy and earthy. He overdoes the pith and the sap; the fist-shaking and the thigh-slapping. He has got too far from them to write of them with ease.

It seems, therefore, that the novelist, and the English novelist in particular, suffers from a disability which affects no other artist to the same extent. His work is influenced by his birth. He is fated to know intimately, and so to describe with understanding, only those who are of his own social rank. He cannot escape from the box in which he has been bred. A bird's-eye view of fiction shows us no gentlemen in Dickens; no working men in Thackeray. One hesitates to call Jane Eyre a lady. The Elizabeths and the Emmas of Miss Austen[2] could not possibly be taken for anything else. It is vain to look for Dukes or for dustmen – we doubt that such extremes are to be found anywhere in fiction. We are, therefore, brought to the melancholy and tantalizing conclusion not only that novels are poorer than they might be, but that we are very largely prevented – for after all, the novelists are the great interpreters – from knowing what is happening either in the heights of Society or in its depths. There is practically no evidence available by which we can guess at the feelings of the highest in the land. What does a King feel? What does a Duke think? We cannot say. For the highest in the land have seldom written at all, and have never written about themselves. We shall never know what the Court of Louis XIV looked like to Louis XIV himself. It seems likely indeed that the English aristocracy will pass out of existence, or be merged with the common people, without leaving any true picture of themselves behind.

But our ignorance of the aristocracy is nothing compared with our ignorance of the working classes. At all times the great families of England and France have delighted to have famous men at their tables, and thus the Thackerays and the Disraelis and the Prousts[3] have been familiar enough with the cut and fashion of aristocratic life to write about it with authority. Unfortunately, however, life is so framed that literary success invariably means a rise, never a fall, and seldom, what is far more desirable, a spread in the social scale. The rising novelist is never pestered to come to gin and winkles with the plumber and his wife. His books never bring him into touch with the cat's-meat man, or start a correspondence with the old lady who sells matches and bootlaces by the gate of the British Museum. He becomes rich; he becomes respectable; he buys an evening suit and dines with peers. Therefore, the later works of successful novelists show, if anything, a slight rise in the social scale. We tend to get more and more portraits of the successful and the distinguished. On the other hand, the old rat-catchers and ostlers of Shakespeare's day are shuffled altogether off the scene, or become, what is far more offensive, objects of pity, examples of curiosity. They serve to show up the rich. They serve to point the evils of the social system. They are no longer, as they used to be when Chaucer wrote, simply themselves. For it is impossible, it would seem, for working men to write in their own language about their own lives. Such education as the act of writing implies at once makes them self-conscious, or class-conscious, or removes them from their own class. That anonymity, in the shadow of which writers write most happily, is the prerogatives of the middle class alone. It is from the middle class that writers spring, because it is in the middle class only that the practice of writing is as natural and habitual as hoeing a field or building a house. Thus it must have been harder for Byron to be a poet than Keats;[4] and it is as impossible to imagine that a Duke could be a great novelist as that *Paradise Lost* could be written by a man behind a counter.

But things change; class distinctions were not always so hard and fast as they have now become. The Elizabethan age was far more elastic in this respect than our own; we, on the other hand, are far less hide-bound than the Victorians. Thus it may well be that we are on the edge of a greater change than any the world has yet known.

In another century or so, none of these distinctions may hold good. The Duke and the agricultural labourer as we know them now may have died out as completely as the bustard[5] and the wild cat. Only natural differences such as those of brain and character will serve to distinguish us. General Ople (if there are still Generals) will visit the niece (if there are still nieces) of the Earl (if there are still Earls) without brushing his coat (if there are still coats). But what will happen to English fiction when it has come to pass that there are neither Generals, nieces, Earls, nor coats, we cannot imagine. It may change its character so that we no longer know it. It may become extinct. Novels may be written as seldom and as unsuccessfully by our descendants as the poetic drama by ourselves. The art of a truly democratic age will be – what?

Foreword to Recent Paintings by Vanessa Bell

> In this foreword Virginia introduced a catalogue of her sister
> Vanessa's paintings, exhibited by the London Artists' Association at the
> Cooling Galleries, 92 Bond Street, from 4 February to 8 March 1930.

That a woman should hold a show of pictures in Bond Street, I said, pausing upon the threshold of Messrs Cooling's gallery,[1] is not usual, nor, perhaps, altogether to be commended. For it implies, I fancy, some study of the nude, and while for many ages it has been admitted that women are naked and bring nakedness to birth, it was held, until sixty years ago that for a woman to look upon nakedness with the eye of an artist, and not simply with the eye of mother, wife or mistress was corruptive of her innocency and destructive of her domesticity. Hence the extreme activity of women in philanthropy, society, religion and all pursuits requiring clothing.

Hence again the fact that every Victorian family has in its cupboard the skeleton of an aunt who was driven to convert the native because her father would have died rather than let her look upon a naked man. And so she went to church; and so she went to China; and so she died unwed; and so there drop out of the cupboard with her bones half a dozen flower pieces done under the shade of a white umbrella in a Surrey garden when Queen Victoria was on the throne.

These reflections are only worth recording because they indicate the vacillations and prevarications (if one is not a painter or a critic of painting) with which one catches at any straw that will put off the evil moment when one must go into the gallery and make up one's mind about pictures. Were it not that Mrs Bell has a certain reputation and is sometimes the theme of argument at dinner-tables, many no doubt would stroll up Bond Street, past Messrs Cooling's, thinking about morality or politics, about grandfathers or great aunts, about anything but pictures as is the way of the English.

But Mrs Bell has a certain reputation it cannot be denied. She is a woman, it is said, yet she has looked on nakedness with a brush in her hand. She is reported (one has read it in the newspapers) to be 'the most considerable painter of her own sex now alive'. Berthe Morisot, Marie Laurencin,[2] Vanessa Bell – such is the stereotyped phrase which comes to mind when her name is mentioned and makes one's predicament in front of her pictures all the more exacting. For whatever the phrase may mean, it must mean that her pictures stand for something, are something and will be something which we shall disregard at our peril. As soon not go to see them as shut the window when the nightingale is singing.

But once inside and surrounded by canvases, this shillyshallying on the threshold seems superfluous. What is there here to intimidate or perplex? Are we not suffused, lit up, caught in a sunny glow? Does there not radiate from the walls a serene yet temperate warmth, comfortable in the extreme after the rigours of the streets? Are we not surrounded by vineyards and olive trees, by naked girls couched on crimson cushions, by naked boys ankle deep in the pale green sea? Even the puritans of the nineteenth century might grant us a moment's respite from the February murk, a moment's liberty in this serene and ordered world. But it is not the puritans who move us on. It is Mrs Bell. It is Mrs Bell who is determined that we shall not loll about juggling with pretty words or dallying with delicious sensations. There is something uncompromising about her art. Ninety-nine painters had nature given them her susceptibility, her sense of the lustre of grass and flower, of the glow of rock and tree, would have lured us on by one refinement and felicity after another to stay and look for ever. Ninety-nine painters again had they possessed that sense of satire which seems to flash its laughter for a moment at those women in Dieppe in the eighties,[3] would have caricatured and illustrated; would have drawn our attention to the antics of parrots, the pathos of old umbrellas, the archness of ankles, the eccentricities of noses. Something would have been done to gratify the common, innocent and indeed very valuable gift which has produced in England so rich a library of fiction. But look round the room: the approach to these pictures is not by that means. No stories are told; no insinuations are made. The hill-side is bare; the group of women is silent; the little boy stands in the sea saying nothing. If portraits there are, they are pictures of flesh which happens from its texture or its modelling to be aesthetically on an equality with the China pot or the chrysanthemum.

Checked at that point in our approach (and the snub is none the less baffling for the beauty with which it is conveyed) one can perhaps draw close from another angle. Let us see if we can come at some idea of Mrs Bell herself and by thus trespassing, crack the kernel of her art. Certainly it would hardly be possible to read as many novels as there are pictures here without feeling our way psychologically over the features of the writer; and the method, if illicit, has its value. But here, for a second time, we are rebuffed. One says, Anyhow Mrs Bell is a woman; and then half way round the room one says, But she may be a man. One says, She is interested in children; one has to add, But she is equally interested in rocks. One asks, Does she show any special knowledge of clothes? One replies, Stark nakedness seems to please her as well. Is she dainty then, or austere? Does she like riding? Is she red haired or brown eyed? Was she ever at a University? Does she prefer herrings or Brussels sprouts? Is she – for our patience is becoming exhausted – not a woman at all, but a mixture of Goddess and peasant, treading the clouds with her feet and with her hands shelling peas? Any writer so ardently questioned would have yielded something to our curiosity. One defies a novelist to keep his life through twenty-seven volumes of fiction safe from our scrutiny. But Mrs Bell says nothing. Mrs Bell is as silent as the grave. Her pictures do not betray her. Their reticence is inviolable.[4] That is why they intrigue and draw us on; that is why, if it be true that they yield their full meaning only to those who can tunnel their way behind the canvas into masses and passages and relations and values of which we know nothing – if it be true that she is a painter's painter – still her pictures claim us and make us stop. They give us an emotion. They offer a puzzle.

And the puzzle is that while Mrs Bell's pictures are immensely expressive, their expressiveness has no truck with words. Her vision excites a strong emotion and yet when we have dramatized it or poetized it or translated it into all the blues and greens, and fines and exquisites and subtles of our vocabulary, the picture itself escapes. It goes on saying something of its own. A good example is to be found in the painting of the Foundling Hospital.[5] Here one says, is the fine old building which has housed a million orphans; here Hogarth painted and kind-hearted Thackeray shed a tear, here

Dickens, who lived down the street on the left-hand side, must often have paused in his walk to watch the children at play. And it is all gone, all perished. Housebreakers have been at work, speculators have speculated. It is dust and ashes – but what has Mrs Bell got to say about it? Nothing. There is the picture, serene and sunny, and very still. It represents a fine eighteenth-century house and an equally fine London plane tree. But there are no orphans, no Thackeray, no Dickens, no housebreakers, no speculators, no tears, no sense that this sunny day is perhaps the last. Our emotion has been given the slip.

And yet somehow our emotion has been returned to us. For emotion there is. The room is charged with it. There is emotion in that white urn; in that little girl painting a picture; in the flowers and the bust; in the olive trees; in the Provençal vineyard; in the English hills against the sky. Here, we cannot doubt as we look is somebody to whom the visible world has given a shock of emotion every day of the week. And she transmits it and makes us share it; but it is always by her means, in her language, with her susceptibility, and not ours. That is why she is so tantalizing, so original, and so satisfying as a painter. One feels that if a canvas of hers hung on the wall it would never lose its lustre. It would never mix itself up with the loquacities and trivialities of daily life. It would go on saying something of its own imperturbably. And perhaps by degrees – who knows? – one would become an inmate of this strange painters' world, in which mortality does not enter, and psychology is held at bay, and there are no words. But is morality to be found there? That was the very question I was asking myself as I came in.

Professions for Women

Virginia Woolf read this lecture to the National Society for Women's Service on 21 January 1931; it was published posthumously in *The Death of the Moth*, 1942.

When your secretary[1] invited me to come here, she told me that your Society is concerned with the employment of women and she suggested that I might tell you something about my own professional experiences. It is true I am a woman; it is true I am employed; but what professional experiences have I had? It is difficult to say. My profession is literature; and in that profession there are fewer experiences for women than in any other, with the exception of the stage – fewer, I mean, that are peculiar to women. For the road was cut many years ago – by Fanny Burney, by Aphra Behn, by Harriet Martineau, by Jane Austen, by George Eliot[2] – many famous women, and many more unknown and forgotten, have been before me, making the path smooth, and regulating my steps. Thus, when I came to write, there were very few material obstacles in my way. Writing was a reputable and harmless occupation. The family peace was not broken by the scratching of a pen. No demand was made upon the family purse. For ten and sixpence one can buy paper enough to write all the plays of Shakespeare – if one has a mind that way. Pianos and models, Paris, Vienna and Berlin, masters and mistresses, are not needed by a writer. The cheapness of writing paper is, of course, the reason why women have succeeded as writers before they have succeeded in the other professions.

But to tell you my story – it is a simple one. You have only got to figure to yourselves a girl in a bedroom with a pen in her hand. She had only to move that pen from left to right – from ten o'clock to one. Then it occurred to her to do what is simple and cheap enough after all – to slip a few of those pages into an envelope, fix a penny stamp in the corner, and drop the envelope into the red box at the corner. It was thus that I became a journalist; and my effort was rewarded on the first day of the following month – a very glorious day it was for me – by a letter from an editor containing a cheque for one pound ten shillings and sixpence. But to show you how little I deserve to be called a professional woman, how little I know of the struggles and difficulties of such lives, I have to admit that instead of spending that sum upon bread and butter, rent, shoes and stockings, or butcher's bills, I went out and bought a cat – a beautiful cat, a Persian cat, which very soon involved me in bitter disputes with my neighbours.

What could be easier than to write articles and to buy Persian cats with the profits? But wait a moment. Articles have to be about something. Mine, I seem to remember, was about a novel by a famous man. And while I was writing this review, I discovered that if I were going to review books I should need to do battle with a certain phantom. And the phantom was a woman, and when I came to know her better I called her after the heroine of a famous poem, The Angel in the House.[3] It was she who used to come between me and my paper when I was writing reviews. It was she who bothered me and wasted my time and so tormented me that at last I killed her. You who come of a younger and happier generation may not have heard of her – you may not know what I mean by the Angel in the House. I will describe her as shortly as I can. She was intensely sympathetic. She was immensely charming. She was utterly unselfish. She excelled in the difficult arts of family life. She sacrificed herself daily. If there was chicken, she took the leg; if there was a draught she sat in it – in short she was so constituted that she never had a mind or a wish of her own, but preferred to sympathize always with the minds and wishes of others. Above all – I need not say it – she was pure. Her purity was supposed to be her chief beauty – her blushes, her great grace. In those days – the last of Queen Victoria – every house had its Angel. And when I came to write I encountered her with the very first words. The shadow of her wings fell on my page; I heard the rustling of her skirts in the room. Directly, that is to say, I took my pen in my hand to review that novel by a famous man, she slipped behind me and whispered: 'My dear, you are a young woman. You are writing about a book that has been written by a man. Be sympathetic; be tender; flatter; deceive; use all the arts and wiles of our sex. Never let anybody guess that you have a mind of your own. Above all, be pure.' And she made as if to guide my pen. I now record the one act for which I take some credit to myself, though the credit rightly belongs to some excellent ancestors of mine who left me a certain sum of money – shall we say five hundred pounds a year? – so that it was not necessary for me to depend solely on charm for my living. I turned upon her and caught her by the throat. I did my best to kill her. My excuse, if I were to be had up in a court of law, would be that I acted in self-defence. Had I not killed her she would have killed me. She would have plucked the heart out of my writing. For, as I found, directly I put pen to paper, you cannot review even a novel without having a mind of your own, without expressing what you think to be the truth about human relations, morality, sex. And all these questions, according to the Angel of the House, cannot be dealt with freely and openly by women; they must charm, they must conciliate, they must – to put it bluntly – tell lies if they are to succeed. Thus, whenever I felt the shadow of her wing or the radiance of her halo upon my page, I took up the inkpot and flung it at her. She died hard. Her fictitious nature was of great assistance to her. It is far harder to kill a phantom than a reality. She was always creeping back when I thought I had despatched her. Though I flatter myself that I killed her in the end, the struggle was severe; it took much time that had better have been spent upon learning Greek grammar; or in roaming the world in search of adventures. But it was a real experience; it was an experience that was bound to befall all women writers at that time. Killing the Angel in the House was part of the occupation of a woman writer.

But to continue my story. The Angel was dead; what then remained? You may say that what remained was a simple and common object – a young woman in a bedroom with an inkpot. In other words, now that she had rid herself of falsehood, that young woman had only to be herself. Ah, but what is 'herself'? I mean, what is a woman? I assure you, I do not know. I do not believe that you know. I do not believe that anybody can know until she has expressed herself in all the arts and professions open to human skill. That indeed is one of the reasons why I have come here – out of respect for you, who are in process of showing us by your experiments what a woman is, who are in process of providing us, by your failures and successes, with that extremely important piece of information.

But to continue the story of my professional experiences. I made one pound ten and six by my first review; and I bought a Persian cat with the proceeds. Then I grew ambitious. A Persian cat is all very well, I said; but a Persian cat is not enough. I must have a motor car. And it was thus that I became a novelist – for it is a very strange thing that people will give you a motor car if you will tell them a story. It is a still stranger thing that there is nothing so delightful in the world as telling stories. It is far pleasanter than writing reviews of famous novels. And yet, if I am to obey your secretary and tell you my professional experiences as a novelist, I must tell you about a very strange experience that befell me as a novelist. And to understand it you must try first to imagine a novelist's state of mind. I hope I am not giving away professional secrets if I say that a novelist's chief desire is to be as unconscious as possible. He has to induce in himself a state of perpetual lethargy. He wants life to proceed with the utmost quiet and regularity. He wants to see the same faces, to read the same books, to do the same things day after day, month after month, while he is writing, so that nothing may break the illusion in which he is living – so that nothing may disturb or disquiet the mysterious nosings about, feelings round, darts, dashes and sudden discoveries of that very shy and illusive spirit, the imagination. I suspect that this state is the same both for men and women. Be that as it may, I want you to imagine me writing a novel in a state of trance. I want you to figure to yourselves a girl sitting with a pen in her hand, which for minutes, and indeed for hours, she never dips into the inkpot. The image that comes to my mind when I think of this girl is the image of a fisherman lying sunk in dreams on the verge of a deep lake with a rod held out over the water. She was letting her imagination sweep unchecked round every rock and cranny of the world that lies submerged in the depths of our unconscious being. Now came the experience, the experience that I believe to be far commoner with women writers than with men. The line raced through the girl's fingers.[4] Her imagination had rushed away. It had sought the pools, the depths, the dark places where the largest fish slumber. And then there was a smash. There was an explosion. There was foam and confusion. The imagination had dashed itself against something hard. The girl was roused from her dream. She was indeed in a state of the most acute and difficult distress. To speak without figure she had thought of something, something about the body, about the passions which it was unfitting for her as a woman to say. Men, her reason told her, would be shocked. The consciousness of what men will say of a woman who speaks the truth about her passions had roused her from her artist's state of unconsciousness. She could write no more. The trance was over. Her imagination could work no longer. This I believe to be a very common experience with women writers – they are impeded by the extreme conventionality of the other sex. For though men sensibly allow themselves great freedom in these respects, I doubt that they realize or can control the extreme severity with which they condemn such freedom in women.

These then were two very genuine experiences of my own. These were two of the adventures of my professional life. The first – killing the Angel in the House – I think I solved. She died. But the second, telling the truth about my own experiences as a body, I do not think I solved. I doubt that any woman has solved it yet. The obstacles against her are still immensely powerful – and yet they are very difficult to define. Outwardly, what is simpler than to write books? Outwardly, what obstacles are there for a woman rather than for a man? Inwardly, I think, the case is very different; she has still many ghosts to fight, many prejudices to overcome. Indeed it will be a long time still, I think, before a woman can sit down to write a book without finding a phantom to be slain, a rock to be dashed against. And if this is so in literature, the freest of all professions for women, how is it in the new professions which you are now for the first time entering?

Those are the questions that I should like, had I time, to ask you. And indeed, if I have laid stress upon these professional experiences of mine, it is because I believe that they are, though in different forms, yours also. Even when the path is nominally open – when there is nothing to prevent a woman from being a doctor, a lawyer, a civil servant – there are many phantoms and obstacles, as I believe, looming in her way. To discuss and define them is I think of great value and importance; for thus only can the labour be shared, the difficulties be solved. But besides this, it is necessary also to discuss the ends and the aims for which we are fighting, for which we are doing battle with these formidable obstacles. Those aims cannot be taken for granted; they must be perpetually questioned and examined. The whole position, as I see it – here in this hall surrounded by women practising for the first time in history I know not how many different professions – is one of extraordinary interest and importance. You have won rooms of your own in the house hitherto exclusively owned by men. You are able, though not without great labour and effort, to pay the rent. You are earning your five hundred pounds a year. But this freedom is only a beginning; the room is your own, but it is still bare. It has to be furnished; it has to be decorated; it has to be shared. How are you going to furnish it, how are you going to decorate it? With whom are you going to share it, and upon what terms? These, I think are questions of the utmost importance and interest. For the first time in history you are able to ask them; for the first time you are able to decide for yourselves what the answers should be. Willingly would I stay and discuss those questions and answers – but not tonight. My time is up; and I must cease.

The London Scene

These are five of a series of six essays commissioned by *Good Housekeeping* and published there in December 1931 and January, March, May and October 1932.

I THE DOCKS OF LONDON

'Whither, O splendid ship,' the poet asked[1] as he lay on the shore and watched the great sailing ship pass away on the horizon. Perhaps, as he imagined, it was making for some port in the Pacific; but one day almost certainly it must have heard an irresistible call and come past the North Foreland and the Reculvers, and entered the narrow waters of the Port of London, sailed past the low banks of Gravesend and Northfleet and Tilbury, up Erith Reach and Barking Reach and Gallion's Reach,[2] past the gas works and the sewage works till it found, for all the world like a car on a parking ground, a space reserved for it in the deep waters of the docks. There it furled its sails and dropped anchor.

However romantic and free and fitful they may seem, there is scarcely a ship on the seas that does not come to anchor in the Port of London in time. From a launch in midstream one can see them swimming up the river with all the marks of their voyage still on them. Liners come, high-decked, with their galleries and their awnings and their passengers grasping their bags and leaning over the rail, while the lascars[3] tumble and scurry below – home they come, a thousand of these big ships every week of the year to anchor in the docks of London. They take their way majestically through a crowd of tramp steamers, and colliers and barges heaped with coal and swaying red sailed boats, which, amateurish though they look, are bringing bricks from Harwich or cement from Colchester[4] – for all is business; there are no pleasure boats on this river. Drawn by some irresistible current, they come from the storms and calms of the sea, its silence and loneliness to their allotted anchorage. The engines stop; the sails are furled; and suddenly the gaudy funnels and the tall masts show up incongruously against a row of workmen's houses, against the black walls of huge warehouses. A curious change takes place. They have no longer the proper perspective of sea and sky behind them, and no longer the proper space in which to stretch their limbs. They lie captive, like soaring and winged creatures who have got themselves caught by the leg and lie tethered on dry land.

With the sea blowing its salt into our nostrils, nothing can be more stimulating than to watch the ships coming up the Thames – the big ships and the little ships, the battered and the splendid ships from India, from Russia, from South America, ships from Australia coming from silence and danger and loneliness past us, home to harbour. But once they drop anchor, once the cranes begin their dipping and their swinging, it seems as if all romance were over. If we turn and go past the anchored ships towards London, we see surely the most dismal prospect in the world. The banks of the river are lined with dingy, decrepit-looking warehouses. They huddle on land that has become flat and slimy mud. The same air of decrepitude and of being run up provisionally stamps them all. If a window is broken, broken it remains. A fire that has lately blackened and blistered one of them seems to have left it no more forlorn and joyless than its neighbours. Behind the masts and funnels lies a sinister dwarf city of workmen's houses. In the foreground cranes and warehouses, scaffolding and gasometers line the banks with a skeleton architecture.

When suddenly, after acres and acres of this desolation one floats past an old stone house standing in a real field, with real trees growing in clumps, the sight is disconcerting. Can it be possible that there is earth, that there once were fields and crops beneath this desolation and disorder? Trees and fields seem to survive incongruously like a sample of another civilization among the wall-paper factories and soap factories that have stamped out old lawns and terraces. Still more incongruously one passes an old grey country church which still rings its bells, and keeps its churchyard green as if country people were still coming across the fields to service. Further down, an inn with swelling bow windows still wears a strange air of dissipation and pleasure making. In the middle years of the nineteenth century it was a favourite resort of pleasure makers, and figured in some of the most famous divorce cases of the time. Now pleasure has gone and labour has come; and it stands derelict like some beauty in her midnight finery looking out over mud flats and candle works, while malodorous mounds of earth, upon which trucks are perpetually tipping fresh heaps, have entirely consumed the fields where, a hundred years ago, lovers wandered and picked violets.

As we go on steaming up the river to London we meet its refuse coming down. Barges heaped with old buckets, razor-blades, fish tails, newspapers and ashes – whatever we leave on our plates and throw into our dustbins – are discharging their cargoes upon the most desolate land in the world. The long mounds have been fuming and smoking and harbouring innumerable rats and growing a rank coarse grass and giving off a gritty, acrid air for fifty years. The dumps get higher and higher, and thicker and thicker, their sides more precipitous with tin cans, their pinnacles more angular with ashes year by year. But then, past all this sordidity, sweeps indifferently a great liner, bound for India. She takes her way through rubbish barges, and sewage barges, and dredgers out to sea. A little further, on the left hand, we are suddenly surprised – the sight upsets all our proportions once more – by what appear to be the stateliest buildings ever raised by the hand of man. Greenwich Hospital with all its columns and domes comes down in perfect symmetry to the water's edge, and makes the river again a stately waterway where the nobility of England once walked at their ease on green lawns, or descended stone steps to their pleasure barges.[5] As we come closer to the Tower Bridge the authority of the city begins to assert itself. The buildings thicken and heap themselves higher. The sky seems laden with heavier, purpler clouds. Domes swell; church spires, white with age, mingle with the tapering, pencil-shaped chimneys of factories. One hears the roar and the resonance of London itself. Here at last, we have landed at that thick and formidable circle of ancient stone, where so many drums have beaten and heads have fallen, the Tower of London itself. This is the knot, the clue, the hub of all those scattered miles of skeleton desolation and ant-like activity. Here growls and grumbles that rough city song that has called the ships from the sea and brought them to lie captive beneath its warehouses.

Now from the dock side we look down into the heart of the ship that has been lured from its voyaging and tethered to the dry land. The passengers and their bags have disappeared; the sailors have gone too. Indefatigable cranes are now at work, dipping and swinging, swinging and dipping. Barrels, sacks, crates are being picked up out of the hold and swung regularly on shore. Rhythmically, dexterously, with an order that has some aesthetic delight in it, barrel is laid by barrel, case by case, cask by cask, one behind another, one on top of another, one beside another in endless array down the aisles and arcades of the immense low-ceiled,[6] entirely plain and unornamented warehouses. Timber, iron, grain, wine, sugar, paper, tallow, fruit – whatever the ship has gathered from the plains, from the forests, from the pastures of the whole world is here lifted from its hold and set in its right place. A thousand ships with a thousand cargoes are being unladen every week. And not only is each package of this vast and varied merchandise picked up and set down accurately, but each is weighed and opened, sampled and recorded, and again stitched up and laid in its place, without haste, or waste, or hurry, or confusion by a very few men in shirt-sleeves, who, working with the utmost organization in the common interest – for buyers will take their word and abide by their decision – are yet able to pause in their work and say to the casual visitor, 'Would you like to see what sort of thing we sometimes find in sacks of cinnamon? Look at this snake!'

A snake, a scorpion, a beetle, a lump of amber, the diseased tooth of an elephant, a basin of quicksilver – these are some of the rarities and oddities that have been picked out of this cast merchandise and stood on a table. But with this one concession to curiosity, the temper of the docks is severely utilitarian. Oddities, beauties, rarities may occur, but if so, they are instantly tested for their mercantile value. Laid on the floor among the circles of elephant tusks is a heap of larger and browner tusks than the rest. Brown they well may be, for these are the tusks of mammoths[7] that have lain frozen in Siberian ice for fifty thousand years; but fifty thousand years are suspect in the eyes of the ivory expert. Mammoth ivory tends to warp; you cannot extract billiard balls from mammoths, but only umbrella handles and the backs of the cheaper kind of hand-glass. Thus if you buy an umbrella or a looking-glass not of the finest quality, it is likely that you are buying the tusk of a brute that roamed through Asian forests before England was an island.

One tusk makes a billiard ball, another serves for a shoe-horn – every commodity in the world has been examined and graded according to its use and value. Trade is ingenious and indefatigable beyond the bounds of imagination. None of all the multitudinous products and waste products of the earth but has been tested and found some possible use for. The bales of wool that are being swung from the hold of an Australian ship are girt, to save space, with iron hoops; but the hoops do not litter the floor; they are sent to Germany and made into safety razors. The wool itself exudes a coarse greasiness. This grease,[8] which is harmful to blankets, serves, when extracted, to make face cream. Even the burrs that stick in the wool of certain breeds of sheep have their use, for they prove that the sheep undoubtedly were fed on certain rich pastures. Not a burr, not a tuft of wool, not an iron hoop is unaccounted for. And the aptness of everything to its purpose, the forethought and readiness which have provided for every process, come, as if by the back door, to provide that element of beauty which nobody in the docks has ever given half a second of thought to. The warehouse is perfectly fit to be a warehouse; the crane to be a crane. Hence beauty begins to steal in. The cranes dip and swing, and there is rhythm in their regularity. The warehouse walls are open wide to admit sacks and barrels; but through them one sees all the roofs of London, its masts and spires, and the unconscious, vigorous movements of men lifting and unloading. Because barrels of wine require to be laid on their sides in cool vaults all the mystery of dim lights, all the beauty of low arches is thrown in as an extra.[9]

The wine vaults present a scene of extraordinary solemnity. Waving long blades of wood to which lamps have been fixed, we peer about, in what seems to be a vast cathedral, at cask after cask lying in a dim sacerdotal atmosphere, gravely maturing, slowly ripening. We might be priests worshipping in the temple of some silent religion and not merely wine tasters and Customs' Officers as we wander, waving our lamps up this aisle, down that. A yellow cat precedes us; otherwise the vaults are empty of all human life. Here side by side the objects of our worship lie swollen with sweet liquor, spouting red wine if tapped. A winy sweetness fills the vaults like incense. Here and there a gas jet flares, not indeed to give light, or because of the beauty of the green and grey arches which it calls up in endless procession, down avenue after avenue, but simply because so much heat is required to mellow the wine. Use produces beauty as a by-product. From the low arches a white cotton-wool-like growth depends. It is a fungus, but whether lovely or loathsome matters not: it is welcome because it proves that the air possesses the right degree of dampness for the health of the precious fluid.

Even the English language has adapted itself to the needs of commerce. Words have formed round objects and taken their exact outline. One may look in the dictionary in vain for the warehouse meaning of 'valinch,' 'shive', 'shirt', and 'flogger,'[10] but in the warehouse they have formed naturally on the tip of the tongue. So too the light stroke on either side of the barrel which makes the bung start has been arrived at by years of trial and experiment. It is the quickest, the most effective of actions. Dexterity can go no further.

The only thing, one comes to feel, that can change the routine of the docks is a change in ourselves. Suppose, for instance, that we gave up drinking claret, or took to using rubber instead of wool for our blankets, the whole machinery of production and distribution would rock and reel and seek about to adapt itself afresh. It is we – our tastes, our fashions, our needs – that make the cranes dip and swing, that call the ships from the sea. Our body is their master. We demand shoes, furs, bags, stoves, oil, rice puddings, candles; and they are brought us. Trade watches us anxiously to see what new desires are beginning to grow in us, what new dislikes. One feels an important, a complex, a necessary animal as one stands on the quayside watching the cranes hoist this barrel, that crate, that other bale from the holds of the ships that have come to anchor. Because one chooses to light a cigarette, all those barrels of Virginian tobacco[11] are swung on shore. Flocks upon flocks of Australian sheep have submitted to the shears because we demand woollen overcoats in winter. As for the umbrella that we swing idly to and fro, a mammoth who roared through the swamps fifty thousand years ago has yielded up its tusk to make the handle.

Meanwhile the ship flying the Blue Peter[12] moves slowly out of the dock; it has turned its bows to India or Australia once more. But in the Port of London, lorries jostle each other in the little street that leads from the dock – for there has been a great sale, and the cart horses are struggling and striving to distribute the wool over England.

II OXFORD STREET TIDE

Down in the docks one sees things in their crudity, their bulk, their enormity. Here in Oxford Street they have been refined and transformed. The huge barrels of damp tobacco have been rolled into innumerable neat cigarettes laid in silver paper. The corpulent bales of wool have been spun into thin vests and soft stockings. The grease of sheep's thick wool has become scented cream[1] for delicate skins. And those who buy and those who sell have suffered the same city change.[2] Tripping, mincing, in black coats, in satin dresses, the human form has adapted itself no less than the animal product. Instead of hauling and heaving, it deftly opens drawers, rolls out silk on counters, measures and snips with yard sticks and scissors.

Oxford Street, it goes without saying, is not London's most distinguished thoroughfare. Moralists have been known to point the finger of scorn at those who buy there, and they have the support of the dandies. Fashion has secret crannies off Hanover Square, round about Bond Street, to which it withdraws discreetly to perform its more sublime rites.[3] In Oxford Street there are too many bargains, too many sales, too many goods marked down to one and eleven three[4] that only last week cost two and six. The buying and selling is too blatant and raucous. But as one saunters towards the sunset – and what with artificial light and mounds of silk and gleaming omnibuses, a perpetual sunset seems to brood over the Marble Arch – the garishness and gaudiness of the great rolling ribbon of Oxford Street has its fascination. It is like the pebbly bed of a river whose stones are forever washed by a bright stream. Everything glitters and twinkles. The first spring day brings out barrows frilled with tulips, violets, daffodils in brilliant layers. The frail vessels eddy vaguely across the stream of the traffic. At one corner seedy magicians are making slips of coloured paper expand in magic tumblers into bristling forests of splendidly tinted flora – a subaqueous flower garden. At another, tortoises[5] repose on litters of grass. The slowest and most contemplative of creatures display their mild activities on a foot or two of pavement, jealously guarded from passing feet. One infers that the desire of man for the tortoise, like the desire of the moth for the star,[6] is a constant element in human nature. Nevertheless, to see a woman stop and add a tortoise to her string of parcels is perhaps the rarest sight that human eyes can look upon.

Taking all this into account – the auctions, the barrows, the cheapness, the glitter – it cannot be said that the character of Oxford Street is refined. It is a breeding ground, a forcing house of sensation.[7] The pavement seems to sprout horrid tragedies; the divorces of actresses, the suicides of millionaires occur here with a frequency that is unknown in the more austere pavements of the residential districts. News changes quicker than in any other part of London. The press of people passing seems to lick the ink off the placards and to consume more of them and to demand fresh supplies of later editions faster than elsewhere. The mind becomes a glutinous slab that takes impressions[8] and Oxford Street rolls off upon it a perpetual ribbon of changing sights, sounds and movement. Parcels slap and hit; motor omnibuses graze the kerb; the blare of a whole brass band in full tongue dwindles to a thin reed of sound. Buses, vans, cars, barrows stream past like the fragments of a picture puzzle; a white arm rises; the puzzle runs thick, coagulates, stops; the white arm sinks, and away it streams again, streaked, twisted, higgledy-piggledy, in perpetual race and disorder. The puzzle never fits itself together, however long we look.

On the banks of this river of turning wheels our modern aristocrats have built palaces just as in ancient days the Dukes of Somerset and Northumberland, the Earls of Dorset and Salisbury lined the Strand with their stately mansions. The different houses of the great firms testify to the courage, initiative, the audacity of their creators much as the great houses of Cavendish and Percy[9] testify to such qualities in some far-away shire. From the loins of our merchants will spring the Cavendishes and the Percys of the future. Indeed, the great Lords of Oxford Street are as magnanimous as any Duke or Earl who scattered gold or doled out loaves to the poor at his gates. Only their largesse takes a different form. It takes the form of excitement, of display, of entertainment, of windows lit up by night, of banners flaunting by day. They give us the latest news for nothing. Music streams[10] from their banqueting rooms free. You need not spend more than one and eleven three to enjoy all the shelter that high and airy halls provide; and the soft pile of carpets, and the luxury of lifts, and the glow of fabrics, and carpets and silver. Percy and Cavendish could give no more. These gifts of course have an object – to entice the shilling and eleven pennies as freely from our pockets as possible; but the Percys and the Cavendishes were not munificent either without hope of some return, whether it was a dedication from a poet or a vote from a farmer. And both the old lords and the new added considerably to the decoration and entertainment of human life.

But it cannot be denied that these Oxford Street palaces are rather flimsy abodes – perching-grounds rather than dwelling-places. One is conscious that one is walking on a strip of wood laid upon steel girders, and that the outer wall, for all its florid stone ornamentation, is only thick enough to withstand the force of the wind. A vigorous prod with an umbrella point might well inflict irreparable damage upon the fabric. Many a country cottage built to house farmer or miller when Queen Elizabeth was on the throne will live to see these palaces fall into the dust. The old cottage walls, with their oak beams and their layers of honest brick soundly cemented together still put up a stout resistance to the drills and bores that attempt to introduce the modern blessing of electricity. But any day of the week one may see Oxford Street vanishing at the tap of a workman's pick as he stands perilously balanced on a dusty pinnacle knocking down walls and façades as lightly as if they were made of yellow cardboard and sugar icing.

And again the moralists point the finger of scorn. For such thinness, such papery stone and powdery brick reflect, they say, the levity, the ostentation, the haste and irresponsibility of our age. Yet perhaps they are as much out in their scorn as we should be if we asked of the lily that it should be cast in bronze, or of the daisy that it should have petals of imperishable enamel. The charm of modern London is that it is not built to last; it is built to pass. Its glassiness, its transparency, its surging waves of coloured plaster give a different pleasure and achieve a different end from that which was desired and attempted by the old builders and their patrons, the nobility of England. Their pride required the illusion of permanence. Ours, on the contrary, seems to delight in proving that we can make stone and brick as transitory as our own desires. We do not build for our descendants, who may live up in the clouds or down in the earth, but for ourselves and our own needs. We knock down and rebuild as we expect to be knocked down and rebuilt. It is an impulse that makes for creation and fertility. Discovery is stimulated and invention on the alert.

The palaces of Oxford Street ignore what seemed good to the Greeks, to the Elizabethan, to the eighteenth-century nobleman; they are overwhelmingly conscious that unless they can devise an architecture that shows off the dressing-case, the Paris frock, the cheap stockings, and the jar of bath salts to perfection, their palaces, their mansions and motor cars and the little villas out at Croydon and Surbiton[11] where their shop assistants live, not so badly after all, with a gramophone and wireless, and money to spend at the movies – all this will be swept to ruin. Hence they stretch stone fantastically; crush together in one wild confusion the styles of Greece, Egypt, Italy, America; and boldly attempt an air of lavishness, opulence, in their effort to persuade the multitude that here unending beauty, ever fresh, ever new, very cheap and within the reach of everybody, bubbles up every day of the week from an inexhaustible well. The mere thought of age, of solidity, of lasting for ever is abhorrent to Oxford Street.

Therefore if the moralist chooses to take his afternoon walk along this particular thoroughfare, he must tune his strain so that it receives into it some queer, incongruous voices. Above the racket of van and omnibus we can hear them crying. God knows, says the man who sells tortoises, that my arm aches; my chance of selling a tortoise is small; but courage! there may come along a buyer; my bed tonight depends on it; so on I must go, as slowly as the police allow, wheeling tortoises down Oxford Street from dawn till dusk. True, says the great merchant, I am not thinking of educating the mass to a higher standard of aesthetic sensibility. It taxes all my wits to think how I can display my goods with the minimum of waste and the maximum of effectiveness. Green dragons on the top of Corinthian columns may help; let us try. I grant, says the middle-class woman, that I linger and look and barter and cheapen and turn over basket after basket of remnants hour by hour. My eyes glisten unseemlily I know, and I grab and pounce with disgusting greed. But my husband is a small clerk in a bank; I have only fifteen pounds a year to dress on; so here I come, to linger and loiter and look, if I can, as well dressed as my neighbours. I am a thief, says a woman of that persuasion, and a lady of easy virtue into the bargain. But it takes a good deal of pluck to snatch a bag from a counter when a customer is not looking; and it may contain only spectacles and old bus tickets after all. So here goes!

A thousand such voices are always crying aloud in Oxford Street. All are tense, all are real, all are urged out of their speakers by the pressure of making a living, finding a bed, somehow keeping afloat on the bounding, careless, remorseless tide of the street. And even a moralist, who is, one must suppose, since he can spend the afternoon dreaming, a man with a balance in the bank – even a moralist must allow that this gaudy, bustling, vulgar street reminds us that life is a struggle; that all building is perishable; that all display is vanity; from which we may conclude – but until some adroit shopkeeper has caught on to the idea and opened cells for solitary thinkers hung with green plush and provided with automatic glow-worms and a sprinkling of genuine[12] death's-head moths to induce thought and reflection, it is vain to try to come to a conclusion in Oxford Street.

III GREAT MEN'S HOUSES

London, happily, is becoming full of great men's houses, bought for the nation and preserved entire with the chairs they sat on and the cups they drank from, their umbrellas and their chests of drawers. And it is no frivolous curiosity that sends us to Dickens's house and Johnson's house and Carlyle's house and Keats's house. We know them from their houses – it would seem to be a fact that writers stamp themselves upon their possessions more indelibly than other people. Of artistic taste they may have none; but they seem always to possess a much rarer and more interesting gift – a faculty for housing themselves appropriately, for making the table, the chair, the curtain, the carpet into their own image.

Take the Carlyles, for instance. One hour spent in 5 Cheyne Row[1] will tell us more about them and their lives than we can learn from all the biographies. Go down into the kitchen. There, in two seconds, one is made acquainted with a fact that escaped the attention of Froude,[2] and yet was of incalculable importance – they had no water laid on. Every drop that the Carlyles used – and they were Scots, fanatical in their cleanliness – had to be pumped by hand from a well in the kitchen. There is the well at this moment and the pump and the stone trough into which the cold water trickled. And here, too, is the wide and wasteful old grate upon which all kettles had to be boiled if they wanted a hot bath; and here is the cracked yellow tin bath, so deep and so narrow, which had to be filled with the cans of hot water that the maid first pumped and then boiled and then carried up three flights of stairs from the basement.

The high old house without water, without electric light, without gas fires, full of books and coal smoke and four poster beds and mahogany cupboards, where two of the most nervous and exacting people of their time lived, year in year out, was served by one unfortunate maid. All through the mid-Victorian age the house was necessarily a battlefield where daily, summer and winter, mistress and maid fought against dirt and cold for cleanliness and warmth. The stairs, carved as they are and wide and dignified, seem worn by the feet of harassed women carrying tin cans. The high panelled rooms seem to echo with the sound of pumping and the swish of scrubbing. The voice of the house – and all houses have voices – is the voice of pumping and scrubbing, of coughing and groaning. Up in the attic under a skylight Carlyle groaned, as he wrestled with his history, on a horsehair chair, while a yellow shaft of London light fell upon his papers and the rattle of a barrel organ and the raucous shouts of street hawkers came through walls whose double thickness distorted but by no means excluded the sound.[3] And the season of the house – for every house has its season – seems to be always the month of February, when cold and fog are in the street and torches flare and the rattle of wheels grows suddenly loud and dies away. February after February Mrs Carlyle lay coughing in the large four-poster hung with maroon curtains in which she was born, and as she coughed the many problems of the incessant battle, against dirt, against cold, came before her. The horsechair couch needed recovering; the drawing-room paper with its small dark pattern needed cleaning; the yellow varnish on the panels was cracked and peeling – all must be stitched, cleansed, scoured with her own hands; and had she, or had she not, demolished the bugs that bred and bred in the ancient wood panelling? So the long watches of the sleepless night passed and then she heard Mr Carlyle stir above her, and held her breath and wondered if Helen were up and had lit the fire and heated the water for his shaving. Another day had dawned and the pumping and the scrubbing must begin again.

Thus number 5 Cheyne Row is not so much a dwelling-place as a battlefield – the scene of labour, effort and perpetual struggle. Few of the spoils of life – its graces and its luxuries – survive to tell us that the battle was worth the effort. The relics of drawing-room and study are like the relics picked up on other battlefields. Here is a packet of old steel nibs; a broken clay pipe; a pen-holder such as schoolboys use; a few cups of white-and-gold china, much chipped; a horsehair sofa and a yellow tin bath. Here, too, is a cast of the thin worn hands that worked here; and of the excruciated and ravished face of Carlyle when his life was done and he lay dead here. Even the garden at the back of the house seems to be not a place of rest and recreation, but another smaller battlefield marked with a tombstone beneath which a dog lies buried. By pumping and by scrubbing, days of victory, evenings of peace and splendour were won, of course. Mrs Carlyle sat, as we see from the picture, in a fine silk dress, in a chair pulled up to a blazing fire and had everything seemly and solid about her; but at what cost had she won it! Her cheeks are hollow; bitterness and suffering mingle in the half-tender, half-tortured expression of the eyes. Such is the effect of a pump in the basement and a yellow tin bath up three pairs of stairs. Both husband and wife had genius: they loved each other; but what can genius and love avail against bugs and tin baths and pumps in the basement?

It is impossible not to believe that half their quarrels might have been spared and their lives immeasurably sweetened if only number 5 Cheyne Row had possessed, as the house agents put it, bath, h.

and c., gas fires in the bedrooms, all modern conveniences[4] and indoor sanitation. But then, we reflect, as we cross the worn threshold, Carlyle with hot water laid on would not have been Carlyle; and Mrs Carlyle without bugs to kill would have been a different woman from the one we know.

An age seems to separate the house in Chelsea where the Carlyles lived from the house in Hampstead which was shared by Keats and Brown and the Brawnes.[5] If houses have their voices and places their seasons, it is always spring in Hampstead as it is always February in Cheyne Row. By some miracle, too, Hampstead has always remained not a suburb or a piece of antiquity engulfed in the modern world, but a place with a character peculiar to itself. It is not a place where one makes money, or goes when one has money to spend. The signs of discreet retirement are stamped on it. Its houses are neat boxes such as front the sea at Brighton with bow windows and balconies and deck-chairs on verandahs. It has style and intention as if designed for people of modest income and some leisure who seek rest and recreation. Its prevailing colours are the pale pinks and blues that seem to harmonize with the blue sea and the white sand; and yet there is an urbanity in the style which proclaims the neighbourhood of a great city. Even in the twentieth century this serenity still pervades the suburb of Hampstead. Its bow windows still look out upon vales and trees and ponds and barking dogs and couples sauntering arm in arm and pausing, here on the hill-top, to look at the distant domes and pinnacles of London, as they sauntered and paused and looked when Keats lived here. For Keats lived up the lane in a little white house behind wooden palings. Nothing has been much changed since his day. But as we enter the house in which Keats lived some mournful shadow seems to fall across the garden. A tree has fallen and lies propped. Waving branches cast their shadows up and down over the flat white walls of the house. Here, for all the gaiety and serenity of the neighbourhood, the nightingale sang; here, if anywhere, fever and anguish had their dwelling and paced this little green plot oppressed with the sense of quick-coming death and the shortness of life[6] and the passion of love and its misery.

Yet if Keats left any impress upon his house it is the impression not of fever, but of that clarity and dignity which come from order and self-control. The rooms are small but shapely; downstairs the long windows are so large that half the wall seems made of light. Two chairs turned together are close to the window as if someone had sat there reading and had just got up and left the room. The figure of the reader must have been splashed with shade and sun as the hanging leaves stirred in the breeze. Birds must have hopped close to his foot. The room is empty save for the two chairs, for Keats had few possessions, little furniture and not more, he said, than one hundred and fifty books. And perhaps it is because the rooms are so empty and furnished rather with light and shadow than with chairs and tables that one does not think of people, here where so many people have lived. The imagination does not evoke scenes. It does not strike one that there must have been eating and drinking here; people must have come in and out; they must have put down bags, left parcels; they must have scrubbed and cleaned and done battle with dirt and disorder and carried cans of water from the basement to the bedrooms. All the traffic of life is silenced. The voice of the house is the voice of leaves brushing in the wind; of branches stirring in the garden. Only one presence – that of Keats himself – dwells here. And even he, though his picture is on every wall, seems to come silently, on the broad shafts of light, without body or footfall. Here he sat on the chair in the window and listened without moving, and saw without starting, and turned the page without haste though his time was so short.

There is an air of heroic equanimity about the house in spite of the death masks and the brittle yellow wreaths and the other grisly memorials which remind us that Keats died young and unknown and in exile.[7] Life goes on outside the window. Behind this calm, this rustling of leaves, one hears the far-off rattle of wheels, the bark of dogs fetching and carrying sticks from the pond. Life goes on outside the wooden paling. When we shut the gate upon the grass and the tree where the nightingale sang we find, quite rightly, the butcher delivering his meat from a small red motor van at the house next door. If we cross the road, taking care not to be cut down by some rash driver – for they drive at a great pace down these wide streets – we shall find ourselves on top of the hill and beneath shall see the whole of London lying below us. It is a view of perpetual fascination at all hours and in all seasons. One sees

London as a whole – London crowded and ribbed and compact, with its dominant domes, its guardian cathedrals; its chimneys and spires; its cranes and gasometers; and the perpetual smoke which no spring or autumn ever blows away. London has lain there time out of mind scarring that stretch of earth deeper and deeper, making it more uneasy, lumped and tumultuous, branding it for ever with an indelible scar. There it lies in layers, in strata, bristling and billowing with rolls of smoke always caught on its pinnacles. And yet from Parliament Hill[8] one can see, too, the country beyond. There are hills on the further side in whose woods birds are singing, and some stoat or rabbit pauses, in dead silence, with paw lifted to listen intently to rustlings among the leaves. To look over London from this hill Keats came and Coleridge and Shakespeare, perhaps. And here at this very moment the usual young man sits on an iron bench clasping to his arms the usual young woman.

IV ABBEYS AND CATHEDRALS

It is a commonplace but we cannot help repeating it, that St Paul's dominates London. It swells like a great grey bubble from a distance; it looms over us, huge and menacing, as we approach. But suddenly St Paul's vanishes. And behind St Paul's, beneath St Paul's, round St Paul's when we cannot see St Paul's, how London has shrunk! Once there were colleges and quadrangles and monasteries with fish ponds and cloisters; and sheep grazing on the greensward; and inns where great poets stretched their legs and talked at their ease. Now all this space has shrivelled. The fields are gone and the fish ponds and the cloisters; even men and women seem to have shrunk and become multitudinous and minute instead of single and substantial. Where Shakespeare and Jonson once fronted each other and had their talk out,[1] a million Mr Smiths and Miss Browns scuttle and hurry, swing off omnibuses, dive into Tubes. They seem too many, too minute, too like each other to have each a name, a character, a separate life of their own.

If we leave the street and step into a city church, the space that the dead enjoy compared with what the living now enjoy, is brought home to us. In the year 1737 a man called Howard died and was buried in St Mary-le-Bow.[2] A whole wall is covered with the list of his virtues. 'He was blessed with a sound and intelligent mind which shone forth conspicuously in the habitual exercise of great and godlike virtues . . . In the midst of a profligate age he was inviolably attached to justice, sincerity and truth.' He occupies space that might serve almost for an office and demand a rent of many hundreds a year. In our day a man of equal obscurity would be allotted one slice of white stone of the regulation size among a thousand others and his great and godlike virtues would have to go unrecorded. Again, in St Mary-le-Bow all posterity is asked to pause and rejoice that Mrs Mary Lloyd 'closed an exemplary and spotless life' without suffering and indeed without regaining consciousness, aged 79 years.

Pause, reflect, admire, take heed of your ways – so these ancient tablets are always advising and exhorting us. One leaves the church marvelling at the spacious days when unknown citizens could occupy so much room with their bones and confidently request so much attention for their virtues when we – behold how we jostle and skip and circumvent each other in the street, how sharply we cut corners, how nimbly we skip beneath motor cars. The mere process of keeping alive needs all our energy. We have no time, we were about to say, to think about life or death either, when suddenly we run against the enormous walls of St Paul's. Here it is again, looming over us, mountainous, immense, greyer, colder, quieter than before. And directly we enter we undergo that pause and expansion and release from hurry and effort which it is in the power of St Paul's, more than any other building in the world, to bestow.

Something of the splendour of St Paul's lies simply in its vast size, in its colourless serenity. Mind and body seem both to widen in this enclosure, to expand under this huge canopy where the light is neither daylight nor lamplight, but an ambiguous element something between the two. One window shakes down a broad green shaft; another tinges the flagstones beneath a cool, pale purple. There is space for each broad band of light to fall smoothly. Very large, very square, hollow-sounding, echoing with a perpetual shuffling and booming, the Cathedral is august in the extreme; but not in the least mysterious. Tombs heaped like majestic beds lie between the pillars. Here is the dignified reposing room to which great statesmen and men of action retire, robed in all their splendour, to accept the thanks and applause of their fellow-citizens. They still wear their stars and garters, their emblems of civic pomp and military pride. Their tombs are clean and comely. No rust or stain has been allowed to spot them. Even Nelson looks a little smug. Even the contorted and agonized figure of John Donne,[3] wrapped in the marble twists of his grave clothes, looks as if it had left the stonemason's yard but yesterday. Yet it has stood here in its agony for three hundred years and has passed through the flames of the fire of London. But death and the corruption of death are forbidden to enter. Here civic virtue and civic greatness are ensconced securely. True, a heavy bossed door has above it the legend that through the gate of death we pass to our joyful resurrection; but somehow the massive portals suggest that they open not upon fields of amaranth and moly[4] where harps sound and heavenly choirs sing, but upon flights of marble steps that lead on to solemn council chambers and splendid halls, loud with trumpets and hung with banners. Effort and agony and ecstasy have no place in this majestic building.

No contrast could be greater than that between St Paul's and Westminster Abbey. Far from being spacious and serene, the Abbey is narrow and pointed, worn, restless and animated. One feels as if one had stepped from the democratic helter-skelter, the hubbub and humdrum of the street, into a brilliant assembly, a select society of men and women of the highest distinction. The company seems to be in full conclave. Gladstone starts forward and then Disraeli.[5] From every corner, from every wall, somebody leans or listens or bends forward as if about to speak. The recumbent even seem to lie attentive, as if to rise next minute. Their hands nervously grasp their sceptres, their lips are compressed for a fleeting silence, their eyes lightly closed as if for a moment's thought. These dead, if dead they are, have lived to the full. Their faces are worn, their noses high, their cheeks hollowed. Even the stone of the old columns seems rubbed and chafed by the intensity of the life that has been fretting it all these centuries. Voice and organ vibrate wirily among the chasings and intricacies of the roof. The fine fans of stone that spread themselves to make a ceiling seem like bare boughs withered of all their leaves and about to toss in the wintry gale. But their austerity is beautifully softened. Lights and shadows are changing and conflicting every moment. Blue, gold and violet pass, dappling, quickening, fading. The grey stone, ancient as it is, changes like a live thing under the incessant ripple of changing light.

Thus the Abbey is no place of death and rest; no reposing-room where the virtuous lie in state to receive the rewards of virtue. Is it, indeed, through their virtues that these dead have come here? Often they have been violent; they have been vicious. Often it is only the greatness of their birth that has exalted them. The Abbey is full of Kings and Queens, Dukes and Princes. The light falls upon gold coronets, and gold still lingers in the folds of ceremonial robes. Reds and yellows still blazon coats of arms and lions and unicorns. But it is full also of another and even more potent royalty. Here are the dead poets, still musing, still pondering, still questioning the meaning of existence. 'Life is a jest and all things show it. I thought so once, and now I know it,' Gay laughs.[6] Chaucer, Spenser, Dryden and the rest still seem to listen with all their faculties on the alert as the clean-shaven clergyman in his spick-and-span red-and-white robes intones for the millionth time the commands of the Bible. His voice rings ripely, authoritatively through the building, and if it were not irreverent one might suppose that Gladstone and Disraeli were about to put the statement just propounded – that children should honour their parents – to the vote. Everybody in this brilliant assembly has a mind and a will of his own. The Abbey is shot with high-pitched voices; its peace is broken by emphatic gestures and characteristic attitudes. Not an inch of its walls but speaks and claims and illustrates. Kings and Queens, poets and statesmen still act their parts and are not suffered to turn quietly to dust. Still in animated debate they rise above the flood and waste of average human life, with their fists clenched and their lips parted, with an orb in one hand, a sceptre in another, as if we had forced them to rise on our behalf and testify that human nature can now and then exalt itself above the humdrum democratic disorder of the hurrying street. Arrested, transfixed, there they stand suffering a splendid crucifixion.

Where then can one go in London to find peace and the assurance that the dead sleep and are at rest? London, after all, is a city of tombs. But London nevertheless is a city in the full tide and race of human life. Even St Clement Danes – that venerable pile planted in the mid-stream of the Strand[7] – has been docked of all those peaceful perquisites – the weeping trees, the waving grasses that the humblest village church enjoys by right. Omnibuses and vans have long since shorn it of these dues. It stands, like an island, with only the narrowest rim of pavement to separate it from the sea. And moreover, St Clement Danes has its duties to the living. As likely as not it is participating vociferously, stridently, with almost frantic joy, but hoarsely as if its tongue were rough with the rust of centuries, in the happiness of two living mortals. A wedding is in progress. All down the Strand St Clement Danes roars its welcome to the bridegroom in tail coat and grey trousers; to the bridesmaids virginal in white; and finally to the bride herself whose car draws up to the porch, and out she steps and passes undulating with a flash of white finery into the inner gloom to make her marriage vows to the roar of omnibuses, while outside the pigeons, alarmed, sweep in circles, and Gladstone's statue is crowded, like a rock with gulls, with nodding, waving, enthusiastic sightseers.

The only peaceful places in the whole city are perhaps those old graveyards which have become gardens and playgrounds. The tombstones no longer serve to mark the graves, but line the walls with their white tablets. Here and there a finely sculptured tomb plays the part of garden ornament. Flowers light up the turf, and there are benches under the trees for mothers and nursemaids to sit on, while the children bowl hoops and play hopscotch in safety. Here one might sit and read *Pamela*[8] from cover to cover. Here one might drowse away the first days of spring or the last days of autumn without feeling too keenly the stir of youth or the sadness of old age. For here the dead sleep in peace, proving nothing, testifying nothing, claiming nothing save that we shall enjoy the peace that their old bones provides for us. Unreluctantly they have given up their human rights to separate names or peculiar virtues. But they have no cause for grievance. When the gardener plants his bulbs or sows his grass they flower again and spread the ground with green and elastic turf. Here mothers and nursemaids gossip; children play; and the old beggar, after eating his dinner from a paper bag, scatters crumbs to the sparrows. These garden graveyards are the most peaceful of our London sanctuaries and their dead the quietest.

V 'THIS IS THE HOUSE OF COMMONS'

Outside the House of Commons[1] stand the statues of great statesmen, black and sleek and shiny as sea lions that have just risen from the water. And inside the Houses of Parliament, in those windy, echoing halls, where people are forever passing and repassing, taking green cards from policemen, asking questions, staring, accosting members, trooping at the heels of schoolmasters, nodding and laughing and running messages and hurrying through swing doors with papers and attaché cases and all the other emblems of business and haste – here, too, are statues – Gladstone, Granville, Lord John Russell[2] – white statues, gazing from white eyes at the old scenes of stir and bustle in which, not so very long ago, they played their part.

There is nothing venerable or timeworn, or musical, or ceremonious here. A raucous voice bawling 'The Speaker!' heralds the tramp of a plain democratic procession whose only pomp is provided by the mace and the Speaker's wig and gown and gold badges of the head waiters. The raucous voice bawls again, 'Hats off, Strangers!' upon which a number of dingy felt hats are flourished obediently and the head waiters bow from the middle downwards. That is all. And yet the bawling voice, the black gown, the tramp of feet on the stone, the mace and the dingy felt hats somehow suggest, better than scarlet and trumpets, that the Commons are taking their seats in their own House to proceed with the business of governing their own country. Vague though our history may be, we somehow feel that we common people won this right centuries ago, and have held it for centuries past, and the mace is our mace and the Speaker is our speaker and we have no need of trumpeters and gold and scarlet to usher our representative into our own House of Commons.

Certainly our own House of Commons from inside is not in the least noble or majestic or even dignified. It is as shiny and as ugly as any other moderate-sized public hall. The oak, of course, is grained yellow. The windows, of course, are painted with ugly coats of arms. The floor, of course, is laid with strips of red matting. The benches, of course, are covered with serviceable leather. Wherever one looks one says, 'of course.' It is an untidy, informal-looking assembly. Sheets of white paper seem to be always fluttering to the floor. People are always coming in and out incessantly. Men are whispering and gossiping and cracking jokes over each other's shoulders. The swing doors are perpetually swinging. Even the central island of control and dignity where the Speaker sits under his canopy, is a perching-ground for casual members who seem to be taking a peep at the proceedings at their ease. Legs rest on the edge of the table where the mace lies suspended; and the secrets which repose in the two brass-bound chests on either side of the table are not immune from the prod of an occasional toe. Dipping and rising, moving and settling, the Commons remind one of a flock of birds settling on a stretch of ploughed land. They never alight for more than a few minutes; some are always flying off, others are always settling again. And from the flock rises the gabbling, the cawing, the croaking of a flock of birds, disputing merrily and with occasional vivacity over some seed, worm, or buried grain.

One has to say to oneself severely, 'But this is the House of Commons. Here the destinies of the world are altered. Here Gladstone fought, and Palmerston and Disraeli.[3] It is by these men that we are governed. We obey their orders every day of the year. Our purses are at their mercy. They decide how fast we shall drive our cars in Hyde Park; also whether we shall have war or peace.' But we have to remind ourselves; for to look at they do not differ much from other people. The standard of dress is perhaps rather high. We look down upon some of the glossiest top hats still to be seen in England. A magnificent scarlet button-hole blazes here and there. Everybody has been well fed and given a good education doubtless. But what with their chatter and laughter, their high spirits, and impatience and irreverence, they are not a whit more judicious, or more dignified, or more respectable-looking than any other assembly of citizens met to debate parish business or to give prizes for fat oxen. This is true; but after a time some curious difference makes itself suspected. We feel that the Commons is a body of a certain character; it has been in existence for a long time; it has its own laws and licences. It is irreverent in a way of its own; and so, presumably, reverent too in its own way. It has somehow a code of its own. People who disregard this code will be unmercifully chastened; those who are in accord with it will be easily condoned. But what it condemns and what it condones, only those who are in the secret of the House can say. All we can be sure of is that a secret there is. Perched up high as we are, under the rule of an official who follows the prevailing informality by crossing his legs and scribbling notes on his knee, we feel sure that nothing could be easier than to say the wrong thing, either with the wrong levity or the wrong seriousness, and that no assurance of virtue, genius, valour is here sure of success if something else – some indefinable quality – is omitted.

But how, one asks, remembering Parliament Square, are any of these competent, well-groomed gentlemen going to turn into statues? For Gladstone, for Pitt, or for Palmerston even, the transition was perfectly easy. But look at Mr Baldwin – he has all the look of a country gentleman poking pigs; how is he going to mount a plinth and wrap himself decorously in a towel of black marble? No statue that did not render the shine of Sir Austen's top hat could do justice to him. Mr Henderson seems constitutionally opposed to the pallor and severity of marble. As he stands there answering questions his fair complexion flushes scarlet, and his yellow hair seems to have been sleeked down with a wet brush ten minutes ago. Sir William Jowitt, it is true, might, if one took off his spruce bow tie, sit to some sculptor for a bust much in the style of the Prince Consort. Ramsay MacDonald has 'features,' as the photographers say, and could fill a marble chair in a public square without looking conspicuously ridiculous.[4] But for the rest, the transition into marble is unthinkable. Mobile, irreverent, commonplace, snub-nosed, red-jowled, squires, lawyers, men of business – their prime quality, their enormous virtue lies surely in the fact that no more normal, average, decent-looking set of human beings could be found in the four kingdoms.[5] The flashing eye, the arched brow, the nervous, sensitive hand – these would be unseemly and out of place here. The abnormal man would be pecked to death by all these cheerful sparrows. Look how irreverently they treat the Prime Minister himself. He has to submit to being questioned and cross-examined by a youth who seems to have rolled out of a punt on the river; or again to be heckled by a stubby little man who, to judge by his accent, must have been shovelling sugar into little blue bags[6] behind a counter before he came to Westminster. Neither shows the least trace of fear or reverence. If the Prime Minister should one of these days turn into a statue, this apotheosis will not be reached here among the irreverent Commons.

All this time the fire of question and answer had popped and cracked incessantly; at last it stopped. The Secretary for Foreign Affairs rose, raised some typewritten sheets and read, clearly and firmly, a statement about some difficulty with Germany. He had seen the German Ambassador at the Foreign Office on Friday; he had said this, he had said that. He had crossed to Paris and seen M. Briand on Monday. They had agreed to this, they had suggested that. A plainer, a graver, a more business-like pronouncement could not be imagined. And as he spoke so directly, so firmly, a block of rough stone seemed to erect itself there on the government benches. In other words, as one listened to the Secretary for Foreign Affairs endeavouring to guide our relations with Germany, it seemed clear that these ordinary-looking business-like men are responsible for acts which will remain when their red cheeks and top hats and check trousers are dust and ashes. Matters of great moment, which affect the happiness of people, the destinies of nations, are here at work chiselling and carving these very ordinary human beings. Down on this stuff of common humanity comes the stamp of a huge machine. And the machine itself and the man upon whom the stamp of the machine descends are both plain, featureless, impersonal.

Time was when the Foreign Secretary manipulated facts, toyed with them, elaborated them, and used all the resources of art and eloquence to make them appear what he chose that they should appear to the people who had to accept his will. He was no common hard-worked man of business, with a small car and a villa and a great longing to get an afternoon off and play golf with his sons and daughters on a Surrey common. The Minister was once dressed to fit his part. Fulminations, perorations shook the air. Men were persuaded, juggled with, played upon. Pitt thundered; Burke was sublime.[7] Individuality was allowed to unfold itself. Now no single human being can withstand the pressure of human affairs. They sweep over him and obliterate him; they leave him featureless, anonymous, their instrument merely. The conduct of affairs has passed from the hands of individuals to the hands of committees.[8] Even committees can only guide them and hasten them and sweep them on to other committees. The intricacies and elegancies of personality are trappings that get in the way of business. The supreme need is despatch.[9] A thousand ships come to anchor in the docks every week; how many thousand causes do not come daily to be decided in the House of Commons? Thus if statues are to be raised, they will become more and more monolithic, plain and featureless. They will cease to record Gladstone's collars, Dizzy's[10] curl and Palmerston's wisp of straw. They will be like granite plinths set on the tops of moors to mark battles. The days of single men and personal power are over.[11] Wit, invective, passion, are no longer called for. Mr MacDonald is addressing not the small separate ears of his audience in the House of Commons, but men and women in factories, in shops, in farms on the veldt, in Indian villages.[12] He is speaking to all men everywhere, not to us sitting here. Hence the clarity, the gravity, the plain impersonality of his statement. But if the days of the small separate statue are over, why should not the age of architecture dawn? That question asks itself as we leave the House of Commons. Westminster Hall raises its immense dignity as we pass out. Little men and women are moving soundlessly about the floor. They appear minute, perhaps pitiable; but also venerable and beautiful under the curve of the vast dome, under the perspective of the huge columns. One would rather like to be a small nameless animal in a vast cathedral. Let us rebuild the world then as a splendid hall; let us give up making statues and inscribing them with impossible virtues.

Let us see whether democracy which makes halls cannot surpass the aristocracy which carved statues. But there are still innumerable policemen. A blue giant stands at every door to see that we do not hurry on with our democracy too fast. 'Admission is on Saturdays only between the hours of ten and twelve.' That is the kind of notice that checks our dreaming progress. And must we not admit a distinct tendency in our corrupt mind soaked with habit to stop and think: 'Here stood King Charles when they sentenced him to death; here the Earl of Essex; and Guy Fawkes; and Sir Thomas More.'[13] The mind, it seems, likes to perch, in its flight through empty space, upon some remarkable nose, some trembling hand; it loves the flashing eye, the arched brow, the abnormal, the particular, the splendid human being. So let us hope that democracy will come, but only a hundred years hence,[14] when we are beneath the grass; or that by some stupendous stroke of genius both will be combined, the vast hall and the small, the particular, the individual human being.

Why Art Today Follows Politics

First appeared in the *Daily Worker* on 14 December 1936.

I have been asked by the Artists' International Association[1] to explain as shortly as I can why it is that the artist at present is interested, actively and genuinely, in politics. For it seems that there are some people to whom this interest is suspect.

That the writer is interested in politics needs no saying. Every publisher's list, almost every book that is now issued, brings proof of the fact.

The historian today is writing not about Greece and Rome in the past, but about Germany and Spain in the present; the biographer is writing lives of Hitler and Mussolini, not of Henry the Eighth and Charles Lamb; the poet introduces Communism and Fascism into his lyrics; the novelist turns from the private lives of his characters to their social surroundings and their political opinions.

Obviously the writer is in such close touch with human life that any agitation in it must change his angle of vision. Either he focuses his sight upon the immediate problem; or he brings his subject matter into relation with the present; or in some cases, so paralysed is he by the agitation of the moment that he remains silent.

But why should this agitation affect the painter and the sculptor, it may be asked? He is not concerned with the feelings of his model, but with its form.

The rose and the apple have no political views. Why should he not spend his time contemplating them, as he has always done, in the cold north light that still falls through his studio window?

To answer this question is not easy, for to understand why the artist – the plastic artist – is affected by the state of society we must try to define the relations of the artist to society, and this is difficult, partly because no such definition has ever been made.

But that there is some sort of understanding between them, most people would agree; and in times of peace it may be said roughly to run as follows: –

The artist on his side held that since the value of his work depended upon freedom of mind; security of person, and immunity from practical affairs – for to mix art with politics he held was to adulterate it – he was absolved from political duties; sacrificed many of the privileges that the active citizen enjoyed; and in return created what is called a work of art.

Society on its side bound itself to run the State in such a manner that it paid the artist a living wage; asked no active help from him; and considered itself repaid by those works of art which have always formed one of its chief claims to distinction.

With many lapses and breaches on both sides the contract has been kept; society has accepted the artist's work in lieu of other services, and the artist, living for the most part precariously on a pittance, has written or painted without regard for the political agitations of the moment.

Thus it would be impossible, when we read Keats, or look at the pictures of Titian and Velasquez, or listen to the music of Mozart or Bach to say what was the political condition of the age or the country in which these works were created.

And if it were otherwise – if the Ode to a Nightingale were inspired by hatred of Germany; if Bacchus and Ariadne symbolized the conquest of Abyssinia; if Figaro[2] expounded the doctrine of Hitler we should feel cheated and imposed upon, as if, instead of bread made with flour, we were given bread made with plaster.

But if it is true that some such contract existed between the artist and society in times of peace it by no means follows that the artist is independent of society. Materially, of course, he depends upon it for his bread and butter.

Art is the first luxury to be discarded in times of stress; the artist is the first of the workers to suffer. But intellectually also he depends upon society.

Society is not only his paymaster, but his patron. If the patron becomes too busy or too distracted to exercise his critical faculty the artist will work in a vacuum and his art will suffer and perhaps perish from lack of understanding.

Again, if the patron is neither poor nor indifferent, but dictatorial – if he will only buy pictures that flatter his vanity or serve his politics – then again the artist is impeded and his work becomes worthless.

And even if there are some artists who can afford to disregard the patron, either because they have private means, or have learnt in the course of time to form their own style and to depend upon tradition, these are for the most part only the older artists, whose work is already done. Even they, however, are by no means immune.

For though it would be easy to stress the point absurdly, still it is a fact that the practice of art, far from making the artist out of touch with his kind, rather increases his sensibility.

It breeds in him a feeling for the passions and needs of mankind in the mass which the citizen whose duty it is to work for a particular country or for a particular party has no time and perhaps no need to cultivate.

Thus even if he be ineffective, he is by no means apathetic. Perhaps, indeed, he suffers more than the active citizen because he has no obvious duty to discharge.

For such reasons then it is clear that the artist is affected as powerfully as other citizens when society is in chaos, although the disturbance affects him in different ways. His studio now is far from being a cloistered spot where he can contemplate his model or his apple in peace.

It is besieged by voices, all disturbing, some for one reason, some for another.

First there is the voice which cries: I cannot protect you; I cannot pay you. I am so tortured and distracted that I can no longer enjoy your works of art.

Then there is the voice which asks for help: Come down from your ivory tower, leave your studio, it cries, and use your gifts as doctor, as teacher, not as artist.

Again there is the voice which warns the artist that unless he can show good cause why art benefits the State he will be made to help it actively – by making airplanes, by firing guns.

And finally, there is the voice which many artists in other countries have already heard and had to obey – the voice which proclaims that the artist is the servant of the politician.

You shall only practise your art, it says, at our bidding. Paint us pictures, carve us statues that glorify our gospels. Celebrate Fascism; celebrate Communism. Preach what we bid you preach. On no other terms shall you exist.

With all these voices crying and conflicting in his ears, how can the artist still remain at peace in his studio contemplating his model or his apple in the cold light that comes through the studio window?

He is forced to take part in politics: he must form himself into societies like the Artists' International Association.

Two causes of supreme importance to him are in peril. The first is his own survival: the other is the survival of his art.

Craftsmanship

This radio talk was broadcast by Woolf in the series *Words Fail Me* on 29 April 1937, and published in the *Listener*, 5 May 1937.

The title of this series is *Words Fail Me*, and this particular talk is called 'Craftsmanship'.[1] We must suppose, therefore, that the talker is meant to discuss the craft of words – the craftsmanship of the writer. But there is something incongruous, unfitting, about the term 'craftsmanship' when applied to words. The English dictionary, to which we always turn in moments of dilemma, confirms us in our doubts. It says that the word 'craft' has two meanings: it means in the first place making useful objects out of solid matter – for example, a pot, a chair, a table. In the second place, the word 'craft' means cajolery, cunning, deceit. Now we know little that is certain about words, but this we do know – words never make anything that is useful; and words are the only things that tell the truth and nothing but the truth. Therefore, to talk of craft in connection with words is to bring together two incongruous ideas, which if they mate can only give birth to some monster fit for a glass case in a museum. Instantly, therefore, the title of the talk must be changed, and for it substituted another – A Ramble round Words, perhaps. For when you cut off the head of a talk it behaves like a hen that has been decapitated. It runs round in a circle till it drops dead – so people say who have killed hens. And that must be the course, or circle, of this decapitated talk. Let us then take for our starting point the statement that words are not useful. This happily needs little proving, for we are all aware of it. When we travel on the Tube, for example, when we wait on the platform for a train, there, hung up in front of us, on an illuminated signboard, are the words 'Passing Russell Square'.[2] We look at those words; we repeat them; we try to impress that useful fact upon our minds; the next train will pass Russell Square. We say over and over again as we pace, 'Passing Russell Square, passing Russell Square'. And then as we say them, the words shuffle and change, and we find ourselves saying, 'Passing away saith the world, passing away ... The leaves decay and fall, the vapours weep their burthen to the ground. Man comes ...' And then we wake up and find ourselves at King's Cross.

Take another example. Written up opposite us in the railway carriage are the words: 'Do not lean out of the window'. At the first reading the useful meaning, the surface meaning, is conveyed; but soon, as we sit looking at the words, they shuffle, they change; and we begin saying, 'Windows, yes windows – casements opening on the foam of perilous seas in faery lands forlorn'.[3] And before we know what we are doing, we have leant out of the window; we are looking for Ruth in tears amid the alien corn. The penalty for that is twenty pounds or a broken neck.

This proves, if it needs proving, how very little natural gift words have for being useful. If we insist on forcing them against their nature to be useful, we see to our cost how they mislead us, how they fool us, how they land us a crack on the head. We have been so often fooled in this way by words, they have so often proved that they hate being useful, that it is their nature not to express one simple statement but a thousand possibilities – they have done this so often that at last, happily, we are beginning to face the fact. We are beginning to invent another language – a language perfectly and beautifully adapted to express useful statements, a language of signs. There is one great living master of this language to whom we are all indebted, that anonymous writer – whether man, woman or disembodied spirit nobody knows – who describes hotels in the Michelin Guide. He wants to tell us that one hotel is moderate, another good, and a third the best in the place. How does he do it? Not with words; words would at once bring into being shrubberies and billiard tables, men and women, the moon rising and the long splash of the summer sea – all good things, but all here beside the point. He sticks to signs; one gable; two gables; three gables. That is all he says and all he needs to say. Baedeker[4] carries the sign language still further into the sublime realms of art. When he wishes to say that a picture is good, he uses one star; if very good, two stars; when, in his opinion, it is a work of transcendent genius, three black stars shine on the page, and that is all. So with a handful of stars and daggers the whole of art criticism, the whole of literary criticism could be reduced to the size of a sixpenny bit[5] – there are moments when one could wish it. But this suggests that in time to come writers will have two languages at their service; one for fact, one for fiction. When the biographer has to convey useful and necessary fact, as, for example, that Oliver Smith went to college and took a third in the year 1892, he will say so with a hollow O on top of the figure five. When the novelist is forced to inform us that John rang the bell; after a pause the door was opened by a parlourmaid who said, 'Mrs Jones is not at home', he will to our great gain and his own comfort convey that repulsive statement not in words, but in signs – say, a capital H on top of the figure three. Thus we may look forward to the day when our biographies and novels will be slim and muscular; and a railway company that says: 'Do not lean out of the window' in words will be fined a penalty not exceeding five pounds for the improper use of language.

Words, then, are not useful. Let us now inquire into their other quality, their positive quality, that is, their power to tell the truth. According once more to the dictionary there are at least three kinds of truth: God's or gospel truth; literary truth; and home truth (generally unflattering). But to consider each separately would take too long. Let us then simplify and assert that since the only test of truth is length of life, and since words survive the chops and changes of time longer than any other substance, therefore they are the truest. Buildings fall; even the earth perishes. What was yesterday a cornfield is today a bungalow. But words, if properly used, seem able to live for ever. What, then, we may ask next, is the proper use of words? Not, so we have said, to make a useful statement; for a useful statement is a statement that can mean only one thing. And it is the nature of words to mean many things. Take the simple sentence 'Passing Russell Square'? That proved useless because besides the surface meaning it contained so many sunken meanings. The word 'passing' suggested the transiency of things, the passing of time and the changes of human life. Then the word 'Russell' suggested the rustling of leaves and the skirt on a polished floor; also the ducal house of Bedford[6] and half the history of England. Finally the word 'Square' brings in the sight, the shape of an actual square combined with some visual suggestion of the stark angularity of stucco. Thus one sentence of the simplest kind rouses the imagination, the memory, the eye and the ear – all combine in reading it.

But they combine – they combine unconsciously together. The moment we single out and emphasize the suggestions as we have done here they become unreal; and we, too, become unreal – specialists, word mongers, phrase finders, not readers. In reading we have to allow the sunken meanings to remain sunken, suggested, not stated; lapsing and flowing into each other like reeds on the bed of a river. But the words in that sentence – Passing Russell Square – are of course very rudimentary words. They show no trace of the strange, of the diabolical power which words possess when they are not tapped out by a typewriter but come fresh from a human brain – the power that is to suggest the writer; his character, his appearance, his wife, his family, his house – even the cat on the hearthrug.[7] Why words do this, how they do it, how to prevent them from doing it nobody knows. They do it without the writer's will; often against his will. No writer presumably wishes to impose his own miserable character, his own private secrets and vices upon the reader. But has any writer, who is not a typewriter, succeeded in being wholly impersonal? Always, inevitably, we know them as well as their books. Such is the suggestive power of words that they will often make a bad book into a very lovable human being, and a good book into a man whom we can hardly tolerate in the room. Even words that are hundreds of years old have this power; when they are new they have it so strongly that they deafen us to the writer's meaning – it is them we see, them we hear. That is one reason why our judgements of living writers are so wildly erratic. Only after the writer is dead do his words to some extent become disinfected, purified of the accidents of the living body.

Now, this power of suggestion is one of the most mysterious properties of words. Everyone who has ever written a sentence must be conscious or half-conscious of it. Words, English words, are full of echoes, of memories, of associations – naturally. They have been out and about, on people's lips, in their houses, in the streets, in the fields for so many centuries. And that is one of the chief difficulties in writing them today – that they are so stored with meanings, with memories, that they have contracted so many famous marriages. The splendid word 'incarnadine'[8] for example – who can use it without remembering also 'multitudinous seas'? In the old days, of course, when English was a new language, writers could invent new words and use them. Nowadays it is easy enough to invent new words – they spring to the lips whenever we see a new sight or feel a new sensation – but we cannot use them because the language is old. You cannot use a brand new word in an old language because of the very obvious yet mysterious fact that a word is not a single and separate entity, but part of other words. It is not a word indeed until it is part of a sentence. Words belong to each other, although, of course, only a great writer knows that the word 'incarnadine' belongs to 'multitudinous seas'. To combine new words with old words is fatal to the constitution of the sentence. In order to use new words properly you would have to invent a new language; and that, though no doubt we shall come to it, is not at the moment our business. Our business is to see what we can do with the English language as it is. How can we combine the old words in new orders so that they survive, so that they create beauty, so that they tell the truth? That is the question.

And the person who could answer that question would deserve whatever crown of glory the world has to offer. Think what it would mean if you could teach, if you could learn, the art of writing. Why, every book, every newspaper would tell the truth, would create beauty. But there is, it would appear, some obstacle in the way, some hindrance to the teaching of words. For though at this moment at least a hundred professors are lecturing upon the literature of the past, at least a thousand critics are reviewing the literature of the present, and hundreds upon hundreds of young men and women are passing examinations in English literature with the utmost credit, still – do we write better, do we read better than we read and wrote four hundred years ago when we were unlectured, uncriticized, untaught? Is our Georgian literature a patch on the Elizabethan? Where then are we to lay the blame? Not on our professors; not on our reviewers; not on our writers; but on words. It is words that are to blame. They are the wildest, freest, most irresponsible, most unteachable of all things. Of course, you can catch them and sort them and place them in alphabetical order in dictionaries. But words do not live in dictionaries; they live in the mind. If you want proof of this, consider how often in moments of emotion when we most need words we find none. Yet there is the dictionary; there at our disposal are some half-a-million words all in alphabetical order. But can we use them? No, because words do not live in dictionaries, they live in the mind. Look again at the dictionary. There beyond a doubt lie plays more splendid than *Antony and Cleopatra*; poems more lovely than the 'Ode to a Nightingale'; novels beside which *Pride and Prejudice* or *David Copperfield*[9] are the crude bunglings of amateurs. It is only a question of finding the right words and putting them in the right order. But we cannot do it because they do not live in dictionaries; they live in the mind. And how do they live in the mind? Variously and strangely, much as human beings live, by ranging hither and thither, by falling in love, and mating together. It is true that they are much less bound by ceremony and convention than we are. Royal words mate with commoners. English words marry French words, German words, Indian words, negro words, if they have a fancy. Indeed, the less we inquire into the past of our dear Mother English the better it will be for that lady's reputation. For she has gone a-roving, a-roving fair maid.[10]

Thus to lay down any laws for such irreclaimable vagabonds is worse than useless. A few trifling rules of grammar and spelling are all the constraint we can put on them. All we can say about them, as we peer at them over the edge of that deep, dark and only fitfully illuminated cavern in which they live – the mind – all we can say about them is that they seem to like people to think and to feel before they use them, but to think and to feel not about them, but about something different. They are highly sensitive, easily made selfconscious. They do not like to have their purity or their impurity discussed. If you start a Society for Pure English, they will show their resentment by starting another for impure English – hence the unnatural violence of much modern speech; it is a protest against the puritans. They are highly democratic, too; they believe that one word is as good as another; uneducated words are as good as educated words, uncultivated words as cultivated words, there are no ranks or titles in their society. Nor do they like being lifted out on the point of a pen and examined separately. They hang together, in sentences, in paragraphs, sometimes for whole pages at a time.

They hate being useful; they hate making money; they hate being lectured about in public. In short, they hate anything that stamps them with one meaning or confines them to one attitude, for it is their nature to change.

Perhaps that is their most striking peculiarity – their need of change. It is because the truth they try to catch is many-sided, and they convey it by being themselves many-sided, flashing this way, then that. Thus they mean one thing to one person, another thing to another person: they are unintelligible to one generation, plain as a pikestaff to the next. And it is because of this complexity that they survive. Perhaps then one reason why we have no great poet, novelist or critic writing today is that we refuse words their liberty. We pin them down to one meaning, their useful meaning, the meaning which makes us catch the train, the meaning which makes us pass the examination. And when words are pinned down they fold their wings and die. Finally, and most emphatically, words, like ourselves, in order to live at their ease, need privacy. Undoubtedly they like us to think, and they like us to feel, before we use them; but they also like us to pause; to become unconscious. Our unconsciousness is their privacy: our darkness is their light . . . That pause was made, that veil of darkness was dropped, to tempt words to come together in one of those swift marriages which are perfect images and create everlasting beauty. But no – nothing of that sort is going to happen tonight. The little wretches are out of temper; disobliging; disobedient; dumb. What is it that they are muttering? 'Time's up! Silence!'

The Art of Biography

First appeared in *Atlantic Monthly*, April 1939, and was reprinted in this version in *The Death of the Moth*, 1942

I

The art of biography, we say – but at once go on to ask, Is biography an art?[1] The question is foolish perhaps, and ungenerous certainly, considering the keen pleasure that biographers have given us. But the question asks itself so often that there must be something behind it. There it is, whenever a new biography is opened, casting its shadow on the page; and there would seem to be something deadly in that shadow, for after all, of the multitude of lives that are written, how few survive!

But the reason for this high death rate, the biographer might argue, is that biography, compared with the arts of poetry and fiction, is a young art. Interest in our selves and in other people's selves is a late development of the human mind. Not until the eighteenth century in England did that curiosity express itself in writing the lives of private people. Only in the nineteenth century was biography fully grown and hugely prolific. If it is true that there have been only three great biographers – Johnson, Boswell, and Lockhart[2] – the reason, he argues, is that the time was short; and his plea, that the art of biography has had but little time to establish itself and develop itself, is certainly borne out by the textbooks. Tempting as it is to explore the reason – why, that is, the self that writes a book of prose came into being so many centuries after the self that writes a poem, why Chaucer preceded Henry James – it is better to leave that insoluble question unasked, and so pass to his next reason for the lack of masterpieces. It is that the art of biography is the most restricted of all the arts. He has his proof ready to hand. Here it is in the preface in which Smith, who has written the life of Jones, takes this opportunity of thanking old friends who have lent letters, and 'last but not least' Mrs Jones, the widow, for that help 'without which,' as he puts it, 'this biography could not have been written.' Now the novelist, he points out, simply says in his foreword, 'Every character in this book is fictitious.' The novelist is free; the biographer is tied.

There, perhaps, we come within hailing distance of that very difficult, again perhaps insoluble, question: What do we mean by calling a book a work of art? At any rate, here is a distinction between biography and fiction – proof that they differ in the very stuff of which they are made. One is made with the help of friends, of facts; the other is created without any restrictions save those that the artist, for reasons that seem good to him, chooses to obey. That is a distinction; and there is good reason to think that in the past biographers have found it not only a distinction but a very cruel distinction.

The widow and the friends were hard taskmasters. Suppose, for example, that the man of genius was immoral, ill-tempered, and threw the boots at the maid's head. The widow would say, 'Still I loved him – he was the father of my children; and the public, who love his books, must on no account be disillusioned. Cover up; omit,' The biographer obeyed. And thus the majority of Victorian biographies are like the wax figures now preserved in Westminster Abbey, that were carried in funeral processions through the street – effigies that have only a smooth superficial likeness to the body in the coffin.

Then, towards the end of the nineteenth century, there was a change. Again for reasons not easy to discover, widows became broader-minded, the public keener-sighted; the effigy no longer carried conviction or satisfied curiosity. The biographer certainly won a measure of freedom. At least he could hint that there were scars and furrows on the dead man's face. Froude's Carlyle is by no means a wax mask painted rosy red. And following Froude there was Sir Edmund Gosse,[3] who dared to say that his own father was a fallible human being. And following Edmund Gosse in the early years of the present century came Lytton Strachey.

II

The figure of Lytton Strachey is so important a figure in the history of biography that it compels a pause. For his three famous books,

Eminent Victorians, Queen Victoria, and *Elizabeth and Essex,*[4] are of a stature to show both what biography can do and what biography cannot do. Thus they suggest many possible answers to the question whether biography is an art, and if not why it fails.

Lytton Strachey came to birth as an author at a lucky moment. In 1918, when he made his first attempt, biography, with its new liberties, was a form that offered great attractions. To a writer like himself, who had wished to write poetry or plays but was doubtful of his creative power, biography seemed to offer a promising alternative. For at last it was possible to tell the truth about the dead; and the Victorian age was rich in remarkable figures many of whom had been grossly deformed by the effigies that had been plastered over them. To recreate them, to show them as they really were, was a task that called for gifts analogous to the poet's or the novelist's, yet did not ask that inventive power in which he found himself lacking.

It was well worth trying. And the anger and the interest that his short studies of Eminent Victorians aroused showed that he was able to make Manning, Florence Nightingale, Gordon, and the rest live as they had not lived since they were actually in the flesh. Once more they were the centre of a buzz of discussion. Did Gordon really drink, or was that an invention? Had Florence Nightingale received the Order of Merit in her bedroom or in her sitting-room? He stirred the public, even though a European war was raging, to an astonishing interest in such minute matters. Anger and laughter mixed; and editions multiplied.

But these were short studies with something of the overemphasis and the foreshortening of caricatures. In the lives of the two great Queens, Elizabeth and Victoria, he attempted a far more ambitious task. Biography had never had a fairer chance of showing what it could do. For it was now being put to the test by a writer who was capable of making use of all the liberties that biography had won: he was fearless; he had proved his brilliance; and he had learned his job. The result throws great light upon the nature of biography. For who can doubt after reading the two books again, one after the other, that the *Victoria* is a triumphant success, and that the *Elizabeth* by comparison is a failure? But it seems too, as we compare them, that it was not Lytton Strachey who failed; it was the art of biography. In the *Victoria* he treated biography as a craft; he submitted to its limitations. In the *Elizabeth* he treated biography as an art; he flouted its limitations.

But we must go on to ask how we have come to this conclusion and what reasons support it. In the first place it is clear that the two Queens present very different problems to their biographer. About Queen Victoria everything was known. Everything she did, almost everything she thought, was a matter of common knowledge. No one has ever been more closely verified and exactly authenticated than Queen Victoria. The biographer could not invent her, because at every moment some document was at hand to check his invention. And, in writing of Victoria, Lytton Strachey submitted to the conditions. He used to the full the biographer's power of selection and relation, but he kept strictly within the world of fact. Every statement was verified; every fact was authenticated. And the result is a life which, very possibly, will do for the old Queen what Boswell did for the old dictionary maker.[5] In time to come Lytton Strachey's Queen Victoria will be Queen Victoria, just as Boswell's Johnson is now Dr Johnson. The other versions will fade and disappear. It was a prodigious feat, and no doubt, having accomplished it, the author was anxious to press further. There was Queen Victoria, solid, real, palpable. But undoubtedly she was limited. Could not biography produce something of the intensity of poetry, something of the excitement of drama, and yet keep also the peculiar virtue that belongs to fact – its suggestive reality, its own proper creativeness?

Queen Elizabeth seemed to lend herself perfectly to the experiment. Very little was known about her. The society in which she lived was so remote that the habits, the motives, and even the actions of the people of that age were full of strangeness and obscurity. 'By what art are we to worm our way into those strange spirits? those even stranger bodies? The more clearly we perceive it, the more remote that singular universe becomes,' Lytton Strachey remarked on one of the first pages. Yet there was evidently a 'tragic history' lying dormant, half revealed, half concealed, in the story of the Queen and Essex. Everything seemed to lend itself to the making of a book that combined the advantages of both worlds, that gave the artist freedom to invent, but helped his invention with the support of facts – a book that was not only a biography but also a work of art.

Nevertheless, the combination proved unworkable; fact and fiction refused to mix. Elizabeth never became real in the sense that Queen Victoria had been real, yet she never became fictitious in the sense that Cleopatra or Falstaff is fictitious. The reason would seem to be that very little was known – he was urged to invent; yet something was known – his invention was checked. The Queen thus moves in an ambiguous world, between fact and fiction, neither embodied nor disembodied. There is a sense of vacancy and effort, of a tragedy that has no crisis, of characters that meet but do not clash.

If this diagnosis is true we are forced to say that the trouble lies with biography itself. It imposes conditions, and those conditions are that it must be based upon fact. And by fact in biography we mean facts that can be verified by other people besides the artist. If he invents facts as an artist invents them – facts that no one else can verify – and tries to combine them with facts of the other sort, they destroy each other.

Lytton Strachey himself seems in the *Queen Victoria* to have realized the necessity of this condition, and to have yielded to it instinctively. 'The first forty-two years of the Queen's life,' he wrote, 'are illuminated by a great and varied quantity of authentic information. With Albert's death a veil descends.' And when with Albert's death the veil descended and authentic information failed, he knew that the biographer must follow suit. 'We must be content with a brief and summary relation,' he wrote; and the last years are briefly disposed of. But the whole of Elizabeth's life was lived behind a far thicker veil than the last years of Victoria. And yet, ignoring his own admission, he went on to write, not a brief and summary relation, but a whole book about those strange spirits and even stranger bodies of whom authentic information was lacking. On his own showing, the attempt was doomed to failure.

III

It seems, then, that when the biographer complained that he was tied by friends, letters, and documents he was laying his finger upon a necessary element in biography; and that it is also a necessary limitation. For the invented character lives in a free world where the facts are verified by one person only – the artist himself. Their authenticity lies in the truth of his own vision. The world created by that vision is rarer, intenser, and more wholly of a piece than the world that is largely made of authentic information supplied by other people. And because of this difference the two kinds of fact will not mix; if they touch they destroy each other. No one, the conclusion seems to be, can make the best of both worlds; you must choose, and you must abide by your choice.

But though the failure of *Elizabeth and Essex* leads to this conclusion, that failure, because it was the result of a daring experiment carried out with magnificent skill, leads the way to further discoveries. Had he lived, Lytton Strachey would no doubt himself have explored the vein that he had opened. As it is, he has shown us the way in which others may advance. The biographer is bound by facts – that is so; but, if it is so, he has the right to all the facts that are available. If Jones threw boots at the maid's head, had a mistress at Islington, or was found drunk in a ditch after a night's debauch, he must be free to say so – so far at least as the law of libel and human sentiment allow.

But these facts are not like the facts of science – once they are discovered, always the same. They are subject to changes of opinion; opinions change as the times change. What was thought a sin is now known, by the light of facts won for us by the psychologists, to be perhaps a misfortune; perhaps a curiosity; perhaps neither one nor the other, but a trifling foible of no great importance one way or the other. The accent on sex has changed within living memory. This leads to the destruction of a great deal of dead matter still obscuring the true features of the human face. Many of the old chapter headings – life at college, marriage, career – are shown to be very arbitrary and artificial distinctions. The real current of the hero's existence took, very likely, a different course.

Thus the biographer must go ahead of the rest of us, like the miner's canary, testing the atmosphere, detecting falsity, unreality, and the presence of obsolete conventions. His sense of truth must be alive and on tiptoe. Then again, since we live in an age when a thousand cameras are pointed, by newspapers, letters, and diaries, at every character from every angle, he must be prepared to admit contradictory versions of the same face. Biography will enlarge its scope by hanging up looking-glasses at odd corners. And yet from all this diversity it will bring out, not a riot of confusion, but a richer unity. And again, since so much is known that used to be unknown, the question now inevitably asks itself, whether the lives of great men only should be recorded. Is not anyone who has lived a life, and left a record of that life, worthy of biography – the failures as well as the successes, the humble as well as the illustrious? And what is greatness? And what smallness? He must revise our standards of merit and set up new heroes for our admiration.

IV

Biography thus is only at the beginning of its career; it has a long and active life before it, we may be sure – a life full of difficulty, danger, and hard work. Nevertheless, we can also be sure that it is a different life from the life of poetry and fiction – a life lived at a lower degree of tension. And for that reason its creations are not destined for the immortality which the artist now and then achieves for his creations.

There would seem to be certain proof of that already. Even Dr Johnson as created by Boswell will not live as long as Falstaff as created by Shakespeare. Micawber and Miss Bates[6] we may be certain will survive Lockhart's Sir Walter Scott and Lytton Strachey's Queen Victoria. For they are made of more enduring matter. The artist's imagination at its most intense fires out what is perishable in fact; he builds with what is durable; but the biographer must accept the perishable, build with it, imbed it in the very fabric of his work. Much will perish; little will live. And thus we come to the conclusion, that he is a craftsman, not an artist; and his work is not a work of art, but something betwixt and between.

Yet on that lower level the work of the biographer is invaluable; we cannot thank him sufficiently for what he does for us. For we are incapable of living wholly in the intense world of the imagination. The imagination is a faculty that soon tires and needs rest and refreshment. But for a tired imagination the proper food is not inferior poetry or minor fiction – indeed they blunt and debauch it

– but sober fact, that 'authentic information' from which, as Lytton Strachey has shown us, good biography is made. When and where did the real man live; how did he look; did he wear laced boots or elastic-sided; who were his aunts, and his friends; how did he blow his nose; whom did he love, and how; and when he came to die did he die in his bed like a Christian, or . . .

By telling us the true facts, by sifting the little from the big, and shaping the whole so that we perceive the outline, the biographer does more to stimulate the imagination than any poet or novelist save the very greatest. For few poets and novelists are capable of that high degree of tension which gives us reality. But almost any biographer, if he respects facts, can give us much more than another fact to add to our collection. He can give us the creative fact; the fertile fact; the fact that suggests and engenders. Of this, too, there is certain proof. For how often, when a biography is read and tossed aside, some scene remains bright, some figure lives on in the depths of the mind, and causes us, when we read a poem or a novel, to feel a start of recognition, as if we remembered something that we had known before.

Reviewing

First published in the Hogarth Sixpenny Pamphlet series on
2 November 1939.

I

In London there are certain shop windows that always attract a crowd. The attraction is not in the finished article but in the worn-out garments that are having patches inserted in them. The crowd is watching the women at work. There they sit in the shop window putting invisible stitches into moth-eaten trousers. And this familiar sight may serve as illustration to the following paper. So our poets, playwrights and novelists sit in the shop window, doing their work under the curious eyes of reviewers. But the reviewers are not content, like the crowd in the street, to gaze in silence; they comment aloud upon the size of the holes, upon the skill of the workers, and advise the public which of the goods in the shop window is the best worth buying. The purpose of this paper is to rouse discussion as to the value of the reviewer's office – to the writer, to the public, to the reviewer and to literature. But a reservation must first be made – by 'the reviewer' is meant the reviewer of imaginative literature – poetry, drama, fiction; not the reviewer of history, politics, economics. His is a different office, and for reasons not to be discussed here he fulfils it in the main so adequately and indeed admirably that his value is not in question. Has the reviewer, then, of imaginative literature any value at the present time to the writer, to the public, to the reviewer and to literature? And, if so, what? And if not, how could his function be changed, and made profitable? Let us broach these involved and complicated questions by giving one quick glance at the history of reviewing, since it may help to define the nature of a review at the present moment.

Since the review came into existence with the newspaper, that history is a brief one. *Hamlet* was not reviewed, nor *Paradise Lost*.

Criticism there was but criticism conveyed by word of mouth, by the audience in the theatre, by fellow writers in taverns and private workshops. Printed criticism came into existence, presumably in a crude and primitive form, in the seventeenth century. Certainly the eighteenth century rings with the screams and catcalls of the reviewer and his victim. But towards the end of the eighteenth century there was a change – the body of criticism then seems to split into two parts. The critic and the reviewer divided the country between them. The critic – let Dr Johnson represent him – dealt with the past and with principles; the reviewer took the measure of new books as they fell from the press. As the nineteenth century drew on, these functions became more and more distinct. There were the critics – Coleridge, Matthew Arnold[1] – who took their time and their space; and there were the 'irresponsible' and mostly anonymous reviewers who had less time and less space, and whose complex task it was partly to inform the public, partly to criticize the book and partly to advertise its existence.

Thus, though the reviewer in the nineteenth century has much resemblance to his living representative, there were certain important differences. One difference is shown by the author of the *Times History*,[2] 'The books reviewed were fewer, but the reviews were longer than now ... Even a novel might get two columns and more.' – he is referring to the middle of the nineteenth century. Those differences are very important as will be seen later. But it is worth while to pause for a moment to examine other results of the review which are first manifest then, though by no means easy to sum up; the effect that is to say of the review upon the author's sales and upon the author's sensibility. A review had undoubtedly a great effect upon sales. Thackeray, for instance, said that *The Times*' review of *Esmond*[3] 'absolutely stopped the sale of the book.' The review also had an immense though less calculable effect upon the sensibility of the author. Upon Keats the effect is notorious; also upon the sensitive Tennyson.[4] Not only did he alter his poems at the reviewer's bidding, but actually contemplated emigration; and was thrown, according to one biographer, into such despair by the hostility of reviewers that his state of mind for a whole decade, and thus his poetry, was changed by them. But the robust and self-confident were also affected. 'How can a man like Macready,'

Dickens demanded,[5] 'fret and fume and chafe himself for such lice of literature as these?' – the 'lice' are writers in Sunday newspapers – 'rotten creatures with men's forms and devils' hearts?' Yet lice as they are, when they 'discharge their pigmy arrows' even Dickens with all his genius and his magnificent vitality cannot help but mind; and has to make a vow to overcome his rage and 'to gain the victory by being indifferent and bidding them whistle on.'

In their different ways then the great poet and the great novelist both admit the power of the nineteenth-century reviewer; and it is safe to assume that behind them stood a myriad of minor poets and minor novelists whether of the sensitive variety or of the robust who were all affected in much the same way. The way was complex; it is difficult to analyse. Tennyson and Dickens are both angry and hurt; they are also ashamed of themselves for feeling such emotions. The reviewer was a louse; his bite was contemptible; yet his bite was painful. His bite injured vanity; it injured reputation; it injured sales. Undoubtedly in the nineteenth century the reviewer was a formidable insect; he had considerable power over the author's sensibility; and upon the public taste. He could hurt the author; he could persuade the public either to buy or to refrain from buying.

II

The figures being thus set in position and their functions and powers roughly outlined, it must next be asked whether what was true then is true now. At first sight there seems to be little change. All the figures are still with us – critic; reviewer; author; public; and in much the same relations. The critic is separate from the reviewer; the function of the reviewer is partly to sort current literature; partly to advertise the author; partly to inform the public. Nevertheless there is a change; and it is a change of the highest importance. It seems to have made itself felt in the last part of the nineteenth century. It is summed up in the words of *The Times*' historian[6] already quoted: '... the tendency was for reviews to grow shorter and to be less long delayed.' But there was another tendency; not only did the reviews become shorter and quicker, but they increased immeasurably in number. The result of these three tendencies was of the highest importance. It was catastrophic indeed; between them they have brought about the decline and fall of reviewing. Because they were quicker, shorter, and more numerous the value of reviews for all parties concerned has dwindled until – is it too much to say until it has disappeared? But let us consider. The people concerned are the author, the reader, and the publisher. Placing them in this order let us ask first how these tendencies have affected the author – why the review has ceased to have any value for him? Let us assume, for brevity's sake, that the most important value of a review to the author was its effect upon him as a writer – that it gave him an expert opinion of his work and allowed him to judge roughly how far as an artist he had failed or succeeded. That has been destroyed almost entirely by the multiplicity of reviews. Now that he has sixty reviews where in the nineteenth century he had perhaps six, he finds that there is no such thing as 'an opinion' of his work. Praise cancels blame; and blame praise. There are as many different opinions of his work as there are different reviewers. Soon he comes to discount both praise and blame; they are equally worthless. He values the review only for its effect upon his reputation and for its effect upon his sales.

The same cause has also lessened the value of the review to the reader. The reader asks the reviewer to tell him whether the poem or novel is good or bad in order that he may decide whether to buy it or not. Sixty reviewers at once assure him that it is a masterpiece – and worthless. The clash of completely contradictory opinions cancel each other out. The reader suspends judgement; waits for an opportunity of seeing the book himself; very probably forgets all about it, and keeps his seven and sixpence[7] in his pocket.

The variety and diversity of opinion affect the publisher in the same way. Aware that the public no longer trusts either praise or blame, the publisher is reduced to printing both side by side: 'This is . . . poetry that will be remembered in hundreds of years time . . .' 'There are several passages that make me physically sick,'* to quote an actual instance; to which he adds very naturally, in his own person, 'Why not read it yourself?' That question is enough by itself to show that reviewing as practised at present has failed in all its

---

* The *New Statesman*, April, 1939.

objects. Why bother to write reviews or to read them or to quote them if in the end the reader must decide the question for himself?

III

If the reviewer has ceased to have any value either to the author or to the public it seems a public duty to abolish him. And, indeed, the recent failure of certain magazines consisting largely of reviews seems to show that whatever the reason, such will be his fate. But it is worth while to look at him in being – a flutter of little reviews is still attached to the great political dailies and weeklies – before he is swept out of existence, in order to see what he is still trying to do; why it is so difficult for him to do it; and whether perhaps there is not some element of value that ought to be preserved. Let us ask the reviewer himself to throw light upon the nature of the problem as it appears to him. Nobody is better qualified to do so than Mr Harold Nicolson. The other day* he dealt with the duties and the difficulties of the reviewer as they appear to him. He began by saying that the reviewer, who is 'something quite different from the critic,' is 'hampered by the hebdomadal[8] nature of his task,' – in other words, he has to write too often and too much. He went on to define the nature of that task. 'Is he to relate every book that he reads to the eternal standards of literary excellence? Were he to do that, his reviews would be one long ululation.[9] Is he merely to consider the library public and to tell people what it may please them to read? Were he to do that, he would be subjugating his own level of taste to a level which is not very stimulating. How does he act?' Since he cannot refer to the eternal standards of literature; since he cannot tell the library public what they would like to read – that would be 'a degradation of the mind' – there is only one thing that he can do: he can hedge. 'I hedge between the two extremes. I address myself to the authors of the books which I review; I want to tell them why I either like or dislike their work; and I trust that from such a dialogue the ordinary reader will derive some information.'

That is an honest statement; and its honesty is illuminating. It

* *Daily Telegraph*, March, 1939.

shows that the review has become an expression of individual opinion, given without any attempt to refer to 'eternal standards' by a man who is in a hurry; who is pressed for space; who is expected to cater in that little space for many different interests; who is bothered by the knowledge that he is not fulfilling his task; who is doubtful what that task is; and who, finally, is forced to hedge. Now the public though crass is not such an ass as to invest seven and sixpence on the advice of a reviewer writing under such conditions; and the public though dull is not such a gull as to believe in the great poets, great novelists and epoch-making works that are weekly discovered under such conditions. Those are the conditions however; and there is good reason to think that they will become more drastic in the course of the next few years. The reviewer is already a distracted tag on the tail of the political kite. Soon he will be conditioned out of existence altogether. His work will be done – in many newspapers it is already done – by a competent official armed with scissors and paste who will be called (it may be) The Gutter.[10] The Gutter will write out a short statement of the book; extract the plot (if it is a novel); choose a few verses (if it is a poem); quote a few anecdotes (if it is a biography). To this what is left of the reviewer – perhaps he will come to be known as the Taster – will fix a stamp – an asterisk to signify approval, a dagger to signify disapproval.[11] This statement – this Gutter and Stamp production – will serve instead of the present discordant and distracted twitter. And there is no reason to think that it will serve two of the parties concerned worse than the present system. The library public will be told what it wishes to know – whether the book is the kind of book to order from the library; and the publisher will collect asterisks and daggers instead of going to the pains to copy out alternate phrases of praise and abuse in which neither he nor the public has any faith. Each perhaps will save a little time and a little money. There remain, however, two other parties to be considered – that is the author and the reviewer. What will the Gutter and Stamp system mean to them?

To deal first with the author – his case is the more complex, for his is the more highly developed organism. During the two centuries or so in which he has been exposed to reviewers he has undoubtedly developed what may be called a reviewer consciousness. There is present in his mind a figure who is known as 'the reviewer.' To Dickens he was a louse armed with pigmy arrows, having the form of a man and the heart of a devil. To Tennyson he was even more formidable. It is true that the lice are so many today and they bite so innumerably that the author is comparatively immune from their poison – no author now abuses reviewers as violently as Dickens or obeys them as submissively as Tennyson. Still, there are eruptions even now in the press which lead us to believe that the reviewer's fang is still poisoned. But what part is affected by his bite? – what is the true nature of the emotion he causes? That is a complex question; but perhaps we can discover something that will serve as answer by submitting the author to a simple test. Take a sensitive author and place before him a hostile review. Symptoms of pain and anger rapidly develop. Next tell him that nobody save himself will read those abusive remarks. In five or ten minutes the pain which, if the attack had been delivered in public, would have lasted a week and bred bitter rancour, is completely over. The temperature falls; indifference returns. This proves that the sensitive part is the reputation; what the victim feared was the effect of abuse upon the opinion that other people had of him. He is afraid, too, of the effect of abuse upon his purse. But the purse sensibility is in most cases far less highly developed than the reputation sensibility. As for the artist's sensibility – his own opinion of his own work – that is not touched by anything good or bad that the reviewer says about it. The reputation sensibility however is still lively; and it will thus take some time to persuade authors that the Gutter and Stamp system is as satisfactory as the present reviewing system. They will say that they have 'reputations' – bladders of opinion formed by what other people think about them; and that these bladders are inflated or deflated by what is said of them in print. Still, under present conditions the time is at hand when even the author will believe that nobody thinks the better or the worse of him because he is praised or blamed in print. Soon he will come to realize that his interests – his desire for fame and money – are as effectively catered for by the Gutter and Stamp system as by the present reviewing system.

But even when this stage is reached, the author may still have some ground for complaint. The reviewer did serve some end besides that of inflating reputations and stimulating sales. And Mr Nicolson has put his finger on it. 'I want to tell them why I either like or dislike their work.' The author wants to be told why Mr Nicolson likes or dislikes his work. This is a genuine desire. It survives the test of privacy. Shut doors and windows; pull the curtains. Ensure that no fame accrues or money; and still it is a matter of the very greatest interest to a writer to know what an honest and intelligent reader thinks about his work.

IV

At this point let us turn once more to the reviewer. There can be no doubt that his position at the present moment, judging both from the outspoken remarks of Mr Nicolson and from the internal evidence of the reviews themselves, is extremely unsatisfactory. He has to write in haste and to write shortly. Most of the books he reviews are not worth the scratch of a pen upon paper – it is futile to refer them to 'eternal standards.' He knows further, as Matthew Arnold has stated,[12] that even if the conditions were favourable, it is impossible for the living to judge the works of the living. Years, many years, according to Matthew Arnold, have to pass before it is possible to deliver an opinion that is not 'only personal, but personal with passion.' And the reviewer has one week. And authors are not dead but living. And the living are friends or enemies; have wives and families; personalities and politics. The reviewer knows that he is hampered, distracted, and prejudiced. Yet knowing all this and having proof in the wild contradictions of contemporary opinion that it is so, he has to submit a perpetual succession of new books to a mind as incapable of taking a fresh impression or of making a dispassionate statement as an old piece of blotting paper on a post office counter. He has to review; for he has to live; and he has to live, since most reviewers come of the educated class, according to the standards of that class. Thus he has to write often, and he has to write much. There is, it seems, only one alleviation of the horror, that he enjoys telling authors why he likes or dislikes their books.

V

The one element in reviewing that is of value to the reviewer himself (independently of the money earned) is the one element that is of value to the author. The problem then is how to preserve this value – the value of the dialogue as Mr Nicolson calls it – and to bring both parties together in a union that is profitable, to the minds and purses of both. It should not be a difficult problem to solve. The medical profession has shown the way. With some differences the medical custom might be imitated – there are many resemblances between doctor and reviewer, between patient and author. Let the reviewers then abolish themselves, or what relic remains of them, as reviewers, and resurrect themselves as doctors. Another name might be chosen – consultant, expositor or expounder; some credentials might be given, the books written rather than the examinations passed; and a list of those ready and authorized to practise made public. The writer then would submit his work to the judge of his choice; an appointment would be made; an interview arranged. In strict privacy, and with some formality – the fee, however, would be enough to ensure that the interview did not degenerate into tea-table gossip – doctor and writer would meet; and for an hour they would consult upon the book in question. They would talk, seriously and privately. This privacy in the first place would be an immeasurable advantage to them both. The consultant could speak honestly and openly, because the fear of affecting sales and of hurting feelings would be removed. Privacy would lessen the shop window temptations – the temptation to cut a figure, to pay off scores. The consultant would have no library public to inform and consider; no reading public to impress and amuse. He could thus concentrate upon the book itself, and upon telling the author why he likes or dislikes it. The author would profit equally. An hour's private talk with a critic of his own choosing would be incalculably more valuable than the five hundred words of criticism mixed with extraneous matter that is now allotted him. He could state his case. He could point to his difficulties. He would no longer feel, as so often at present, that the critic is talking about something that he has not written. Further, he would have the advantage of coming into touch with a well-stored mind, housing other books and even other literatures, and thus other standards; with a live human being, not with a man in a mask. Many bogeys would lose their horns. The louse would become a man. By degrees the writer's 'reputation' would drop off. He would become quit of that tiresome appendage and its irritable consequences – such are a few of the obvious and indisputable advantages that privacy would ensure.

Next there is the financial question – would the profession of expositor be as profitable as the profession of reviewer? How many authors are there who would wish to have an expert opinion on their work? The answer to this is to be heard crying daily and crying loudly in any publisher's office or in any author's post bag. 'Give me advice,' they repeat, 'give me criticism.' The number of authors seeking criticism and advice genuinely, not for advertising purposes but because their need is acute, is an abundant proof of the demand. But would they pay the doctor's fee of three guineas?[13] When they discovered, as certainly they would, how much more an hour of talk holds, even if it costs three guineas, than the hurried letter which they now extort from the harassed publisher's reader, or the five hundred words which is all they can count on from the distracted reviewer, even the indigent would think it an investment worth making. Nor is it only the young and needy who seek advice. The art of writing is difficult; at every stage the opinion of an impersonal and disinterested critic would be of the highest value. Who would not spout the family tea pot[14] in order to talk with Keats for an hour about poetry, or with Jane Austen about the art of fiction?

VI

There remains finally the most important, but the most difficult of all these questions – what effect would the abolition of the reviewer have upon literature? Some reasons for thinking that the smashing of the shop window would make for the better health of that remote goddess have already been implied. The writer would withdraw into the darkness of the workshop; he would no longer carry on his difficult and delicate task like a trouser mender in Oxford Street, with a horde of reviewers pressing their noses to the glass and commenting to a curious crowd upon each stitch. Hence his self-consciousness would diminish and his reputation would shrivel. No longer puffed this way and that, now elated, now depressed, he could attend to his work. That might make for better writing. Again the reviewer, who must now earn his pence by cutting shop window capers to amuse the public and to advertise his skill, would have only the book to think of and the writer's needs. That might make for better criticism.

But there might be other and more positive advantages. The Gutter and Stamp system by eliminating what now passes for literary criticism – those few words devoted to 'why I like or dislike this book' – will save space. Four or five thousand words, possibly, might be saved in the course of a month or two. And an editor with that space at his disposal might not only express his respect for literature, but actually prove it. He might spend that space, even in a political daily or weekly, not upon stars and snippets, but upon unsigned and uncommercial literature – upon essays, upon criticism. There may be a Montaigne[15] among us – a Montaigne now severed into futile slices of one thousand to fifteen hundred words weekly. Given time and space he might revive, and with him an admirable and now almost extinct form of art. Or there may be a critic among us – a Coleridge, a Matthew Arnold. He is now frittering himself away, as Mr Nicolson has shown, upon a miscellaneous heap of poems, plays, novels, all to be reviewed in one column by Wednesday next. Given four thousand words, even twice a year, the critic might emerge, and with him those standards, those 'eternal standards,' which if they are never referred to, far from being eternal cease to exist. Do we not all know that Mr A writes better or it may be worse than Mr B. But is that all we want to know? Is that all we ought to ask?

But to sum up, or rather to heap a little cairn of conjectures and conclusions at the end of these scattered remarks for somebody else to knock down. The review it is contended increases self-consciousness and diminishes strength. The shop window and the looking-glass inhibit and confine. By putting in their place discussion – fearless and disinterested discussion – the writer would gain in range, in depth, in power. And this change would tell eventually upon the public mind. Their favourite figure of fun, the author, that hybrid between the peacock and the ape,[16] would be removed from their derision, and in his place would be an obscure workman doing his job in the darkness of the workshop and not unworthy of respect. A new relationship might come into being, less petty and less personal than the old. A new interest in literature, a new respect for literature might follow. And, financial advantages apart, what a ray of light that would bring, what a ray of pure sunlight a critical and hungry public would bring into the darkness of the workshop!

The Dream

This review of George Bullock's *Marie Corelli: The Life and Death of a Best Seller* (Constable, 1940) was published in the *Listener*, 15 February 1940.

This is a depressing book.[1] It leaves one with a feeling not of humiliation, that is too strong a word, nor of disgust, that is too strong also. It makes us feel – it is to Mr Bullock's credit as a biographer – that we have been watching a stout white dog performing tricks in front of an audience which eggs it on, but at the same time jeers. There is nothing in the life and death of a best seller that need cause us this queasiness. The lives of those glorious geese Florence Barclay and Ella Wheeler Wilcox[2] can be read without a blush for them or for ourselves. They were performers too – conjurors who tumbled bank notes, billiard balls, fluttering pigeons out of very seedy hats. But they lived, and they lived with such gusto that no one can fail to share it. With Marie Corelli it was different.

Her life began with a trick and rather a shady trick. The editor of the *Illustrated London News*, a married man, 'wandering round Stratford-on-Avon church' fell in love with a woman. That bald statement must be draped. Dr Mackay committed an immoral act with a female who was not of his own social standing. 'This unwelcome flowering of his lighter moments', as Mr Bullock puts it – Corelliism is catching – was a child. But she was not called Marie and she was not called Corelli. Those were names that she invented later to drape the fact. Most of her childhood was spent draping facts in the 'Dream Hole', a mossy retreat in a dell at Box Hill.[3] Sometimes George Meredith appeared for a moment among the tendrils. But she never saw him. Wrapped in what she called later 'the flitting phantasmagoria of the universal dream' she saw only one person – herself. And that self, sometimes called Thelma, sometimes Mavis Clare, draped in white satin, hung with pure lilies, and exhibited twice a year in stout volumes for which the public

THE DREAM

paid her ten thousand pounds apiece, is as damning an indictment of Victorian taste in one way as the Albert Memorial[4] is in another. Of those two excrescences, perhaps that which we call Marie Corelli is the more painful. The Albert Memorial is empty; but within the other erection was a live human being. It was not her fault; society blew that golden bubble, as Miss Corelli herself might have written, from the black seed of shame. She was ashamed of her mother. She was ashamed of her birth. She was ashamed of her face, of her accent, of her poverty. Most girls, as empty-headed and commonplace as she was, would have shared her shame, but they would have hidden it – under the table cloth, behind the chiffonier.[5] But nature had endowed her with a prodigious power of making public confession of this small ignoble vice. Instead of hiding herself, she exposed herself. From her earliest days she had a rage for publicity. 'I'll be "somebody"', she told her governess. 'I'll be as unlike anybody else as I can!' 'That would hardly be wise', said Miss Knox placidly. 'You would then be called eccentric'. But Miss Knox need not have been afraid. Marie Corelli did not wish to be unlike anybody else; she wanted to be as like everybody else in general and the British aristocracy in particular as it was possible to be. But to attain that object she had only one weapon – the dream. Dreams, apparently, if made of the right material, can be astonishingly effective. She dreamt so hard, she dreamt so efficiently, that with two exceptions all her dreams came true. Not even Marie Corelli could dream her shifty half-brother into the greatest of English poets, though she worked hard to 'get him made Poet Laureate', or transform her very dubious father into an eminent Victorian man of letters. All that she could do for Dr Mackay was to engage the Caledonian pipers to play at his funeral and to postpone that function from a foggy day to a fine one in order that his last appearance might be given full publicity. Otherwise all her dreams materialized. Ponies, motor cars, dresses, houses furnished 'like the tea lounge at the Earl's Court Exhibition',[6] gondolas, expensively bound editions of Shakespeare – all were hers. Cheques accumulated. Invitations showered. The Prince of Wales held her hand in his. 'Out of small things what wonders rise', he murmured. Gladstone called on her and stayed for two hours. '*Ardath*', he is reported to have said, 'is a magnificent conception'. On Easter Sunday the

Dean of Westminster quoted *Barabbas* from the pulpit. No words, the Dean said, could be more beautiful. Rostand[7] translated her novels. The whole audience at Stratford-on-Avon rose to its feet when she came into the theatre.

All her dreams came true. But it was the dream that killed her. For inside that ever thickening carapace of solid dream the commonplace vigorous little woman gradually ceased to live. She became harder, duller, more prudish, more conventional; and at the same time more envious and more uneasy. The only remedy that revived her was publicity. And like other drug-takers she could only live by increasing the dose. Her tricks became more and more extravagant. On May Day she drove through the streets behind ponies wreathed in flowers; she floated down the Avon in a gondola called *The Dream* with a real gondolier in a scarlet sash. The press resounded with her lawsuits, her angry letters, her speeches. And then even the press turned nasty. They omitted to say that she had been present at the Braemar gathering.[8] They gave full publicity to the fact that she had been caught hoarding sugar.

For her there is some excuse. But how are we to excuse the audience that applauded the exhibition? Queen Victoria and Mr Gladstone can be excepted. The taste of the highly exalted is apt to become dropsical. And there is excuse for 'the million', as Marie Corelli called them – if her books saved one working man from suicide, or allowed a dressmaker's drudge here and there to dream that she, too, was Thelma or Mavis Clare, there were no films then to sustain them with plush and glow and rapture after the day's work. But what are we to say of Oscar Wilde? His compliments may have been ambiguous; but he paid them, and he printed her stories. And what are we to say of the great ladies of her adored aristocracy? 'She is a common little thing', one of them remarked. But no lunch or dinner party was complete without her. And what are we to say of Mr Arthur Severn? 'Pendennis'[9] she called him. He accepted her hospitality, tolerated that effusion which she was pleased to call her passion, and then made fun of her accent. 'Ouwels' she said instead of 'owls', and he laughed at her. And what are we to say of the press that levelled all its cameras at the stout ugly old woman who was ashamed of her face; and because she was ashamed of her birth, 'got busy' about the mother – was her name Cody, or was it Kirtland – was she a bricklayer's daughter or an Italian countess? – who had borne this illegitimate child?

But though it would be a relief to end in a burst of righteous indignation, the worst of this book is that it provokes no such glow, but only the queasiness with which we watch a decked-up dog performing rather ordinary tricks. It is a relief when the performance is over. Only, unfortunately, that is not altogether the fact. For still at Stratford-on-Avon Mason Croft is kept precisely as it was when Marie Corelli lived there. There is the silver inkpot still full of ink as she left it; the hands of the clock still point to 7.15 as they did when she died; all her manuscripts are carefully preserved under glass cases; and 'the large empty bed, covered with a heavy white quilt, which is more awe-inspiring than a corpse, as a scarcely clothed dancer excites more than does a nude' awaits the dreamer. So Stratford-on-Avon, along with other relics, preserves a lasting monument to the taste of the Victorian age.

Thoughts on Peace in an Air Raid

This essay, originally intended as a contribution to a Women's
Symposium in the USA, was first published in *New Republic*,
New York, 21 October 1940, and reprinted in this version in
The Death of the Moth, 1942.

The Germans were over this house last night and the night before that.[1] Here they are again. It is a queer experience, lying in the dark and listening to the zoom of a hornet which may at any moment sting you to death. It is a sound that interrupts cool and consecutive thinking about peace. Yet it is a sound – far more than prayers and anthems – that should compel one to think about peace. Unless we can think peace into existence we – not this one body in this one bed but millions of bodies yet to be born – will lie in the same darkness and hear the same death rattle overhead. Let us think what we can do to create the only efficient air-raid shelter while the guns on the hill go pop pop pop and the searchlights finger the clouds and now and then, sometimes close at hand, sometimes far away, a bomb drops.

Up there in the sky young Englishmen and young German men are fighting each other. The defenders are men, the attackers are men. Arms are not given to Englishwomen either to fight the enemy or to defend herself. She must lie weaponless tonight. Yet if she believes that the fight going on up in the sky is a fight by the English to protect freedom, by the Germans to destroy freedom, she must fight, so far as she can, on the side of the English. How far can she fight for freedom without firearms? By making arms, or clothes or food. But there is another way of fighting for freedom without arms; we can fight with the mind. We can make ideas that will help the young Englishman who is fighting up in the sky to defeat the enemy.

But to make ideas effective, we must be able to fire them off. We must put them into action. And the hornet in the sky rouses another hornet in the mind. There was one zooming in *The Times*

THOUGHTS ON PEACE IN AN AIR RAID

this morning – a woman's voice saying, 'Women have not a word to say in politics.' There is no woman in the Cabinet; nor in any responsible post. All the idea-makers who are in a position to make ideas effective are men. That is a thought that damps thinking, and encourages irresponsibility. Why not bury the head in the pillow, plug the ears, and cease this futile activity of idea-making? Because there are other tables besides officer tables and conference tables. Are we not leaving the young Englishman without a weapon that might be of value to him if we give up private thinking, tea-table thinking, because it seems useless? Are we not stressing our disability because our ability exposes us perhaps to abuse, perhaps to contempt? 'I will not cease from mental fight,'[2] Blake wrote. Mental fight means thinking against the current, not with it.

That current flows fast and furious. It issues in a spate of words from the loudspeakers and the politicians. Every day they tell us that we are a free people, fighting to defend freedom. That is the current that has whirled the young airman up into the sky and keeps him circling there among the clouds. Down here, with a roof to cover us and a gas mask handy, it is our business to puncture gas bags and discover seeds of truth. It is not true that we are free. We are both prisoners tonight – he boxed up in his machine with a gun handy; we lying in the dark with a gas mask handy. If we were free we should be out in the open, dancing, at the play, or sitting at the window talking together. What is it that prevents us? 'Hitler!' the loudspeakers cry with one voice. Who is Hitler? What is he? Aggressiveness, tyranny, the insane love of power made manifest, they reply. Destroy that, and you will be free.

The drone of the planes is now like the sawing of a branch overhead. Round and round it goes, sawing and sawing at a branch directly above the house. Another sound begins sawing its way in the brain. 'Women of ability' – it was Lady Astor[3] speaking in *The Times* this morning – 'are held down because of a subconscious Hitlerism in the hearts of men.' Certainly we are held down. We are equally prisoners tonight – the Englishmen in their planes, the Englishwomen in their beds. But if he stops to think he may be killed; and we too. So let us think for him. Let us try to drag up into consciousness the subconscious Hitlerism that holds us down. It is the desire for aggression; the desire to dominate and enslave.

Even in the darkness we can see that made visible. We can see shop windows blazing; and women gazing; painted women; dressed-up women; women with crimson lips and crimson fingernails. They are slaves who are trying to enslave.[4] If we could free ourselves from slavery we should free men from tyranny. Hitlers are bred by slaves.

A bomb drops. All the windows rattle. The anti-aircraft guns are getting active. Up there on the hill under a net tagged with strips of green and brown stuff to imitate the hues of autumn leaves guns are concealed. Now they all fire at once. On the nine o'clock radio we shall be told 'Forty-four enemy planes were shot down during the night, ten of them by anti-aircraft fire.' And one of the terms of peace, the loudspeakers say, is to be disarmament. There are to be no more guns, no army, no navy, no air force in the future. No more young men will be trained to fight with arms. That rouses another mind-hornet in the chambers of the brain – another quotation. 'To fight against a real enemy, to earn undying honour and glory by shooting total strangers, and to come home with my breast covered with medals and decorations, that was the summit of my hope ... It was for this that my whole life so far had been dedicated, my education, training, everything ...'

Those were the words of a young Englishman[5] who fought in the last war. In the face of them, do the current thinkers honestly believe that by writing 'Disarmament' on a sheet of paper at a conference table they will have done all that is needful? Othello's occupation will be gone;[6] but he will remain Othello. The young airman up in the sky is driven not only by the voices of loudspeakers; he is driven by voices in himself – ancient instincts, instincts fostered and cherished by education and tradition. Is he to be blamed for those instincts? Could we switch off the maternal instinct at the command of a table full of politicians? Suppose that imperative among the peace terms was: 'Childbearing is to be restricted to a very small class of specially selected women,' would we submit? Should we not say, 'The maternal instinct is a woman's glory. It was for this that my whole life has been dedicated, my education, training, everything ...' But if it were necessary, for the sake of humanity, for the peace of the world, that childbearing, should be restricted, the maternal instinct subdued, women would attempt it. Men would help them. They would honour them for their refusal to bear children. They would give them other openings for their creative power. That too must make part of our fight for freedom. We must help the young Englishmen to root out from themselves the love of medals and decorations. We must create more honourable activities for those who try to conquer in themselves their fighting instinct, their subconscious Hitlerism. We must compensate the man for the loss of his gun.

The sound of sawing overhead has increased. All the searchlights are erect. They point at a spot exactly above this roof. At any moment a bomb may fall on this very room. One, two, three, four, five, six . . . the seconds pass. The bomb did not fall. But during those seconds of suspense all thinking stopped. All feeling, save one dull dread, ceased. A nail fixed the whole being to one hard board. The emotion of fear and of hate is therefore sterile, unfertile. Directly that fear passes, the mind reaches out and instinctively revives itself by trying to create. Since the room is dark it can create only from memory. It reaches out to the memory of other Augusts – in Bayreuth, listening to Wagner; in Rome,[7] walking over the Campagna; in London. Friends' voices come back. Scraps of poetry return. Each of those thoughts, even in memory, was far more positive, reviving, healing and creative than the dull dread made of fear and hate. Therefore if we are to compensate the young man for the loss of his glory and of his gun, we must give him access to the creative feelings. We must make happiness. We must free him from the machine. We must bring him out of his prison into the open air. But what is the use of freeing the young Englishman if the young German and the young Italian remain slaves?

The searchlights, wavering across the flat, have picked up the plane now. From this window one can see a little silver insect turning and twisting in the light. The guns go pop pop pop. Then they cease. Probably the raider was brought down behind the hill. One of the pilots landed safe in a field near here the other day. He said to his captors, speaking fairly good English, 'How glad I am that the fight is over!' Then an Englishman gave him a cigarette, and an Englishwoman made him a cup of tea. That would seem to show that if you can free the man from the machine, the seed does not fall upon altogether stony ground. The seed may be fertile.

At last all the guns have stopped firing. All the searchlights have been extinguished. The natural darkness of a summer's night returns. The innocent sounds of the country are heard again. An apple thuds to the ground. An owl hoots, winging its way from tree to tree. And some half-forgotten words of an old English writer come to mind: 'The huntsmen are up in America ...'[8] Let us send these fragmentary notes to the huntsmen who are up in America, to the men and women whose sleep has not yet been broken by machine-gun fire, in the belief that they will rethink them generously and charitably, perhaps shape them into something serviceable. And now, in the shadowed half of the world, to sleep.

Ellen Terry

First published in the *New Statesman and Nation*, 8 February 1941.

When she came on to the stage as Lady Cicely in *Captain Brassbound's Conversion*,[1] the stage collapsed like a house of cards and all the limelights were extinguished. When she spoke it was as if someone drew a bow over a ripe, richly seasoned cello; it grated, it glowed and it growled. Then she stopped speaking. She put on her glasses. She gazed intently at the back of a settee. She had forgotten her part. But did it matter? Speaking or silent, she was Lady Cicely – or was it Ellen Terry? At any rate, she filled the stage and all the other actors were put out, as electric lights are put out in the sun.

Yet this pause when she forgot what Lady Cicely said next was significant. It was a sign not that she was losing her memory and past her prime, as some said. It was a sign that Lady Cicely was not a part that suited her. Her son, Gordon Craig,[2] insists that she only forgot her part when there was something uncongenial in the words, when some speck of grit had got into the marvellous machine of her genius. When the part was congenial, when she was Shakespeare's Portia, Desdemona, Ophelia,[3] every word, every comma was consumed. Even her eyelashes acted. Her body lost its weight. Her son, a mere boy, could lift her in his arms. 'I am not myself,' she said. 'Something comes upon me ... I am always-in-the-air, light and bodiless.' We, who can only remember her as Lady Cicely on the little stage at the Court Theatre, only remember what, compared with her Ophelia or her Portia, was as a picture postcard compared with the great Velasquez[4] in the gallery.

It is the fate of actors to leave only picture postcards behind them. Every night when the curtain goes down the beautiful coloured canvas is rubbed out. What remains is at best only a wavering, insubstantial phantom – a verbal life on the lips of the living. Ellen Terry was well aware of it. She tried herself, overcome by the greatness of Irving as Hamlet and indignant at the caricatures of his detractors, to describe what she remembered. It was in vain.

She dropped her pen in despair. 'Oh God, that I were a writer!' she cried. 'Surely a *writer* could not string words together about Henry Irving's Hamlet and say *nothing, nothing*.' It never struck her, humble as she was, and obsessed by her lack of book learning, that she was, among other things, a writer. It never occurred to her when she wrote her autobiography, or scribbled page after page to Bernard Shaw late at night, dead tired after a rehearsal, that she was 'writing.'[5] The words in her beautiful rapid hand bubbled off her pen. With dashes and notes of exclamation she tried to give them the very tone and stress of the spoken word. It is true, she could not build a house with words, one room opening out of another, and a staircase connecting the whole. But whatever she took up became in her warm, sensitive grasp a tool. If it was a rolling-pin, she made perfect pastry. If it was a carving knife, perfect slices fell from the leg of mutton. If it were a pen, words peeled off, some broken, some suspended in mid-air, but all far more expressive than the tappings of the professional typewriter.[6]

With her pen then at odds and ends of time she has painted a self-portrait. It is not an Academy portrait,[7] glazed, framed, complete. It is rather a bundle of loose leaves upon each of which she has dashed off a sketch for a portrait – here a nose, here an arm, here a foot, and there a mere scribble in the margin. The sketches done in different moods, from different angles, sometimes contradict each other. The nose cannot belong to the eyes; the arm is out of all proportion to the foot. It is difficult to assemble them. And there are blank pages, too. Some very important features are left out. There was a self she did not know, a gap she could not fill. Did she not take Walt Whitman's words for a motto? 'Why, even I myself, I often think, know little or nothing of my real life. Only a few hints – a few diffused faint clues and indirections ... I seek ... to trace out here?'[8]

Nevertheless, the first sketch is definite enough. It is the sketch of her childhood. She was born to the stage. The stage was her cradle, her nursery. When other little girls were being taught sums and pot hooks she was being cuffed and buffeted into the practice of her profession. Her ears were boxed, her muscles suppled. All day she was hard at work on the boards. Late at night when other children were safe in bed she was stumbling along the dark streets wrapped in her father's cloak. And the dark street with its curtained windows was nothing but a sham to that little professional actress, and the rough-and-tumble life on the boards was her home, her reality. 'It's all such sham there,' she wrote – meaning by 'there' what she called 'life lived in houses' – 'sham – cold – hard – pretending. It's not sham here in our theatre – here all is real, warm and kind – we live a lovely spiritual life here.'

That is the first sketch. But turn to the next page. The child born to the stage has become a wife. She is married at sixteen to an elderly famous painter.[9] The theatre has gone; its lights are out and in its place is a quiet studio in a garden. In its place is a world full of pictures and 'gentle artistic people with quiet voices and elegant manners.' She sits mum in her corner while the famous elderly people talk over her head in quiet voices. She is content to wash her husband's brushes; to sit to him; to play her simple tunes on the piano to him while he paints. In the evening she wanders over the downs with the great poet, Tennyson. 'I was in Heaven,' she wrote. 'I never had one single pang of regret for the theatre.' If only it could have lasted! But somehow – here a blank page intervenes – she was an incongruous element in that quiet studio. She was too young, too vigorous, too vital, perhaps. At any rate, the marriage was a failure.

And so, skipping a page or two,[10] we come to the next sketch. She is a mother now. Two adorable children claim all her devotion. She is living in the depths of the country, in the heart of domesticity. She is up at six. She scrubs, she cooks, she sews. She teaches the children. She harnesses the pony. She fetches the milk. And again she is perfectly happy. To live with children in a cottage, driving her little cart about the lanes, going to church on Sunday in blue and white cotton – that is the ideal life! She asks no more than that it shall go on like that for ever and ever. But one day the wheel comes off the pony cart. Huntsmen in pink leap over the hedge. One of them dismounts and offers help. He looks at the girl in a blue frock and exclaims: 'Good God! It's Nelly!' She looks at the huntsman in pink and cries, 'Charles Reade!'[11] And so, all in a jiffy, back she goes to the stage, and to forty pounds a week. For – that is the reason she gives – the bailiffs are in the house. She must make money.

At this point a very blank page confronts us. There is a gulf which we can only cross at a venture. Two sketches face each other; Ellen Terry in blue cotton among the hens; Ellen Terry robed and crowned as Lady Macbeth on the stage of the Lyceum. The two sketches are contradictory yet they are both of the same woman. She hates the stage; yet she adores it. She worships her children; yet she forsakes them. She would like to live for ever among pigs and ducks in the open air; yet she spends the rest of her life among actors and actresses in the limelight. Her own attempt to explain the discrepancy is hardly convincing. 'I have always been more woman than artist,' she says. Irving put the theatre first. 'He had none of what I may call my bourgeois qualities – the love of being in love, the love of a home, the dislike of solitude.' She tries to persuade us that she was an ordinary woman enough; a better hand at pastry than most; an adept at keeping house; with an eye for colour, a taste for old furniture, and a positive passion for washing children's heads. If she went back to the stage it was because – well, what else could she do when the bailiffs were in the house?

This is the little sketch that she offers us to fill in the gap between the two Ellen Terrys – Ellen the mother, and Ellen the actress. But here we remember her warning: 'Why, even I myself know little or nothing of my real life.' There was something in her that she did not understand; something that came surging up from the depths and swept her away in its clutches. The voice she heard in the lane was not the voice of Charles Reade; nor was it the voice of the bailiffs. It was the voice of her genius; the urgent call of something that she could not define, could not suppress, and must obey. So she left her children and followed the voice back to the stage, back to the Lyceum, back to a long life of incessant toil, anguish and glory.

But, having gazed at the full-length portrait of Ellen Terry as Sargent[12] painted her, robed and crowned as Lady Macbeth, turn to the next page. It is done from another angle. Pen in hand, she is seated at her desk. A volume of Shakespeare lies before her. It is open at *Cymbeline*, and she is making careful notes in the margin. The part of Imogen presents great problems. She is, she says, 'on the rack' about her interpretation. Perhaps Bernard Shaw can throw light upon the question? A long letter from the brilliant young critic of the *Saturday Review*[13] lies beside Shakespeare. She has never met him, but for years they have written to each other, intimately, ardently, disputatiously, some of the best letters in the language. He says the most outrageous things. He compares dear Henry to an ogre, and Ellen to a captive chained in his cage. But Ellen Terry is quite capable of holding her own against Bernard Shaw. She scolds him, laughs at him, fondles him, and contradicts him. She has a curious sympathy for the advanced views that Henry Irving abominated. But what suggestions has the brilliant critic to make about Imogen? None apparently that she has not already thought for herself. She is as close and critical a student of Shakespeare as he is. She has studied every line, weighed the meaning of every word; experimented with every gesture. Each of those golden moments when she becomes bodyless, not herself, is the result of months of minute and careful study. 'Art,' she quotes, 'needs that which we can give her, I assure you.'[14] In fact this mutable woman, all instinct, sympathy and sensation, is as painstaking a student, and as careful of the dignity of her art as Flaubert[15] himself.

But once more the expression on that serious face changes. She works like a slave — none harder. But she is quick to tell Mr Shaw that she does not work with her brain only. She is not in the least clever. Indeed, she is happy she tells him, '*not to be clever*.' She stresses the point with a jab of her pen. 'You clever people,' as she calls him and his friends, miss so much, mar so much. As for education, she never had a day's schooling in her life. As far as she can see, but the problem baffles her, the main spring of her art is imagination. Visit mad-houses, if you like; take notes; observe; study endlessly. But first, imagine. And so she takes her part away from the books out into the woods. Rambling down grassy rides, she lives her part until she is it. If a word jars or grates, she must re-think it, re-write it. Then when every phrase is her own, and every gesture spontaneous out she comes on to the stage and is Imogen, Ophelia, Desdemona.

But is she, even when the great moments are on her, a great actress? She doubts it. 'I cared more for love and life,' she says. Her face, too, has been no help to her. She cannot sustain emotion. Certainly she is not a great tragic actress. Now and again, perhaps, she has acted some comic part to perfection. But even while she analyses herself, as one artist to another, the sun slants upon an old kitchen chair. 'Thank the Lord for my eyes!' she exclaims. What a world of joy her eyes have brought her! Gazing at the old 'rush-bottomed, sturdy-legged, and wavy-backed' chair, the stage is gone, the limelights are out, the famous actress is forgotten.

Which, then, of all these women is the real Ellen Terry? How are we to put the scattered sketches together? Is she mother, wife, cook, critic, actress, or should she have been, after all, a painter? Each part seems the right part until she throws it aside and plays another. Something of Ellen Terry it seems overflowed every part and remained unacted. Shakespeare could not fit her; nor Ibsen; nor Shaw. The stage could not hold her; nor the nursery. But there is, after all, a greater dramatist than Shakespeare, Ibsen or Shaw. There is nature. Hers is so vast a stage, and so innumerable a company of actors, that for the most part she fobs them off with a tag or two. They come on and they go off without breaking the ranks. But now and again nature creates a new part, an original part. The actors who act that part always defy our attempts to name them. They will not act the stock parts – they forget the words, they improvise others of their own. But when they come on the stage falls like a pack of cards and the limelights are extinguished. That was Ellen Terry's fate – to act a new part. And thus while other actors are remembered because they were Hamlet, Phèdre or Cleopatra,[16] Ellen Terry is remembered because she was Ellen Terry.

The Death of the Moth

First published posthumously in the book of this title, 1942.

Moths that fly by day are not properly to be called moths; they do not excite that pleasant sense of dark autumn nights and ivy-blossom which the commonest yellow-underwing asleep in the shadow of the curtain never fails to rouse in us. They are hybrid creatures, neither gay like butterflies nor sombre like their own species. Nevertheless the present specimen, with his narrow hay-coloured wings, fringed with a tassel of the same colour, seemed to be content with life. It was a pleasant morning, mid-September, mild, benignant, yet with a keener breath than that of the summer months. The plough was already scoring the field opposite the window, and where the share had been, the earth was pressed flat and gleamed with moisture. Such vigour came rolling in from the fields and the down beyond that it was difficult to keep the eyes strictly turned upon the book. The rooks too were keeping one of their annual festivities; soaring round the tree tops until it looked as if a vast net with thousands of black knots in it had been cast up into the air; which, after a few moments sank slowly down upon the trees until every twig seemed to have a knot at the end of it. Then, suddenly, the net would be thrown into the air again in a wider circle this time, with the utmost clamour and vociferation, as though to be thrown into the air and settle slowly down upon the tree tops were a tremendously exciting experience.

The same energy which inspired the rooks, the ploughmen, the horses, and even, it seemed, the lean bare-backed downs, sent the moth fluttering from side to side of his square of the window-pane. One could not help watching him. One was, indeed, conscious of a queer feeling of pity for him. The possibilities of pleasure seemed that morning so enormous and so various that to have only a moth's part in life, and a day moth's at that, appeared a hard fate, and his zest in enjoying his meagre opportunities to the full, pathetic. He flew vigorously to one corner of his compartment, and, after waiting there a second, flew across to the other. What remained for him but to fly to a third corner and then to a fourth? That was all he could do, in spite of the size of the downs, the width of the sky, the far-off smoke of houses, and the romantic voice, now and then, of a steamer out at sea. What he could do he did. Watching him, it seemed as if a fibre, very thin but pure, of the enormous energy of the world had been thrust into his frail and diminutive body. As often as he crossed the pane, I could fancy that a thread of vital light became visible. He was little or nothing but life.

Yet, because he was so small, and so simple a form of the energy that was rolling in at the open window and driving its way through so many narrow and intricate corridors in my own brain and in those of other human beings, there was something marvellous as well as pathetic about him. It was as if someone had taken a tiny bead of pure life and decking it as lightly as possible with down and feathers, had set it dancing and zigzagging to show us the true nature of life. Thus displayed one could not get over the strangeness of it. One is apt to forget all about life, seeing it humped and bossed and garnished and cumbered so that it has to move with the greatest circumspection and dignity. Again, the thought of all that life might have been had he been born in any other shape caused one to view his simple activities with a kind of pity.

After a time, tired by his dancing apparently, he settled on the window ledge in the sun, and, the queer spectacle being at an end, I forgot about him. Then, looking up, my eye was caught by him. He was trying to resume his dancing, but seemed either so stiff or so awkward that he could only flutter to the bottom of the window-pane; and when he tried to fly across it he failed. Being intent on other matters I watched these futile attempts for a time without thinking, unconsciously waiting for him to resume his flight, as one waits for a machine, that has stopped momentarily, to start again without considering the reason of its failure. After perhaps a seventh attempt he slipped from the wooden ledge and fell, fluttering his wings, on to his back on the window-sill. The helplessness of his attitude roused me. It flashed upon me that he was in difficulties; he could no longer raise himself; his legs struggled vainly. But, as I stretched out a pencil, meaning to help him to right himself, it came over me that the failure and awkwardness were the approach of death. I laid the pencil down again.

The legs agitated themselves once more. I looked as if for the enemy against which he struggled. I looked out of doors. What had happened there? Presumably it was midday, and work in the fields had stopped. Stillness and quiet had replaced the previous animation. The birds had taken themselves off to feed in the brooks. The horses stood still. Yet the power was there all the same, massed outside indifferent, impersonal, not attending to anything in particular. Somehow it was opposed to the little hay-coloured moth. It was useless to try to do anything. One could only watch the extraordinary efforts made by those tiny legs against an oncoming doom which could, had it chosen, have submerged an entire city, not merely a city, but masses of human beings; nothing, I knew, had any chance against death. Nevertheless after a pause of exhaustion the legs fluttered again. It was superb this last protest, and so frantic that he succeeded at last in righting himself. One's sympathies, of course, were all on the side of life. Also, when there was nobody to care or to know, this gigantic effort on the part of an insignificant little moth, against a power of such magnitude, to retain what no one else valued or desired to keep, moved one strangely. Again, somehow, one saw life, a pure bead. I lifted the pencil again, useless though I knew it to be. But even as I did so, the unmistakable tokens of death showed themselves. The body relaxed, and instantly grew stiff. The struggle was over. The insignificant little creature now knew death. As I looked at the dead moth, this minute wayside triumph of so great a force over so mean an antagonist filled me with wonder. Just as life had been strange a few minutes before, so death was now as strange. The moth having righted himself now lay most decently and uncomplainingly composed. O yes, he seemed to say, death is stronger than I am.

Notes

THE WAR FROM THE STREET

1. *August 4, 1914*: the date of the assassination in Sarajevo of the Austrian Archduke Ferdinand by an agent of the Black Hand, a Serbian liberation organization. It was this incident that led to the First World War.
2. *a vast, featureless, almost shapeless jelly ... taking the reflection of the things*: there is a comparable formulation concerning the press (in both senses) and its impact on readers in *Jacob's Room* (1922; Penguin Books, 1992, p. 84):

   > These pinkish and greenish newspapers are thin sheets of gelatine pressed nightly over the brain and heart of the world. They take the impression of the whole. Jacob cast his eye over it. A strike, a murder, football, bodies found ...

   See also 'Oxford Street Tide' in 'The London Scene' (p. 114 and note 8, p. 205).

MODERN FICTION

1. *an improvement upon the old*: this essay seems to have had its origin in Woolf's thoughts on completing her second novel, *Night and Day* (1919; Penguin Books, 1992):

   > [A]s the current answers don't do, one has to grope for a new one; & the process of discarding the old, when one is by no means certain what to put in their place, is a sad one. Still, if you think of it, what answers do Arnold Bennett or Thackeray, for instance, suggest? Happy ones – satisfactory solutions – answers one would accept, if one had the least respect for one's soul? (*Diary*, I, 27 March 1919, p. 259).

2. *making motor cars*: the comparison for this analogy about modernization has itself been modernized from the 1919 version of the essay, where it was 'making bicycles'.

3. *Mr Wells ... Galsworthy*: H. G. Wells (1866–1946), Arnold Bennett (1867–1931) and John Galsworthy (1867–1933) belonged to an older generation of novelists, often mocked by Woolf for their concern with realism.
4. *Mr Hardy ... Long Ago*: Thomas Hardy (1840–1928) and Joseph Conrad (1857–1924) were novelists much admired by Woolf. W. H. Hudson (1841–1922) was a naturalist, author of *The Purple Land* (1885), *Green Mansions* (1904) and an autobiography, *Far Away and Long Ago* (1918), which Woolf reviewed (*Essays*, II, pp. 290–302). In her essay 'How It Strikes a Contemporary', she juxtaposes it with Joyce's *Ulysses* (see pp. 26–7).
5. *The Old Wives' Tale, George Cannon, Edwin Clayhanger*: Bennett's *The Old Wives' Tale* was published in 1908; George Cannon, like Edwin Clayhanger, is a character in a trilogy, consisting of *Clayhanger* (1910), *Hilda Lessways* (1911) and *These Twain* (1916). These novels were largely set in 'the Five Towns' – Tunstall, Burslem, Hanley, Stoke and Longton – a centre for the pottery industry in the West Midlands.
6. *his Joans and his Peters*: an allusion to Wells's novel *Joan and Peter* (1918), reviewed by Woolf (*Essays*, II, pp. 294–7).
7. *the life of Monday or Tuesday*: Woolf published a collection of short stories entitled *Monday or Tuesday* in 1921 (the allusion was added when the essay was revised for *The Common Reader*, and this paragraph was considerably expanded).
8. *gig lamps*: either the lamps on each side of a gig, i.e. a light, two-wheeled horse-drawn carriage, or possibly a pair of spectacles (slang, in use since the mid-nineteenth century).
9. *A Portrait of the Artist as a Young Man ... Little Review*: James Joyce's *A Portrait* had been published in 1916, and in 1919, when the first version of this essay appeared, *Ulysses* was appearing in episodes in the *Little Review*. It was published in its entirety in 1922, having at an early stage been offered to the Hogarth Press. The scene in the cemetery, mentioned below, is the Hades episode (ch. 6).
10. *Youth ... Casterbridge*: *Youth* is a novel by Conrad, published in 1902 and reviewed by Woolf in 1917 (*Essays*, II, pp. 158–60). *The Mayor of Casterbridge* is a novel by Hardy, published in 1886.
11. *Tristram ... Pendennis*: Woolf draws a comparison between Sterne's *Tristram Shandy* (1767) and *Ulysses* because both novelists show concern with the body and its functions. In her reading notebook, she wonders 'Would my objection apply to T.[ristram] S.[handy]?

NOTES

I believe Johnson was outraged by TS. T.S. has a warmer temperature than Ulysses.' (Brenda Silver: *Virginia Woolf's Reading Notebooks*, Princeton, 1983, p. 156) She reread Thackeray's *Pendennis* (1850) in August or September of 1922, at the same time as *Ulysses*, and told T. S. Eliot that in respect of psychology 'I had found Pendennis more illuminating' (*Diary*, II, 26 Sept. 1922, p. 203).

12. *Gusev*: Chekhov's short story of 1890 had been translated by Constance Garnett in a collection entitled *The Witch and Other Stories*, published in 1918, and reviewed by Woolf (*Essays*, II, pp. 244–7).
13. *Learn to make yourself* . . .: the quotation is from Elena Militsina, 'The Village Priest', in a collection of that title reviewed by Woolf in 1918 (*Essays*, II, pp. 341–3).
14. *Meredith*: George Meredith, poet and novelist (1828–1909).

THE ROYAL ACADEMY

1. *The motor cars . . . knight of Belgium*: this essay describes the Royal Academy's Summer Exhibition of 1919. The pictures were displayed in Burlington House, off Piccadilly, approached through a courtyard where an equestrian statue of the Belgian King Albert was on display as part of the Exhibition; so were a number of expensive motor cars, which were not.
2. *the brae-side . . . Buck Royal*: the Duke talks about a deer-shooting party in the Scottish Highlands – the brae-side is the hillside; kickshaws are toys or foibles.
3. *The Guard dies . . . to look upon*: the Duke moves on from hunting to regimental sentiments: 'The Guard dies . . .' was attributed to General Cambronne, 'Up, Guards . . .' to Wellington, both from the Battle of Waterloo. On seeing him reduced to tears, the rest of the officers politely turn their backs.
4. *Rudyard Kipling*: (1865–1936) poet and short-story writer, preoccupied with male camaraderie. He often set scenes in the Officers' Mess, though Woolf does not seem to have a particular story in mind.
5. *The picture, no. 306*: *The Wonders of the Deep* by John R. Reid. In a letter to Vanessa, Woolf mocks the Academy's enthusiasm for genre painting, the old-fashioned 'every picture tells a story' style of painting:

> I get an immense deal of pleasure from working out the pictures, but I mustn't tell you, or you won't read my article. I can't settle down to write it, though, because I always remember pictures that I haven't quite worked out, and I have to go back again ... I think Cocaine [by Alfred Priest] is one of the best, but there is a marine piece which is also very good.
> (*Letters*, II, 17 July 1919, pp. 377–8)

6. *Lord Chancellor ... Mr Balfour*: the Lord Chancellor was Lord Birkenhead (F. E. Smith, 1872–1930); Mr Balfour was James Balfour, an MP and cabinet minister.
7. *Sargent ... Gassed*: John Singer Sargent (1856–1925), a highly successful American painter.
8. *Roger Fry*: (1866–1934) art critic, and advocate of post-impressionism. A close friend of Woolf, who published his biography in 1940.

GOTHIC ROMANCE

1. *waste-paper baskets*: Woolf's regular literalization of the selection process by which some works survive, and others fade into obscurity (cf. the use of 'trash' in the following paragraph).
2. *the aesthetic value of shock and terror*: this continues a question opened up in aesthetics at about the time of, though not in relation to, the Gothic novelists, when Edmund Burke and Immanuel Kant, to name the most influential, wrote about the sublime as an experience of being overwhelmed. In making the link to a popular genre, Woolf also anticipates the interest shown since in the social and psychological operations of horror and melodrama, much of it focusing on the new media of film and, later, television. Woolf here takes up a discussion begun in 'Across the Border', her review of Dorothy Scarborough's *The Supernatural in Modern Fiction* (*Essays*, II, pp. 217–20).
3. *the taste which demands this particular stimulus*: Woolf's use of the term 'stimulus' here is derived from contemporary behavioural psychology, as with the habit/impulse opposition she sometimes adopts.
4. *Clara Reeve ... Wilkinson*: Clara Reeve (1729–1807), author of *The Old English Baron* (1778); Mrs Ann Radcliffe (1764–1823), author of *The Romance of the Forest* (1791), *The Mysteries of Udolpho* (1794), etc.; Matthew Lewis, author of *The Monk* (1796); Charles Maturin

(1782–1824), author of *Melmoth the Wanderer* (1820), and Sarah Wilkinson, author of *Adeline, or the Victim of Seduction* (1828), and other romances.
5. *the day of publication*: published in 1797.
6. *Johnson's ... Man*: *The Vanity of Human Wishes* appeared in 1749; Gray's poems were mainly written between 1742 and 1761, Richardson's novel *Clarissa* was published in 1747–8, Addison's play *Cato* in 1713 and Pope's poem *An Essay on Man* in 1733–4.
7. *Walpole ... Radcliffe*: Horace Walpole (1719–97) was the author of *The Castle of Otranto* (1764), perhaps the earliest Gothic novel. The quotations below from Radcliffe's *The Mysteries of Udolpho* (1794) and Wilkinson's *Adeline, or the Victim of Seduction* (1828) are taken from Birkhead.
8. *Scott ... Peacock*: Walter Scott (1771–1832) wrote introductions to *The Castle of Otranto* and Ann Radcliffe's novels; Jane Austen parodied the Gothic novel in *Northanger Abbey* (1818) as did Thomas Love Peacock in such novels as *Nightmare Abbey* (1818).
9. *use of emotion*: the lines are:

> But oh! that deep romantic chasm ...
> A savage place! as holy and enchanted
> As e'er beneath a waning moon was haunted
> By woman wailing for her demon-lover!

10. *The Turn of the Screw*: James's novel was published in 1898. At the end of 1921, Woolf published an essay on 'Henry James's Ghost Stories' in *The Times Literary Supplement* (*Essays*, III, pp. 319–25).

HOW IT STRIKES A CONTEMPORARY

1. *How it Strikes a Contemporary*: the title is that of a poem by Robert Browning in *Men and Women* (1855). Rereading *The Common Reader* in 1929, Woolf judged this essay harshly.

> I am horrified by my own looseness. This is partly that I don't think things out first; partly that I stretch my style to take in crumbs of meaning. But the result is wobble & diffusity & breathlessness which I detest. (*Diary*, III, 23 June 1929, p. 235)

2. *Robert Elsmere ... Stephen Phillips*: *Robert Elsmere* was a bestselling

novel by Mrs Humphrey Ward, published in 1888; Stephen Phillips (1864–1915) wrote plays in verse – both were briefly fashionable.

3. *ten and sixpence*: the price of a novel when this essay was written; it is the same as half a guinea (a guinea being twenty-one shillings, or one pound one shilling), mentioned a little further on.

4. *the Dryden ... the Arnold*: John Dryden (1631–1700); Samuel Johnson (1709–84); S. T. Coleridge (1772–1834); Matthew Arnold (1822–88).

5. *praise and blame**: Woolf's footnote quotes from a contemporary review of Rose Macaulay's *Told by an Idiot* (1923), which compares it favourably in some respects to works by Shakespeare and Swift, and then from a review of T. S. Eliot's poem *The Waste Land* (published by the Woolfs at the Hogarth Press, 1923), which dismisses it as worthless.

6. *Reviewers we have but no critic*: the distinction between reviewer and critic corresponds to Woolf's regular polemics against the professionalization of literary criticism.

7. *Dryden ... Coleridge*: all were practising writers as well as critics.

8. *Hardy ... Conrad*: Thomas Hardy (1840–1928) had published his last novels in 1897; Joseph Conrad (1857–1924) was Polish by birth and his novels were strongly influenced by the Russian tradition.

9. *Waverley ... Unbound*: *Waverley*, a novel by Scott (1814); *The Excursion* by Wordsworth (1814), 'Kubla Khan' by Coleridge (1816) and *Don Juan* by Byron (1819–24) are all poems; most of Hazlitt's essays appeared between 1817 and 1825; *Pride and Prejudice* is a novel by Jane Austen (1813); *Hyperion* by Keats (1820) and *Prometheus Unbound* by Shelley (1820) are poems.

10. *Yeats ... Ulysses*: W. B. Yeats (1865–1939) was (in 1923) only halfway through his poetic career; W. H. Davies (1871–1940) and Walter de la Mare (1873–1956) were poets, D. H. Lawrence (1885–1930) a novelist, Max Beerbohm (1872–1956) an essayist and parodist. W. H. Hudson's autobiography *Far Away and Long Ago* was published in 1918 and James Joyce's *Ulysses* in 1922. Fittingly, Woolf's estimate of the future reputations of these writers perfectly illustrates her general point about the impossibility of assessing the work of contemporaries.

11. *shorthand*: a frequent metaphor in Woolf for the combination of abbreviation and speed she sees as characteristic of the conditions of modern writing. It is expanded later in the present essay by an opposition between 'notebooks' (like Bernard's, in *The Waves* (1931;

Penguin Books, 1992)) as typical of the present age, and lasting works of literature.
12. *The Watsons*: an early work by Jane Austen, first published in 1871, and recently reprinted, 1923.
13. *We enter ... passion*: the quotation is from Arnold's essay 'The Study of Poetry' in *The English Poets*, I, ed. T. H. Ward (1880).
14. *the Byron centenary*: the centenary of Byron's death fell in 1924. Byron had left England in 1816 supposedly because of the scandal of his relationship with his half-sister Augusta Leigh.
15. *from notebooks of the present*: earlier, Woolf entertained the possibility that the modern period, by virtue of being more 'cut off' from its past than any past period had been, might be subject to unprecedented conditions, which would render the search for new masterpieces both anachronistic and unattainable: modernity would be incompatible with literature in the traditional sense. But now, she reverts to a more cyclical view, seeing the necessary fragmentation of the present as preparatory to an age which will be creative in a historically recognizable way.
16. *Lady Hester Stanhope*: (1776–1839) was a deeply eccentric Englishwoman who spent much of her life travelling and later living in the Holy Land (see 'Lady Hester Stanhope', *Essays*, I, pp. 325–9).

TO SPAIN

1. *Dieppe*: the French coastal town at which ferries from Newhaven, near the Woolfs' house in Sussex, arrive. In 1923 the Woolfs took their first holiday abroad since their honeymoon in 1912, crossing to France on 27 March and travelling by train to Madrid and Granada. Woolf's letters convey her excitement: 'I felt a kind of levity and frivolity and congeniality upon me with the first sight of Dieppe. How much more enjoyable in some queer way France is than England!' (*Letters*, III, 30 March 1923, p. 23, to Jacques Raverat; see also pp. 24–6, 29–30).
2. *Sud Express*: the train from Paris down to Spain and Portugal.
3. *Sierra Nevada*: this was where Gerald Brenan's house was. Leonard and Virginia stayed with him there at Yegen from 5 to 13 April, and then made their way back through Spain and France to Paris. Leonard returned to England a few days before Virginia to take up his new job as literary editor of the *Nation*. This piece appeared in the first edition he prepared.

THUNDER AT WEMBLEY

1. *Wembley*: the north London stadium had been specially built for the British Empire Exhibition in 1924–5, which this piece describes. The Woolfs visited it on 29 May 1924, a month after it opened. In the run-up to its opening, a great deal of attention was directed towards the technological innovations it was to utilize, in particular the broadcasting throughout the country of the inaugural speech by King George V. The following extract brings out the fascination with possibilities that were soon to take on associations of mass manipulation, rather than national participation (see Woolf's negative references, in essays like 'Thoughts on Peace in an Air Raid' (p. 168ff) and 'The Leaning Tower' (*A Woman's Essays*, Penguin Books, 1992, pp. 159ff), to the loudspeaker and the megaphone and Hitler's voice eerily speaking in every home):

> Just above and to the left of the King's head is seen a microphone ... by means of which the royal words reached, by radio, a vast audience listening all over the country. At the top of the photograph ... are three rectangular 'loudspeakers', through which the speeches were distributed to the great crowd present in the Stadium ... (*Illustrated London News*, 26 April 1924)

With these inverted commas honouring the newness of the new means of communication, it is as if the magic attributed to the royal person had given way to an aura now attached to his detachable, technically transmitted words, 'distributed' to the people like multiplying loaves and fishes. The previous week, readers were given an indication of new priorities with the information that 'Loudspeakers installed in numerous cities and towns will convey his Majesty's words to many of the public who, in addition to hearing the King's voice, may experience listening to broadcasts for the first time' (19 April 1924).

The content of the King's speech itself celebrates what is at once the self-contained artificial environment to which Woolf's essay alludes ('It is nature that is the ruin of Wembley'), and the capacity of its simulation in miniature to draw together the heterogeneous elements of the Empire: 'The Exhibition may be said to reveal to us the whole Empire in little, containing within its 220 acres of ground a vivid model of the architecture, art and industry of all the races which come under the British flag'. In that 'vivid model' are

contained the beginnings of the 'global village' of later twentieth-century mass culture – Wembley rock concerts included.
2. *Lord Stevenson, Lieut.-General Sir Travers Clarke, and the Duke of Devonshire*: Lord Stevenson was chairman of the Exhibition board, Sir Travers Clarke its chief administrative officer; the Duke of Devonshire was at that time Secretary of State for the Colonies and deeply involved in the organization and finance of the Exhibition.
3. *Earl's Court and the White City ... brilliant*: Earl's Court had become a year-round showplace in the nineties, following J. R. Whitley's canny development of derelict ground between railway lines. It had permanent fairground features, notably a Great Wheel, and also annual exhibitions and 'spectaculars' such as Buffalo Bill's Wild West Show (the present Earl's Court building dates from 1937). The White City, occupying a site in Shepherd's Bush, stole Earl's Court's thunder after it opened in 1908. In contrast with these, Wembley had new improved lighting, featured in a special photograph in the *Illustrated London News* (3 May 1924), to which the caption reads: 'Man-made "moonlight" at Wembley: some of the great "flood lights" (170 in all) on the roof of the stadium, which help to illuminate the Exhibition grounds at night'.
4. *a guinea*: one pound one shilling, over three times as much as the six shillings and eightpence (exactly a third of a pound, or twenty shillings) mentioned jokingly below as the quintessential middle-range price. The price of entry to the Exhibition was 1/6d (one shilling and sixpence) for adults, and ninepence (half that sum) for children.
5. *motor cars ... not flimsy and cheap*: the going rate for the cheapest new motor cars that year was £235.
6. *old masters*: i.e. *not* old masters.
7. *rattans*: small canes or walking-sticks made of rattan, the wood from a kind of palm tree.
8. *mowing machines*: new developments in this line also feature in the first part of *To the Lighthouse* (1927; Penguin Books, 1992), where James Ramsay is cutting out pictures of products from the Army & Navy Stores catalogue. Motor lawnmowers were expensive acquisitions selling for around £65 in 1924; an advertisement in the week the Exhibition opened for the 'Governor' brand emphasizes the saving of time and money:

> [A] boy can quickly learn to operate it and with it can do as much work as would be done by a large horse-drawn machine

in the same time. The saving of time and the upkeep of a horse alone enables the 'GOVERNOR' to pay for its first cost – in but one season ... (*Illustrated London News*, 26 April 1924)

At this time, then, the labour-saving aspect did not directly benefit the prospective owner, but was translated into the saving of 'upkeep' for beasts or boys.

9. *rosy Burma*: one of the exhibiting countries, like 'sand-coloured Canada', below. There was also a replica of the tomb of Tutankhamen, much in the news at the time; and South Africa's exhibit included 'real diamond-seeking', for which thousands of tons of blue soil were specially brought over from the mines. This was 'expected to yield thousands of pounds' worth of stones, which will be cut and polished in public at Wembley'.

ON BEING ILL

1. *Considering how common illness is*: Woolf wrote this essay during a long illness in the autumn of 1925. In September she had received a letter from T. S. Eliot 'that fawns & flatters, implores me to write for his new 4ly' (i.e. the *New Criterion*). She was ill during October and November, but wrote about the experience. A diary entry for 7 December records: 'there is Tom's postcard about *On Being Ill* – an article which I, & Leonard too, thought one of my best: to him characteristic &c: I mean he is not enthusiastic; so, reading the proof just now, I saw wordiness, feebleness, & all the vices in it' (*Diary*, III, 14 Sept., 7 Dec., pp. 41, 49. See also *Letters*, III, to T. S. Eliot, pp. 203, 220; Lytton Strachey likes it, and so does Edward Sackville-West, pp. 236, 239–40).
2. *confuse his ... welcome us*: in her diary, Woolf wrote of having a tooth out: 'The queer little excursion into the dark world of gas always interests me ... Suppose one woke instead to find the deity himself by one's side!' (*Diary*, I, 7 March 1919, p. 250). See also her essay on 'Gas', written in 1929 (*CE*, II, pp. 298–300).
3. *The Opium Eater*: De Quincey's *Confessions of an English Opium Eater* appeared in 1822.
4. *the pages of Proust*: the publication of the sixteen volumes of *A la recherche du temps perdu*, begun in 1913, was completed in 1927.
5. *Babel*: Gen. 11 – when its builders tried to make the tower of Babel

NOTES

reach Heaven, God punished them by creating different languages, so that they no longer understood one another.

6. *the Americans*: the same point about the inventiveness of American English is made in the essay 'American Fiction': 'the Americans are doing what the Elizabethans did – they are coining new words. They are instinctively making the language adapt itself to their needs' (*CE*, II, p. 120).

7. *Chloral*: chloral hydrate, much used as a sedative and anaesthetic.

8. *Wisest Fate ... no*: 'But wisest Fate says no,/This must not yet be so,' lines 149–50 of Milton's 'Ode on the Morning of Christ's Nativity' (1629).

9. *in whom the obsolete exists so strangely side by side with anarchy and newness*: this extraordinary, enigmatic parenthesis might serve as an encapsulation of Woolf's far from simple view of her sex.

10. *C. L. ...*: these and the following characters seem to be imaginary, identified by their initials alone, and may be part of a pastiche of the allusiveness of eighteenth-century journalism, in keeping with the anachronistic subject matter of the whole paragraph.

11. *a giant tortoise ... a theorbo*: tortoises could be quite easily obtained at the time. A theorbo is a large double-necked lute, very fashionable in the seventeenth century; Samuel Pepys (see below, note 14) learned to play one.

12. *Wonderful to relate*: a conventional translation of, and allusion to, the phrase *mirabile dictu* from Virgil's *Aeneid*.

13. *Beachy Head*: outside Eastbourne in Sussex, a point renowned for its view and its suitability for a fatal leap.

14. *Pepys in Heaven*: Samuel Pepys (1633–1703), civil servant, most famous as a diarist.

15. *Pericles ... the Fourth*: Pericles (*c.* 500–429 BC) was an Athenian statesman; Arthur was a mythical British king, supposed to have lived in the 6th century AD; Charlemagne (742–814) was a legendary Frankish king; George IV reigned from 1820 to 1830.

16. *The Decline ... Bovary*: *The Decline and Fall of the Roman Empire* (1776–88) by Edward Gibbon; *The Golden Bowl* (1904) by Henry James; *Madame Bovary* (1856) by Gustave Flaubert.

17. *and oft at eve ... wind*: 'and oft at eve ...': from Milton's *Comus* (1637); 'wandering in thick flocks ...': from Shelley's *Prometheus Unbound* (1820).

18. *a whole three-volume novel ... Bruyère*: the standard nineteenth-century format for a newly published novel was the 'three-decker'; Thomas

Hardy (1840–1928) was a poet and novelist, Jean de la Bruyère (1645–96) a French moralist and satirist.
19. *we dip in Lamb's Letters*: the quotation is from a letter to Bernard Barton of 25 July 1829. Lamb's *Letters*, ed. Alfred Ainger (1888).
20. *O saisons ... défauts*: from *Une saison en enfer*, 1873.
21. *Mallarmé or Donne*: Stéphane Mallarmé (1842–98), French symbolist poet; John Donne (1572–1631), English metaphysical poet.
22. *Foreigners ...*: exactly the opposite point is made in 'On Not Knowing Greek', where Woolf sees lack of familiarity with the language as a barrier, not an aid, to understanding its poetry (*A Woman's Essays*, Penguin Books, 1992, p. 103): 'We can never hope to get the whole fling of a sentence in Greek as we do in English. We cannot hear it ...'
23. *flyblown*: tainted, putrid.
24. *Coleridge himself squeaks*: Coleridge gave several sets of lectures on Shakespeare.
25. *Augustus Hare ... not the peer of Boswell*: Augustus Hare was the author of *Two Noble Lives. Being Memorials of Charlotte, Countess Canning, and Louisa, Marchioness of Waterford* (3 vols, 1891–3). The rest of this essay gives highlights from their stories, and that of their parents, Lord and Lady Stuart. Woolf's reading notes suggest that she had read this book a year earlier, perhaps intending to include the sisters in a projected 'history of England in one obscure life after another' (*Diary*, III, 20 July 1925, p. 37). James Boswell's *The Life of Samuel Johnson* (1791) is often considered the greatest English biography.
26. *Beckford's mania ... castle building*: William Beckford (1759–1844), author of *Vathek*, redesigned his house, Fonthill Abbey, in an extravagant Gothic style.
27. *great Watts ... master*: G. F. Watts (1817–1904), Victorian painter, briefly married to Ellen Terry (see note 9, p. 215). His comparison of Lady Waterford's sketches with the work of Titian and Raphael, the greatest of the Renaissance old masters, was absurd.

THE CINEMA

1. *hubble-bubble ... simmer*: 'Double, double, toil and trouble;/Fire burn, and cauldron bubble', are the words recited by the witches over their cauldron in *Macbeth* (IV. i. 10–11).
2. *There is the King ... Horner*: until television took over this function,

cinema programmes began with newsreels of current events. The King was George V; Sir Thomas Lipton (1850–1931) established a chain of highly successful grocery stores; Jack Horner won the Grand National in 1926.
3. *Prince of Wales . . . Circus*: the Prince of Wales later became Edward VIII, and then abdicated; the Mile End Road runs eastwards out of London; Piccadilly Circus is the hub of London's West End.
4. *to this moment*: 'to' is an unusual variant for 'at' in this phrase.
5. *Anna Karenina*: Tolstoy's novel (1873–7) was first filmed in Russia in 1910, and altogether some fifteen film versions have since been made (two of them starring Greta Garbo, in 1927 and 1935, so too late for this piece). Anna abandons her husband and child for her lover Vronsky, and eventually commits suicide.
6. *performance of Dr Caligari*: screenings at this time included live musical accompaniment. *The Cabinet of Dr Caligari* (1919), directed by Robert Wiene and influenced by Expressionism, explores the boundary between madness and sanity in the switches between the doctor, his somnambulist patient Cesare (played by Conrad Veidt), and the hero-narrator.
7. *My luve's like a red, red rose . . . June*: the first line of Robert Burns's poem.
8. *the very slightest help from words or music*: Woolf is writing before the invention of soundtracks for film (introduced in 1929).
9. *Vesuvius*: volcano near what is now Naples, whose eruption in AD 79 destroyed the city of Pompeii.
10. *Tolstoy . . . Anna*: the contrasting sub-plot of *Anna Karenina* concerns the happy marriage of Konstantin Levin and his search for the simple life.

HOW SHOULD ONE READ A BOOK?

1. *end of my title*: this piece was first written to be read to schoolchildren at Hayes Court School near Bromley, where the daughter of her friend Mary Hutchinson was enrolled. Woolf was driven over there by Mary, with Vanessa Bell and Duncan Grant. She described the occasion in a letter of 31 January to Vita Sackville-West (who was in Persia):

> Do you by any chance remember Kent? After all, I did go down in Mary's motor, with Nessa and Duncan . . . this

analysing reminds me of my lecture, which I am infinitely sick of – To explain different kinds of novels to children – to make little anecdotes out of it – that took me more time and trouble than to write 6 Times leaders. But it was all right – 60 nice children: a large Georgian country house; immense cedars; angular open minded school mistresses: a drive home in the dark with Nessa and Duncan, who pour out pure gaiety and pleasure in life...' (*Letters*, III, pp. 236–7; see also *Diary*, III, pp. 57, 237)

2. *blue-books*: official parliamentary reports.
3. *Defoe ... Crusoe*: Daniel Defoe (1660–1731); Jane Austen (1775–1817); Thomas Hardy (1840–1928). Defoe's *Robinson Crusoe* was published in 1719.
4. *Peacock ... Meredith*: Thomas Love Peacock (1785–1866); Anthony Trollope (1815–82); Walter Scott (1771–1832); George Meredith (1828–1909).
5. *that curiosity which possesses us sometimes ... being*: Woolf's novels, in particular *Night and Day* (1919; Penguin Books, 1992), contain a number of such voyeuristic scenes, where a character is outside on the street in the dark, imagining the activities going on behind the blinds of a window.
6. *Donne ... Park*: after 1606 John Donne (1572–1631) lived in poverty in a cottage at Mitcham with his wife and growing family. Twickenham Park was the home of his patroness, Lucy Countess of Bedford, from 1607 to 1618.
7. *Sidney ... sister*: Sir Philip Sidney (1554–86) lived at Wilton, and wrote the pastoral romance *Arcadia* for his sister, the Countess of Pembroke, in about 1580.
8. *Lady Pembroke ... Spenser*: Anne Clifford, a later Countess of Pembroke (1590–1676), was a diarist, who as Countess of Dorset had lived at Knole, Vita Sackville-West's ancestral house; she later made her home in the north. Gabriel Harvey was an Elizabethan scholar, and friend of the poet Edmund Spenser (*c*.1552–99), author of *The Faerie Queene* (see also 'The Strange Elizabethans', *CE*, III, pp. 32–43).
9. *Temples ... St Johns*: Sir William Temple (1628–99), statesman and author; his wife Dorothy Osborne was famous for her letters (see 'Dorothy Osborne's Letters', *A Woman's Essays*, Penguin Books, 1992, pp. 126–32); Jonathan Swift (1667–1745), satirist and author of *Gulliver's Travels*; Robert Harley, Earl of Oxford (1661–1724),

NOTES

Tory politician; Henry St John, Viscount Bolingbroke (1678–1751), friend and patron of Swift and Pope.

10. *Samuel Johnson . . . Garrick*: Samuel Johnson (1709–84), dictionary maker and great man of letters; Oliver Goldsmith (1731–74), dramatist and novelist; David Garrick (1717–79), friend of Johnson, and the greatest actor of his day.

11. *Voltaire . . . Deffand*: Voltaire (1694–1778), a great French philosopher and writer in many genres; Denis Diderot (1713–84), a philosopher and novelist; Madame du Deffand (1697–1780), famous as a wit, hostess, correspondent.

12. *Twickenham . . . Hill*: Alexander Pope (1688–1744) lived at Twickenham in the first half of the eighteenth century, and Horace Walpole (1717–97) lived there in the second, redesigning his house at Strawberry Hill in a Gothic style. Friendship with Miss Berry connects him with the Victorian novelist William Thackeray (1811–63). (He, in turn, was connected with Woolf through his daughter Minny, who had been Leslie Stephen's first wife.)

13. *Tate . . . Rishy*: Tate Wilkinson's *Memoirs of his Own Life* (1790) relate the story of Captain Jones who was rescued from poverty by becoming heir to a great fortune, left to him by a chance acquaintance (see 'Jones and Wilkinson', *CE*, III, pp. 207–12); the young subaltern was Henry Edward Bunbury (1778–1860), later to become Lt.-General (his memoirs were edited by Sir Charles Bunbury in 1868); Maria Allen, Dr Burney's stepdaughter, eloped with Martin Rishton (see 'Fanny Burney's Half-sister', *CE*, III, pp. 147–57).

14. *Western wind . . . again*: anonymous lyric, first recorded in the early sixteenth century. Louis quotes a slightly different version repeatedly to himself in *The Waves* (1931; Penguin Books, 1992, pp. 153–6).

15. *I shall fall . . . grieve*: Beaumont and Fletcher, *The Maid's Tragedy* (1610), (IV. i. 219–20).

16. *Minutes are numbered . . . rest*: John Ford, *The Lover's Melancholy* (1628), (IV. iii. 57–64).

17. *whether we be young . . . to be*: William Wordsworth, *The Prelude* (1850 version), (VI. 603–8).

18. *The moving Moon . . . beside*: S. T. Coleridge, 'The Rime of the Ancient Mariner' (1798), lines 255–8.

19. *And the woodland haunter . . . the shade*: Ebenezer Jones (1820–60), 'When the World is Burning', lines 21–7.

20. *Robinson . . . Prelude*: references, other than those already mentioned, are to *Emma* (1816) by Jane Austen; *The Return of the Native* (1878)

by Thomas Hardy; *King Lear* (1605) by Shakespeare; *Phèdre* (1677) by Racine.
21. *then perhaps the Agamemnon*: Woolf discusses Aeschylus's play further in 'On Not Knowing Greek' (*A Woman's Essays*, Penguin Books, 1992, p. 99).
22. *Coleridge ... Johnson*: S. T. Coleridge (1772–1834), John Dryden (1631–1700), and Samuel Johnson (1696–1772) were regarded as the founders of literary criticism.

STREET HAUNTING; A LONDON ADVENTURE

1. *rambling the streets of London*: 'Street Haunting' was written during the winter of 1926/7. On 11 December 1926 Woolf jotted down 'A few thoughts to fill up time waiting for dinner. An article all about London'. On 28 February 1927 she planned to 'spend this week in long romantic London walks' (*Diary*, III, pp. 118, 129). On 29 March she wrote to Helen McAfee of the *Yale Review* offering her the article. She was still correcting proofs on 5 August when she wrote to Vita Sackville-West, 'I've a very low opinion of my writing at the moment. This comes of correcting proofs: its all bounce and jerk; I want to spin a thread like a spider' (*Letters*, III, pp. 356–7, 407).
2. *grateful*: welcome.
3. *Mr Lloyd George*: Liberal Prime Minister from 1916 to 1922, and a controversial figure.
4. *excreted*: expelled, or extruded.
5. *stone-blind*: completely blind.
6. *between Holborn and Soho*: a shabby area of central London.
7. *shores of Oxford Street*: Cf. 'Oxford Street Tide' in 'The London Scene', p. 113ff.
8. *Princess Mary's garden wall*: the Princess Royal and Viscount Lascelles lived at Chesterfield House, South Audley Street, in Mayfair.
9. *Brixton; she must have a bit of green to look at*: Brixton was a south London suburb, known for this feature at the time.
10. *three and sixpence*: eighteenpence was the same as one shilling and sixpence, slightly less than half of three (shillings) and sixpence.
11. *puce-bound*: in a purplish brown binding.
12. *innumerable ... Laura*: volumes of Victorian novels; in particular, Arthur and Laura are the hero and heroine of Thackeray's *Pendennis* (1850).

NOTES

13. *worth a penny stamp*: letters cost a penny to post.
14. *over the Strand . . . Waterloo Bridge*: the route from central London to Waterloo, one of the main stations for commuters travelling south. Barnes and Surbiton are suburbs to the south-west of London.
15. *frontispiece . . . folio*: a later reference in this paragraph to 'Ben Jonson's title-page' makes it clear that Woolf was thinking of Jonson's portrait in his *Works* (1616).
16. *the Temple*: one of the Inns of Court, to which lawyers were professionally attached.

EVENING OVER SUSSEX: REFLECTIONS IN A MOTOR CAR

1. *Sussex*: Leonard and Virginia Woolf lived partly at Monk's House in the Sussex village of Rodmell, near Lewes. Eastbourne, Bexhill and St Leonards, mentioned below, are nearby seaside towns.
2. *char-à-bancs*: predecessors of the modern bus or coach, they transported holiday-makers to the seaside.
3. *when William came over*: in 1066, to win the Battle of Hastings (also on the Sussex coast). The small town of Battle, mentioned further on, stands near the actual site.
4. *red villas*: many bungalows, designed as inexpensive homes for retirement from urban regions were constructed along the Sussex coast during the inter-war period.
5. *air balls*: balloons.
6. *I cannot hold this*: the movement here, from a sense of being overwhelmed by nature to a need to grasp and communicate it, follows that of Romantic ideas of the sublime.
7. *the power to convey*: cf. Woolf's posthumously published essay, 'Reading': 'perhaps one of the invariable properties of beauty is that it leaves in the mind a desire to impart' (*CE*, II, p. 33).
8. *the self splits up*: a number of other essays, such as 'Ellen Terry' (p. 173ff) and 'Street Haunting' (p. 70ff), play with this notion of multiple selves, involving not so much the fragmentation of an original unity, but the proliferaton of a potentially infinite number of 'I's.

THE SUN AND THE FISH

1. *Athens; Segesta*: Segesta was a Sicilian city in classical time. Perhaps

the point of these pictures in the mind's eye is their very arbitrariness or lack of point.

2. *When one says ... to sort*: Woolf was currently writing about Queen Victoria and that 'most heterogeneous collection of objects' for ch. 5 of *Orlando* (1928; Penguin Books, 1993, p. 160).

3. *morganatically*: a morganatic marriage was one in which a man of higher status married a woman of lower status, denying her and her children any claim on his possessions or title (such as Orlando's marriage to Pepita in Woolf's novel, or that of Vita Sackville-West's grandfather; difference of class was also an aspect of Woolf's relationship to Vita).

4. *the eclipse*: a complete eclipse of the sun occurred early on the morning of 29 June 1927. Virginia, Leonard, their nephew Quentin Bell, Vita Sackville-West, Harold Nicolson and various other friends travelled up on one of the trains laid on to take southerners to Barden Fell in Yorkshire, from where it would be visible. There is a full account in the diary entry for 30 June (*Diary*, III, pp. 142–4), which this essay draws on.

5. *Euston Railway Station*: their destination was Richmond in Yorkshire, and the station was King's Cross, as the diary correctly records, not Euston.

6. *Stonehenge*: 'I thought how we were like very old people, in the birth of the world – druids on Stonehenge' (*Diary*, III, p. 143).

7. *convalescences*: cf. 'On Being Ill' (p. 43ff) for a further exploration of the relations between sickness or recovery and seeing anew. In her diary, Woolf wrote: 'It was like recovery. We had been much worse than we had expected. We had seen the world dead. This was within the power of nature' (*Diary*, III, p. 144).

8. *the Zoological Gardens*: Woolf had first described the exotic fish in the new aquarium at London Zoo two years earlier (*Essays*, III, pp. 404–5). On 12 July, twelve days after their trip to Yorkshire for the eclipse, Vita and Virginia spent an afternoon at the zoo, and Vita later wrote to Virginia after her article appeared: 'I can't tell you how much I like "The Sun and the Fish" (all the more because it is about things we did together) ...' (*The Letters of Vita Sackville-West to Virginia Woolf*, eds. L. DeSalvo & Mitchell A. Leaska, Hogarth Press, 1984, pp. 234, note 2; 269). The article may pick up a private joke between them, since Virginia liked to compare Vita to 'a porpoise in a fishmonger's shop'.

NOTES

THE NIECE OF AN EARL

1. *Meredith ... Camper*: *The Case of General Ople and Lady Camper* (1890) is a novella by George Meredith (1828–1909), particularly concerned with social difference. It is reprinted in *The Tale of Chloe and Other Stories* (Ward, Lock and Bowden, 1894), and this sentence is from ch. ii, p. 266. In February of 1928 Woolf had written a reassessment of 'The Novels of George Meredith' (*CE*, II, pp. 23–7).
2. *Jane Eyre ... Austen*: *Jane Eyre* (1847) is the titular heroine of Charlotte Brontë's novel. Elizabeth (Bennet) is the heroine of Jane Austen's novel *Pride and Prejudice* (1813), and *Emma* is the heroine of the novel of that name (1816).
3. *Thackerays ... Prousts*: William Makepeace Thackeray (1811–63), English novelist and satirist, author of *Vanity Fair*; Benjamin Disraeli (1804–81), novelist and Prime Minister, later made Earl of Beaconsfield; Marcel Proust (1871–1922), French novelist familiar with high life.
4. *Byron ... Keats*: George Gordon, Lord Byron (1788–1824) was 6th Baron of Rochdale; John Keats (1795–1821) was the eldest son of a livery-stable keeper.
5. *bustard*: a large swift-running bird, now extinct.

FOREWORD TO
RECENT PAINTINGS BY VANESSA BELL

1. *Cooling's gallery*: twenty-seven of Vanessa Bell's paintings were exhibited at the Cooling Galleries, 92 New Bond Street, from 4 February to 8 March 1930. They were priced between 18 and 50 guineas.
2. *Berthe Morisot, Marie Laurencin*: Berthe Morisot (1841–95), the first woman French Impressionist, exhibited at all the Impressionist Exhibitions except the fourth. Marie Laurencin (1885–1956), another French woman painter, mainly of young girls, using a naïve, decorative style.
3. *Dieppe in the eighties*: one of the paintings exhibited.
4. *Their reticence is inviolable*: Woolf here recalls the view of the art critic Roger Fry, who in 1926 had written of Vanessa's paintings, 'Her great distinction lies in her reticence and her frankness. Complete frankness of statement, but with never a hint of how she arrived at her conviction ... You are left with the completest statement she can contrive, to make what you can of it or nothing

at all, as the case may be' (cited by Frances Spalding in her biography *Vanessa Bell*, Macmillan, 1983, p. 235).
5. *the painting of the Foundling Hospital*: the Foundling Hospital (now renamed the Coram Trust) stood on the corner of Guilford Street, at the heart of Bloomsbury. It provided a home for illegitimate children. The painter Hogarth had been a strong supporter, painting it and its founder Captain Coram. Charles Dickens had lived close by at 48 Doughty Street from 1837 to 1839 and Thackeray had lived at Coram Street in 1840. In *Jacob's Room* the Hospital is associated with the abandoned Fanny Elmer, who may herself be pregnant (1922; Penguin Books, 1992, pp. 105, 122).

PROFESSIONS FOR WOMEN

1. *your secretary*: i.e. Pippa (Philippa) Strachey (1872–1968). Writing this lecture gave Woolf the idea for the two major books that followed *The Waves*, as a diary entry for 20 January 1931 reveals:

   > I have this moment, while having my bath, conceived an entire new book – a sequel to a Room of One's Own – about the sexual life of women: to be called Professions for Women perhaps – Lord how exciting! This sprang out of my paper to be read on Wednesday to Pippa's society (*Diary*, IV, p. 6).

   The books eventually became *The Years* (1937; Penguin Books, 1968; reprinted 1993) and *Three Guineas* (1938; Penguin Books, 1977; reprinted 1993). A diary entry for 23 January records that her lecture had been attended by 'Two hundred people; well dressed, keen, and often beautiful young women. Ethel [Smyth] in her blue kimono & wig' (*Diary*, IV, pp. 6–7). Vera Brittain wrote an account of it for the *New Statesman and Nation*, 31 January 1931, reprinted in *The Pargiters* (eds. Mitchell A. Leaska, Hogarth Press, 1978, p. xxxv), which also provides a much fuller text of this lecture, derived from a typescript in the Berg Collection, New York.
2. *Fanny Burney ... George Eliot*: Fanny Burney (1752–1840) was a novelist and diarist; Aphra Behn (1640–89), a poet, novelist and playwright, while Harriet Martineau (1802–76) wrote on a wide range of issues. Woolf had discussed women writers and the need to 'think back through our mothers' in *A Room of One's Own* (1929; Penguin Books, 1945; reprinted 1993, esp. p. 69).

NOTES

3. *The Angel in the House*: a verse celebration of married love by Coventry Patmore (1823–96), idealizing women in the domestic role. A cancelled sentence in the longer version of the text defines her as 'the woman that men wished women to be' (*The Pargiters*, p. xxix).
4. *The line raced ... fingers*: Woolf had described thinking as a process analogous to fishing in *A Room of One's Own* (1929; Penguin Books, 1993 edn, p. 5ff). In the longer version of the text the woman fishing is angrier at the repression of her forbidden thought. She is directed to wait 'until men have become so civilized that they are not shocked when a woman speaks the truth about her body' (*The Pargiters*, p. xl).

THE LONDON SCENE

Early in 1931 Woolf was commissioned to write six articles for *Good Housekeeping* (see *Diary*, IV, 17 Feb. 1931, p. 12). Although the pieces were not published until December and the following year, she seems to have done much of the preparation for them in the second half of March 1931: she planned to visit Carlyle's and Keats's house on 16 March; she visited the docks on 20 March and the House of Commons on 30 March (*Diary*, IV, pp. 13, 15, 16).

I THE DOCKS OF LONDON

1. *Whither, O splendid ship ... asked*: from 'A Passer-by', probably the best-known lyric of the Poet Laureate, Robert Bridges (1844–1930):

    > Whither, O splendid ship, thy white sails crowding,
    > Leaning across the bosom of the urgent West,
    > That fearest nor sea rising, nor sky clouding,
    > Whither away, fair rover, and what thy quest?

    Woolf visited the docks in a Port of London Authority launch, in a party which included Leonard, Vita Sackville-West and the Persian ambassador; she returned with Harold Nicolson (*Diary*, IV, p. 15).
2. *North Foreland ... Gallion's Reach*: Woolf names the places passed by a ship sailing into the Port of London: North Foreland is the westernmost point of Kent; Reculver is in north Kent; thereafter

the ship sails into the mouth of the Thames, passing Tilbury on the north bank and Gravesend and Northfleet on the south. Stretches of the Thames as it passes Erith are known as Erith Reach, then Barking Reach (where the sewage works and power station are) and finally Gallion's Reach, where the river narrows and becomes less navigable.

3. *lascars*: Indian sailors.
4. *Harwich . . . Colchester*: ports north of London, on the Essex coast.
5. *stateliest . . . domes . . . a stately waterway . . . pleasure barges*: Greenwich Hospital, now the Royal Naval College, was completed by Christopher Wren in 1705. The vocabulary of this description is reminiscent of the opening of Coleridge's poem 'Kubla Khan' (1797):

> In Xanadu did Kubla Khan
> A stately pleasure-dome decree:
> Where Alph, the sacred river, ran . . .

6. *low-ceiled*: i.e. having a low ceiling.
7. *mammoths*: this creature (who also appears in *Between the Acts* (1941; Penguin Books, 1992, p. 8) is Woolf's favourite marker of a prehistoric period, especially at points where she is making a contrast between the present built-up state of the city and its origins as a swamp.
8. *This grease*: i.e. lanolin.
9. *thrown in as an extra*: this expression is itself an example of what Woolf goes on to describe as the English language's adaptation to 'the needs of commerce'.
10. *valinch . . . flogger*: these are technical terms used in the storing of liquor. The 'valinch' is a sampling tube, used for drawing wine from a cask through a bunghole; a 'shive' is a specially thin bung for sealing a cask; a 'shirt' seems to be the term for an inner casing or lining, and a 'flogger' is the instrument used to strike the cask in order to open the bung – as in the following sentence.
11. *Virginian tobacco*: in a recent radio programme (*Kaleidoscope*, 19 July 1992) Lottie Hope, who worked for Woolf, described her as rolling her own cigarettes and using a brand of tobacco called 'Virginia'.
12. *the Blue Peter*: a flag with a white square, hoisted before sailing.

II OXFORD STREET TIDE

1. *scented cream*: this efficiently picks up on the example of waste-free

utilization of lanolin used in the previous essay (p. 111, and note 8, above).
2. *city change*: the phrase 'city change' adapts Shakespeare's 'a sea-change' from Ariel's song in *The Tempest* (I. ii. 401).
3. *more sublime rites*: to the south of Oxford Street lie Hanover Square and Bond Street, famous for their fashion shops.
4. *one and eleven three*: i.e. one shilling and eleven pence three-farthings (i.e. not quite two shillings); two and six (two shillings and sixpence) was 'half a crown', a much-used coin worth an eighth of a pound.
5. *tortoises*: freely available for sale when Woolf was writing, they are mentioned as possible objects of convalescent desire in 'On Being Ill' (see p. 46).
6. *the desire of the moth for the star*: a line from Shelley's 'One word is too often profaned', defined as 'The devotion to something afar/From the sphere of our sorrow.'
7. *sensation*: as today, news headlines were displayed on boards on the pavement, next to vendors.
8. *a glutinous slab that takes impressions*: for this association of mental impressionability, the 'press', and jelly, cf. 'The War from the Street' (see p. 3 and note 2, p. 183).
9. *the great houses of Cavendish and Percy*: the family names of the Dukes of Devonshire and Northumberland. Somerset House still stands in the Strand.
10. *the latest news ... Music streams*: department stores offered free facilities such as reading rooms and concerts to their clientele.
11. *Croydon and Surbiton*: suburbs to the south and south-west of London, respectively.
12. *automatic ... genuine*: these two adjectives are typical of advertising copy of the time. Vanity here means emptiness, vain means pointless. The shopkeepers are imagined as producing artificial aids to melancholy.

III GREAT MEN'S HOUSES

1. *5 Cheyne Row*: (it had been renumbered 24). Thomas Carlyle (1795–1881) and his wife Jane (1801–66) had lived there from 1834 to the end of their lives. Woolf's earliest diary describes her father taking her to see it (*A Passionate Apprentice*, 29 Jan. 1897, p. 24), and it may have been the house she imagined for the Hilberys in *Night and Day* (1919; Penguin Books, 1992). On 16 March 1931 she recorded her

intention of visiting Carlyle's and Keats's house that afternoon; a footnote adds that Leonard drove her to Keats Grove (*Diary*, IV, p. 13).
2. *the attention of Froude*: as Carlyle's literary executor, J. A. Froude published *Reminiscences* (1881) and a four-volume biography (1884), and edited Jane Carlyle's *Letters and Memorials* (1883). Woolf had written about Jane's *Letters* (*Essays*, I, pp. 54–7) and on her friendship with Geraldine Jewsbury (*CE*, IV, pp. 27–39).
3. *excluded the sound*: Carlyle's attic study with its double walls, installed in 1853 in an attempt to shut out the noise, was a great feature of the house.
4. *as the house agents put it . . . conveniences*: Woolf's interest in the new language of estate agents' descriptions emerges also in *The Years* (1937; Penguin Books, 1968; reprinted, 1993). 'Modern conveniences' referred to such amenities as electricity and flushing toilets.
5. *Keats and Brown and the Brawnes*: Keats lived with Charles Armitage Brown from 1818 to 1820 at Wentworth Place in what is now Keats Grove, Hampstead. Here he was to fall in love with Fanny Brawne when she and her mother moved into the other half of this semi-detached house in 1819.
6. *nightingale . . . shortness of life*: Keats heard the nightingale that inspired his ode (May 1819) in the garden of Wentworth Place. He was already ill with tuberculosis, and died two years later at the age of 27.
7. *in exile*: Keats died in Rome.
8. *Parliament Hill*: a hill to the south-east of Hampstead Heath, with a panoramic view over London. Coleridge lived at nearby Highgate for nearly 20 years.

IV ABBEYS AND CATHEDRALS

1. *Shakespeare and Jonson . . . talk out*: Woolf is apparently in Cheapside, one of the oldest streets in the city, looking towards St Paul's Cathedral. The Mermaid Tavern, where Shakespeare and Jonson drank together, had once stood here, close to the corner of Bread Street.
2. *St Mary-le-Bow*: this church, designed by Christopher Wren, is slightly further along Cheapside. To be born within the sound of Bow bells is to qualify as a cockney, i.e. a true Londoner.
3. *Nelson . . . Donne*: the monument to Lord Nelson is in the south transept, while that of Donne, a sculpture of the poet in his shroud,

is in the south choir aisle. The latter was virtually the only monument to survive the burning down of the old cathedral by the Great Fire of London, 1666.
4. *fields of ... moly*: amaranth is an imaginary flower that never fades, associated with immortality; moly is a magical herb, used in Homer's *Odyssey* to disenchant Circe's victims.
5. *Gladstone ... Disraeli*: visitors enter Westminster Abbey at the north transept, where there are a series of monuments to eminent statesmen including Gladstone (1809–98) and Disraeli (1804–87).
6. *Gay laughs*: epitaph of John Gay, poet and playwright (1685–1732); with other poets, he is buried or memorialized at Poets' Corner in the south transept.
7. *St Clement Danes ... Strand*: St Clement Danes Church, designed and built by Christopher Wren, stands in the middle of the Strand. There is a memorial to Gladstone outside the west front. On 31 March 1931 Woolf attended a memorial service there for the novelist Arnold Bennett (*Diary*, IV, p. 16).
8. *Pamela*: (1740–1); a novel by Samuel Richardson.

V 'THIS IS THE HOUSE OF COMMONS'

1. *Outside the House of Commons*: Sidney and Beatrice Webb, old friends of the Woolfs, took them to the House of Commons as their guests on 30 March 1931 (*Diary*, IV, p. 16). This piece describes a debate that took place that day on the projected Customs Union between Austria and Germany, and whether it violated Austria's economic integrity, as established by the Geneva Protocol of 1922. Arthur Henderson, as Foreign Secretary in this Labour administration (Ramsay MacDonald was Prime Minister), took a prominent part. The leader in the *New Statesman and Nation* on the following Friday violently objected to what it saw as the craziness of the French opposition – 'her terror of, and animosity against, Germany ... her worship of the "security" fetish' – and saw this as personified by its principal Foreign Minister, Aristide Briand, who 'indulged in big and dangerous talk in Paris the other day. Objurgations and threats, references to 1914 and hints at another war – these are the words of maniacs'. But subsequent events were to justify the minister's fears.
2. *Gladstone, Granville, Lord John Russell*: statues in Parliament Square – for Gladstone, see note 5 above; George Leveson-Gower, Earl of Granville, Whig-Liberal statesman (1851–91), Foreign

Secretary, 1851; Lord John Russell (1792–1878), leading Victorian statesman.
3. *Gladstone ... Disraeli*: the great Prime Ministers of the previous century (see note 5, p. 207); Lord Palmerston (1784–1865).
4. *Mr Baldwin ... conspicuously ridiculous*: for Arthur Henderson and Ramsay MacDonald, see note 1 above; Stanley Baldwin (1867–1947), leader of the Conservatives in opposition, had been Prime Minister from 1924 to 1929, and would be so again in 1935; Sir Austen Chamberlain (1863–1937) was a Conservative MP who, as Foreign Secretary, had pursued pro-French policies; Sir William Jowitt (1885–1957) was Labour Attorney-General. In a similar passage in the last chapter of *Jacob's Room*, Woolf contrasts the modern statesmen who were taking the decision to declare war on Germany in 1914 with the busts of their greater predecessors (1922; Penguin Books, 1992, pp. 151–2).
5. *the four kingdoms*: i.e. England, Ireland, Scotland and Wales.
6. *out of a punt ... shovelling sugar into little blue bags*: the hecklers resemble a university undergraduate ('out of a punt') or a grocer (this was before the time of prepacked brand-name sugar). As opposed to the admiration expressed earlier for the efficient, virile work of the dockers, Woolf shows scorn for this kind of shop labour.
7. *Fulminations ... sublime*: fulminations are verbal explosions or thunderings; perorations are summings up or conclusions of speeches. William Pitt (1708–78) and Edmund Burke (1729–97) were great eighteenth-century statesmen, famous for their eloquence.
8. *from the hands of individuals to the hands of committees*: Woolf's reflections here on bureaucratization and the de-individualization of politics may be compared with the satiric look at government in the penultimate chapter of *Jacob's Room* (1922; Penguin Books, 1992, pp. 150–2).
9. *despatch*: prompt settlement, efficiency.
10. *Dizzy*: Disraeli's nickname.
11. *The days of single men and personal power are over*: a comment that Woolf might not have made five years later, when Hitler and Mussolini dominated European politics.
12. *on the veldt, in Indian villages*: both South Africa (where the veldt is the open, uncultivated land) and India were then part of the British Empire.
13. *Here stood ... More*: all these were traditionally sentenced to death in Westminster Hall; Charles I in 1649; the Earl of Essex during

NOTES

Elizabeth's reign, in 1601; Guy Fawkes in 1606, for his attempt to blow up James I and the Houses of Parliament; Sir Thomas More in 1535, for his refusal to acknowledge Henry VIII as supreme head of the English Church.

14. *let us hope that democracy will come, but only a hundred years hence*: Woolf tends to project a democracy she nevertheless wishes into the fairly remote future. She speculated on the possible art of a classless society at the end of 'The Leaning Tower', written almost ten years later, and there the terms are reversed. Instead of associating democracy with homogenization, she sees it as a chance for greater individuality: 'The novelist will have more interesting people to describe – people who have had a chance to develop their humour, their gifts, their tastes; real people, not people cramped and squashed into featureless masses' (*A Woman's Essays*, Penguin Books, 1992, p. 176).

WHY ART TODAY FOLLOWS POLITICS

1. *the Artists' International Association*: this group, founded in 1933, was pacifist and anti-Fascist in outlook. Vanessa Bell and Duncan Grant were also members.
2. *Keats ... Figaro*: John Keats wrote 'Ode to a Nightingale' (1819); Titian painted *Bacchus and Ariadne* (in the National Gallery); Mozart composed the opera *The Marriage of Figaro* (1786).

CRAFTSMANSHIP

1. *talk is called 'Craftsmanship'*: Woolf's radio talk gave her much anxiety before the event: 'What a mercy to use this page to uncramp in! after squeezing drop by drop into my 17 minute BBC: wh. is alternately 25 & then 15 minutes. Curse the BBC ... Never again will I read even one talk.' Her first reaction after she had given it was gloomy ('I have just done my BBC. Never again never again'), but next day she reported more cheerfully:

> The BBC was moderately succesful: that is I got my pecker up, & read with ease & emotion; was then checked by the obvious fact that my emotion did not kindle ... But the bright bubble, the fly in the eye, & all the other effects –

premonitory shivers & disgusts of that BBC gently subsided & vanished as I walked home through the cold streets alone, & thought that very few people had listened: the world much as usual. So great was the relief that I was very cordial to Barnes [the producer], & would have agreed to do another had he asked me. Remember, however, to refrain from that folly. (*Diary*, V, 21, 27, 29, 30 April 1937, pp. 80–83)

2. *Passing Russell Square*: Woolf imagines herself travelling home on the underground from the West End via the Piccadilly Line. She would have waited for a train that passed Russell Square Station, closest to her home at 52 Tavistock Square. Had she forgotten to get out there, she would have arrived at King's Cross Station. 'Passing away saith the world' may be a variant on 1 John i. 17, 'And the world passeth away', while the following words recall the opening lines of Tennyson's poem 'Tithonus' (1833):

> The woods decay, the woods decay and fall,
> The vapours weep their burthen to the ground,
> Man comes and tills the field and lies beneath,
> And after many a summer dies the swan.

3. *Windows . . . forlorn*: the train windows suggest the seventh stanza of Keats's 'Ode to a Nightingale' (1819):

> Perhaps the self-same song that found a path
> Through the sad heart of Ruth, when, sick for home,
> She stood in tears amid the alien corn;
> The same that oft-times hath
> Charm'd magic casements, opening on the foam
> Of perilous seas, in faery lands forlorn.

4. *the Michelin Guide . . . Baedeker*: tourist guides to the Continent: Baedeker was mainly concerned with architecture, art galleries and museums, Michelin Guides with finding accommodation.
5. *the size of a sixpenny bit*: the smallest silver coin, similar to a dime or a five pence piece.
6. *ducal house of Bedford*: since Russell was their family name.
7. *his character . . . the hearthrug*: the assumed accoutrements of a writer are revealingly male.
8. *incarnadine*: Woolf alludes to the words spoken by Macbeth after his murder of Duncan:

NOTES

> Will all great Neptune's ocean wash this blood
> Clean from my hand? No, this my hand will rather
> The multitudinous seas incarnadine,
> Making the green one red.
>
> (*Macbeth*, II. ii. 60–63)

9. *Pride ... Copperfield*: *Pride and Prejudice* (1813), by Jane Austen; *David Copperfield* (1850), by Charles Dickens.
10. *she has gone a-roving ... fair maid*: a line from a sea shanty.

THE ART OF BIOGRAPHY

1. *Is biography an art?*: Woolf herself was currently engaged in writing a biography of the art critic Roger Fry, who had died in 1934. In doing so, she was partly prompted by the wishes of his partner, Helen Anrep, whose student daughter Baba (Anastasia) partly occasioned this essay: a diary entry for 14 November 1938 records 'spending my morning writing Biography for America in order to pay off Baba's debts. So it seems' (*Diary*, V, p. 186).
2. *biographers ... Lockhart*: Johnson wrote a collection of *Lives of the Poets* (1781): Boswell, Johnson's friend, wrote *The Life of Samuel Johnson* (1791); Lockhart, who married Scott's daughter, wrote *Memoirs of the Life of Sir Walter Scott* (1838).
3. *Froude's Carlyle ... Gosse*: J. A. Froude wrote *The Life of Thomas Carlyle* (1884); Edmund Gosse was the author of *Father and Son* (1907).
4. *Lytton ... Essex*: Lytton Strachey (1880–1932) had been a close friend of the Woolfs. His *Eminent Victorians* was published in 1918; it gave brief lives of Cardinal Manning, Florence Nightingale, General Gordon and others; *Queen Victoria* was published in 1921 and *Elizabeth and Essex* in 1928.
5. *the old dictionary maker*: Dr Johnson, whose *A Dictionary of the English Language* was published in 1755.
6. *Micawber ... Bates*: Micawber is a character from Charles Dickens's *David Copperfield* (1850), Miss Bates from Jane Austen's *Emma* (1816).

REVIEWING

1. *Dr Johnson ... Coleridge, Matthew Arnold*: the major names in the tradition of English criticism. See note 4, p. 188, on 'How It Strikes a Contemporary'.
2. *the Times History*: Woolf quotes from the second volume of *The History of the Times, 1841–84* (published by *The Times*, London, 1939, ch. xxii, 'Reviewers of *The Times*', p. 468).
3. *Thackeray ... Esmond*: on 27 December 1858 Thackeray advised G. F. Atkinson, 'As for that little hint about Printing House Square ... a request for a notice might bring a slasher down upon you, such as I once had in the Times for one of my own books (Esmond), of wh[ich] the sale was absolutely stopped by a Times article.' The letter was first reproduced in facsimile in *The Leisure Hour* (1883), p. 561, and subsequently in various biographies (e.g. that by Lewis Melville in 1899). *The History of the Times*, II, also refers to this review, p. 488.
4. *Upon Keats ... Tennyson*: although Keats died of consumption, Shelley's preface to his elegy *Adonais* attributed his death to adverse criticism. Byron commented:

    > 'Tis strange the mind, that very fiery particle,
    > Should let itself be snuff'd out by an article.

    The Scottish critic J. G. Lockhart was responsible for attacks on both Keats and Tennyson: his review of Tennyson's *Poems 1832* in *The Quarterly* had a drastic effect on him, according to his biographer Harold Nicolson – see *Tennyson: Aspects of his Life, Character and Poetry* (Constable, 1923, esp. pp. 117, 118).
5. *How can a man ... Dickens demanded*: the source of this quotation has not been located. It is just possible that Woolf made it up.
6. *Times' historian*: in *The History of the Times*, II, p. 468.
7. *seven and sixpence*: a typical price for a book in 1940, it would be equivalent to thirty-eight pence in decimal currency.
8. *hebdomadal*: weekly.
9. *ululation*: howl.
10. *The Gutter*: the 'gutter press' supposedly caters for crude or low taste.
11. *an asterisk ... a dagger*: an asterisk (*) and a dagger (†) are printer's indicators.
12. *Matthew Arnold has stated*: in 'The Study of Poetry'. Woolf made this point with the same quotation in 'How It Strikes a Contemporary' – see note 13, p. 189.

NOTES

13. *the doctor's fee of three guineas?*: professional people were paid in guineas, one guinea being equivalent to one pound and one shilling (or one pound and five pence in decimal currency). Woolf's feminist polemic *Three Guineas*, published the previous year (1938), had offered a prescription for contemporary problems.
14. *spout the family tea pot*: i.e. pawn the family tea pot.
15. *Montaigne*: Woolf greatly admired the Renaissance French philosopher and essayist Michel de Montaigne; her essay on him appears in *A Woman's Essays* (Penguin Books, 1992, pp. 56–64).
16. *the peacock and the ape*: the peacock traditionally figures self-display, the ape, imitation.

THE DREAM

1. *a depressing book*: Woolf's diary records that she was offered this book to review on 26 January 1940; 'came home to type out my ten guinea Corelli' (31 January); and received 'A letter from Joe Ackerley approving my Corelli' on 9 February (*Diary*, V, pp. 260, 262, 265).
2. *Florence Barclay and Ella Wheeler Wilcox*: Florence Barclay (1862–1921) was a popular English novelist, sentimental and religiose; Ella Wheeler Wilcox (1850–1919) was an American poet (see 'Wilcoxiana', *Essays*, II, pp. 97–101).
3. *Box Hill*: in Surrey; the Victorian novelist George Meredith (1828–1909) had a house near by.
4. *the Albert Memorial*: Woolf loved to hate this object, which was designed by Gilbert Scott, completed in 1872, and stands in Hyde Park, facing the Albert Hall. It included numerous statues of the virtues and sciences, as well as a frieze with 170 life-size figures.
5. *chiffonier*: a narrow Victorian sideboard.
6. *the Earl's Court Exhibition*: a permanent site for London outings from the nineties (see note 3, p. 191).
7. *Ardath ... Rostand*: *Ardath* was published in 1889, *Barabbas* in 1893. Edmond Rostand (1868–1918) was a French poet and playwright.
8. *Braemar gathering*: i.e. the Highland Games.
9. *Pendennis*: after Arthur Pendennis, hero of Thackeray's novel (1850).

THOUGHTS ON PEACE IN AN AIR RAID

1. *and the night before that*: this piece was written in late summer 1940, when the war in the air was at its height. Woolf received a request 'to contribute to some Womens Symposium in USA' on 12 June and there are further references on 25 July and 6 August to 'the American lady'. On 31 August she was working on 'that infernal bomb article' (*Diary*, V, pp. 295, 305, 310, 314). During this period, Woolf was living at Rodmell, Sussex rather than in London, though she and Leonard made regular day trips to the city. The air raids were very heavy during August and diary entries record, 'The sound was like someone sawing in the air just above us', and the 'pop pop pop' of the guns (*Diary*, V, 16, 19 Aug., pp. 311, 312), anticipating this essay. On 20 October, the day before this piece appeared, Woolf described a visit to see the bomb damage to their house in London, and Woolf salvaged her old diaries (*Diary*, V, pp. 330–32).
2. *I will not cease from mental fight*: from Blake's 'Jerusalem' (the preface to his poem *Milton* (1804–8)).
3. *Lady Astor*: Nancy Astor (1879–1964) was the first woman to sit in Parliament in 1919; she was a champion of women's causes and strongly anti-Nazi. The relation between women's enslavement within a patriarchy and Nazism had been one of the central themes in Woolf's *Three Guineas* (1938; Penguin Books, 1977; reprinted 1993).
4. *Even in the darkness . . . enslave*: these sentences hover shadily between images of shoppers and images of prostitutes, as though to make the point that both the lady and the whore are placed in the same situation of being enslaving slaves. The night-time phantasmagoria is reinforced by rhythm, rhyming and repetition: 'blazing . . . gazing'; 'women; women'; 'crimson . . . crimson'.
5. *a young Englishman*: Frank Lushington in his autobiography, *Portrait of a Young Man* (Faber & Faber, 1940, pp. 251, 259).
6. *Othello's occupation will be gone*: see *Othello*, III. iii. 358.
7. *Bayreuth . . . Rome*: Woolf had visited Bayreuth in August 1909, and Rome in March 1927 and again in May 1935 (Germany and Italy were now both at war with England).
8. *The huntsmen are up in America . . .*: from Sir Thomas Browne (1605–82), *The Garden of Cyrus*, ch. 5.

ELLEN TERRY

1. *Captain Brassbound's Conversion*: (1900) written by George Bernard Shaw for Ellen Terry (1847–1928); she performed as Lady Cicely in 1906, 1907 and 1908. Woolf wrote this essay in late November and early December 1940 for the New York *Harper's Bazaar*, prompted by interest in the subject (she had first written of Ellen Terry in her comedy *Freshwater* (ed. L. P. Ruotolo, 1976)), but also with some misgiving: 'I'm not sure of my audience in Harper's' – and later, 'Exhausted with the long struggle of writing 2,000 about Ellen Terry.' In the event, it was turned down by *Harper's* (26 January 1941) and appeared in the *New Statesman and Nation*, 8 February 1941 (*Diary*, V, pp. 330, 342, 343, 354).
2. *Her son, Gordon Craig*: author of *Ellen Terry and her Secret Self* (1931), and editor with C. St John of her posthumous *Memoirs* (1933), both books read by Woolf in preparing this article (*Diary*, V, p. 342, note 17).
3. *Portia, Desdemona, Ophelia*: heroines in Shakespeare's *The Merchant of Venice, Othello* and *Hamlet*. From 1878 to 1902, Ellen Terry worked with Henry Irving, the greatest Shakespearian actor of his day.
4. *Velasquez, Diego Rodriguez de Silva y*: Spanish court painter (1599–1660) whose portraits were often life size or even larger.
5. *she was 'writing'*: Terry wrote *The Story of My Life* (1908, 2nd ed. 1922) and her correspondence with Shaw was published posthumously, edited by C. St John (1931).
6. *typewriter*: here, the typist, rather than the machine.
7. *not an Academy portrait*: for Woolf's views on Royal Academy taste, see 'The Royal Academy' (p. 13ff).
8. *Why, even I myself . . . trace out here*: from Whitman's 'When I Read the Book' (1847); used as an epigraph in her autobiography.
9. *an elderly famous painter*: George Frederic Watts (1817–1904); Ellen Terry was thirty years younger than Watts when she married him in 1864. Woolf's comedy *Freshwater* (ed. L. P. Ruotolo, 1976) is set on the Isle of Wight at the house of her great-aunt, Julia Margaret Cameron: it includes Tennyson, Watts, Ellen Terry and her young lover, John Craig, as characters.
10. *skipping a page or two*: during which Terry eloped with the architect Edward Godwin, and returned to the stage briefly in 1867 before leading a pastoral life in Harpenden, Hertfordshire.
11. *Charles Reade*: a popular Victorian novelist (1814–84).

12. *Sargent*: see note 7 on 'The Royal Academy', p. 186.
13. *Saturday Review*: George Bernard Shaw worked for this paper from 1895.
14. *I assure you*: the words of the actress Anne Oldfield (1683–1730), quoted by Terry in her autobiography.
15. *Flaubert*: the French novelist Gustave Flaubert (1821–1880) was totally committed to the craft of writing.
16. *Phèdre or Cleopatra*: the heroines of plays by Racine and Shakespeare.

READ MORE IN PENGUIN

In every corner of the world, on every subject under the sun, Penguin represents quality and variety – the very best in publishing today.

For complete information about books available from Penguin – including Puffins, Penguin Classics and Arkana – and how to order them, write to us at the appropriate address below. Please note that for copyright reasons the selection of books varies from country to country.

In the United Kingdom: Please write to *Dept. JC, Penguin Books Ltd, FREEPOST, West Drayton, Middlesex UB7 0BR*

If you have any difficulty in obtaining a title, please send your order with the correct money, plus ten per cent for postage and packaging, to *PO Box No. 11, West Drayton, Middlesex UB7 0BR*

In the United States: Please write to *Penguin USA Inc., 375 Hudson Street, New York, NY 10014*

In Canada: Please write to *Penguin Books Canada Ltd, 10 Alcorn Avenue, Suite 300, Tororto, Ontario M4V 3B2*

In Australia: Please write to *Penguin Books Australia Ltd, 487 Maroondah Highway, Ringwood, Victoria 3134*

In New Zealand: Please write to *Penguin Books (NZ) Ltd, 182–190 Wairau Road, Private Bag, Takapuna, Auckland 9*

In India: Please write to *Penguin Books India Pvt Ltd, 706 Eros Apartments, 56 Nehru Place, New Delhi 110 019*

In the Netherlands: Please write to *Penguin Books Netherlands B.V., Keizersgracht 231 NL–1016 DV Amsterdam*

In Germany: Please write to *Penguin Books Deutschland GmbH, Friedrichstrasse 10–12, W–6000 Frankfurt/Main 1*

In Spain: Please write to *Penguin Books S. A., C. San Bernardo 117–6º E–28015 Madrid*

In Italy: Please write to *Penguin Italia s.r.l., Via Felice Casati 20, I–20124 Milano*

In France: Please write to *Penguin France S. A., 17 rue Lejeune, F–31000 Toulouse*

In Japan: Please write to *Penguin Books Japan, Ishikiribashi Building, 2–5–4, Suido, Tokyo 112*

In Greece: Please write to *Penguin Hellas Ltd, Dimocritou 3, GR–106 71 Athens*

In South Africa: Please write to *Longman Penguin Southern Africa (Pty) Ltd, Private Bag X08, Bertsham 2013*

BY THE SAME AUTHOR

THE DIARIES OF VIRGINIA WOOLF

Volume 1: 1915–19

'Splendid in expression as in vision it is an almost unequalled account of the imagination working' – Stuart Hampshire

'In calling it a masterpiece I mean to indicate that it is a literary achievement equal to, though very different from, *The Waves*, or *To the Lighthouse*, having the same accurate beauty of writing but also an immediacy such as one finds only in diaries' – from the Introduction by Quentin Bell

Volume 2: 1920–24

'More alive than most living voices . . . it is the map of a mind struggling against madness and reaching the equilibrium which made her great novels possible. On every page the sharp twin edges of intelligence and abnormally acute senses make their impress' – Claire Tomalin

Volume 3: 1925–30

'Three qualities of the great diarists – Pepys, Greville or Kilvert – she certainly has. She is interested in everything she sets down . . . she writes for, and talks to, each reader directly . . . she moves back and forth between the ridiculous and the sublime with no loss of authenticity or humour . . . She offers rich and inexhaustible companionship'
– Michael Ratcliffe

Volume 4: 1931–35

'One of the most important and also one of the most readable books of the twentieth century' – Anthony Curtis

'Brilliantly subtle, yet direct . . . But it is the balance between the outer and the inner life which is unique; the implicit understanding of the way they replenish one another' – Rosemary Dinnage

Volume 5: 1936–41

'As an account of the intellectual and cultural life of our century, Virginia Woolf's diaries are invaluable; as the record of one bruised and unquiet mind, they are unique' – Peter Ackroyd in the *Sunday Times*

BY THE SAME AUTHOR

The Waves
Edited with an Introduction and Notes by Kate Flint

The Waves, more than any of Virginia Woolf's novels, conveys the complexities of human experience. Tracing the lives of a group of friends, *The Waves* follows their development from childhood to youth and middle age. While social events, individual achievements and disappointments form the outer structure of the book, it is most remarkable for the rich poetic language that conveys the inner life of its characters: their aspirations, their triumphs and regrets, their awareness of unity and isolation. Separately and together, they query the relationship of past to present, and the meaning of life itself. 'A book of great beauty and a prose poem of genius' – Stephen Spender

Night and Day
Edited with an Introduction and Notes by Julia Briggs

Night and Day, Virginia Woolf's second novel, opens in Chelsea, at the house of the Hilberys, a family dominated by the memory of their great Victorian ancestor, the poet Richard Alardyce. It centres on Katharine Hilbery, a young woman who at first acquiesces in favour of marriage to William Rodney, rejecting Ralph Denham for whom she feels a more profound and more disturbing affinity. As its crisis deepens, the novel searches beyond the accepted goals of marriage and work to probe the shifting reality of feelings, 'the things one doesn't say'. In that sense, although set in upper-class Edwardian drawing rooms before the First World War, *Night and Day* brilliantly and movingly brings into question the values that had been fought for. 'A love story . . . so exciting that to read it is to pass through a keen emotional experience' – *The Times Literary Supplement*

BY THE SAME AUTHOR

To the Lighthouse
Edited by Stella McNichol with an Introduction and Notes by Hermione Lee

Based on the author's childhood experiences, the novel tells the story of the Ramsay family on holiday in Skye and of a promised journey to the lighthouse that only takes place years later. Written with an astonishing and beautiful lyricism, it is told almost entirely through the reflections of its characters. '*To the Lighthouse* is the story of a marriage and a childhood. It is a lamentation of loss and grief for powerful, loved, dead, parents ... It is, less apparently, about the English class-structure and its radical break with Victorianism after the First World War' – Hermione Lee

Between the Acts
Edited with an Introduction and Notes by Gillian Beer

Outwardly a novel about country-house life, set in a house in whose grounds there is to be a pageant, *Between the Acts* is a powerful evocation of English experience in the months leading up to the Second World War. The present moment is seen as possibly the last instant of civilization, causing the humdrum and the everyday to become alive with meaning. 'Her posthumous novel ... suggests several new directions ... Its weave of past and present, quotidian reality and imminent catastrophe, the thin line between civilization and barbarism, its erotic overtones and continual humour make a powerful and prophetic statement' – Richard Shone in *The Times*

BY THE SAME AUTHOR

A Room of One's Own
Edited with an Introduction and Notes by Michèle Barrett

A Room of One's Own grew out of a lecture that Virginia Woolf had been invited to give at Girton College, Cambridge in 1928. Ranging over Jane Austen and Charlotte Brontë and why neither of them could have written *War and Peace*, over the silent fate of Shakespeare's gifted (and imaginary) sister, over the effects of poverty and chastity on female creativity, she gives us one of the greatest feminist polemics of the century.

The Voyage Out
Edited with an Introduction and Notes by Jane Wheare

The Voyage Out opens with a party of English people aboard the *Euphrosyne* bound for South America. Among them is Rachel Vinrace, a young girl, innocent and wholly ignorant of the world of politics and society, books, sex, love and marriage. She is a free spirit half-caught, momentarily and passionately, by Terence Hewet, an aspiring writer met in Santa Marina. But their engagement is to end abruptly, not in marriage but in tragedy.

Orlando
Edited by Brenda Lyons with an Introduction and Notes by Sandra M. Gilbert

'You have invented a new form of Narcissism, – I confess, – I am in love with Orlando – this is a complication I had not forseen', wrote Vita Sackville-West to the author. Sliding in and out of three centuries, and slipping between genders, *Orlando* is a sparkling incarnation of Vita's personality as Virginia Woolf saw it. Described by Bernard Blackstone as 'First masculine, then feminine, first in love, and then loved; first jilting and then jilted, a man of action, a poet, a woman of fashion and a Victorian lady', Orlando triumphs over anatomy in her ability to choose her own sexual destiny. Clever, witty, ornate, a shade mocking and brilliantly perceptive, it is a delight to read.

BY THE SAME AUTHOR

Jacob's Room
Edited with an Introduction and Notes by Sue Roe

Set in the halcyon days of pre-war innocence *Jacob's Room* follows the progress of a young man as he passes from adolescence to adulthood in a hazy rite of passage. Wandering through the windswept shores of Cornwall to the sunscorched landscape of Greece, his character is revealed in a stream of loosely related incidents, thoughts and impressions. As Sue Roe writes in her Introduction, 'Subtle, delicate and tantalizingly suggestive, *Jacob's Room* is the novel in which Woolf examines for the first time the relationship between memory and desire.'

Mrs Dalloway
Edited by Stella McNichol with an Introduction and Notes by Elaine Showalter

Mrs Dalloway portrays the life of Clarissa Dalloway, the elegant and vivacious wife of a Member of Parliament, during a summer's day in London at the end of the First World War. Mrs Dalloway is preparing for a party that evening; her old lover Peter Walsh has just returned from India. In another part of London Septimus Warren Smith is going mad with shell-shock. Into their day and the novel Virginia Woolf poured all her passionate sense of how other people live, remember and love as well as hate, and in prose of astonishing beauty she struggled to catch, impression by impression and minute by minute, the feel of life itself.

and:

The Years
A Woman's Essays
Selected Short Stories